5.99.

YORK MANUSCRIPTS CONFERENCES: PROCEEDINGS SERIES
University of York, Centre for Medieval Studies

VOLUME III

LATE-MEDIEVAL RELIGIOUS TEXTS AND THEIR TRANSMISSION

Essays in Honour of
A. I. Doyle

This collection of new essays constitutes the proceedings of the sixth York Manuscripts Conference, held at the University of York in July 1991. The guest of honour on that occasion was Dr Ian Doyle, to whom this volume is dedicated, in deep appreciation of the extraordinary contribution he has made to the study of religious texts and their histories of transmission. Dr Doyle's lively introductory address is followed by eleven studies which range widely over the different types and genres of religious literature which were produced in late-medieval England, paying attention to both verse and prose, and representing the three literary languages of the time, English, French and Latin, though concentrating on texts in English. Discussions are provided of the *Ancrene Wisse*, the *South English Legendary*, Anglo-Norman Saints' Lives, Middle English Penitential Lyrics, the *Lay Folk's Catechism*, *Piers Plowman*, Wyclif's Latin Sermons, the English sermons in MS Sidney Sussex 74, Osbern Bokenham's Middle English collection of the lives of female saints (the *Legendys of Hooly Wummen*), and the Middle English religious texts in the 'Lincoln Thornton' manuscript.

YORK MANUSCRIPTS CONFERENCES: PROCEEDINGS SERIES
University of York, Centre for Medieval Studies
(General Editor: A. J. Minnis)

ISSN 0955-9663

Published Proceedings of Previous Conferences

LATE-MEDIEVAL RELIGIOUS TEXTS AND THEIR TRANSMISSION

Essays in Honour of
A. I. Doyle

Edited by
A. J. MINNIS

D. S. BREWER

First published 1994 by D. S. Brewer, Cambridge

D. S. Brewer is an imprint of Boydell & Brewer Ltd
PO Box 9, Woodbridge, Suffolk IP12 3DF, UK
and of Boydell & Brewer Inc.
PO Box 41026, Rochester, NY 14604-4126, USA

ISBN 0 85991 386 4

British Library Cataloguing-in-Publication Data
Late-medieval Religious Texts and Their Transmission: Essays in
Honour of A. I. Doyle. – (York Manuscripts Conferences:
Proceedings Series, ISSN 0955-9663; Vol. 3)
I. Minnis, A. J. II. Series
820.9001
ISBN 0-85991-386-4

Library of Congress Cataloging-in-Publication Data
Late-medieval religious texts and their transmission : essays in honour of A. I.
Doyle / edited by A. J. Minnis.
p. cm. – (York manuscripts conferences, ISSN 0955-9663 ; v. 3)
ISBN 0-85991-386-4 (alk. paper)
1. English literature – Middle English, 1100-1500 – Criticism, Textual –
Congresses. 2. Christian literature, English (Middle) – Criticism, Textual –
Congresses. 3. Christian literature, Latin (Medieval and modern) – England –
Criticism, Textual – Congresses. 4. Books and reading – England –
History – Congresses. 5. Manuscripts, Medieval – England – Congresses.
6. Paleography, English – Congresses. 7. Scriptoria – England – Congresses.
I. Doyle, A. I. (Anthony Ian), 1925-   . II. Minnis, A. J. (Alastair J.)
III. Series.
PR275.T45L37   1994
274.2 – dc20   93-25077

This publication is printed on acid-free paper

Printed in Great Britain by
St Edmundsbury Press Ltd, Bury St Edmunds, Suffolk

CONTENTS

LIST OF ILLUSTRATIONS

A Hive of Industry or a Hornets' Nest

Osbern Bokenham's Legendys of Hooly Wummen

PREFACE

In July 1991 over a hundred scholars came together for the Sixth Manuscripts Conference at the University of York, to honour Dr Ian Doyle for the extraordinary contribution he has made to the study of medieval religious texts and their histories of transmission. This collection of some of the papers from that conference is dedicated to Ian, with much affection, and with deep appreciation both of his publications and of the advice which he has given and continues to give with such unstinting generosity. It has not been possible to cover all his areas of interest in this book – that would require several volumes rather than just one – but we have sought to do justice to at least some of them.

Ian Doyle's own introductory address, which provides much food for thought about the current state of Medieval Studies, is followed by eleven studies which range widely over the different types and genres of religious literature which were produced in late-medieval England. Attention is paid to both verse and prose, and the three literary languages of the time, English, French and Latin, are all represented, though in accordance with the tradition of the York Manuscripts Conferences we have concentrated on texts in English. Discussions are provided of the *Ancrene Wisse*, the *South English Legendary*, Anglo-Norman Saints' Lives, Middle English Penitential Lyrics, the *Lay Folks' Catechism*, *Piers Plowman*, Wyclif's Latin Sermons, the English sermons in MS Sidney Sussex 74, Osbern Bokenham's Middle English collection of the lives of female saints (the *Legendys of Hooly Wummen*), and the Middle English religious texts in the 'Lincoln Thornton' manuscript. Here are no 'substitutes for thoughtful and sensitive response' of the kind which Ian Doyle deplores, but excellent examples of the thing itself.

Throughout this volume Ian Doyle's much-quoted Cambridge thesis is dated as 1954, this being the year in which its two volumes became available in Cambridge University Library and received their accession numbers (cf. Ian Doyle's own usage on p. 1, n. 1).

We are grateful to the following Libraries and Institutions for permission to publish the following photographs of manuscripts in their collections:

Plates 1 and 2: By permission of the Master and Fellows of Sidney Sussex College, Cambridge.
Plates 3 and 4: By permission of the Board of Trinity College, Dublin.
Plate 5: By permission of the Master and Fellows of Magdalene College, Cambridge.
Plate 6: By permission of the Management Committee of the Wisbech and Fenland Museum.
Plates 7, 8 and 9: By permission of the British Library.

A special word of thanks is due to Dr Alan Fletcher, for allowing us to use his photograph of Ian Doyle as our frontispiece.

A. J. Minnis
Centre for Medieval Studies
University of York
December 1992

ABBREVIATIONS

EETS ES	Early English Text Society, Extra Series
EETS OS	Early English Text Society, Original Series
EETS SS	Early English Text Society, Supplementary Series
IMEVC	Brown and R.H. Robbins, *The Index of Middle English Verse* (New York, 1943); *Supplement* by R.H. Robbins and J.L. Cutler (Lexington, Ky., 1965)
JEGP	*Journal of English and Germanic Philology*
JWCI	*Journal of the Warburg and Courtauld Institutes*
MED	*Middle English Dictionary* (Ann Arbor)
OED	*Oxford English Dictionary*
PL	*Patrologia Latina*, ed. J.-P. Migne (Paris, 1844–64)
PMLA	*Publications of the Modern Language Association of America*
RES	*Review of English Studies*
SATF	Société des anciens textes français

Ian Doyle pictured at
the 1991 York Manuscripts Conference

INTRODUCTORY ADDRESS:
YORK MANUSCRIPTS CONFERENCE, JULY 1991

A. I. Doyle

When I agreed rather rashly to Alastair Minnis's proposal that I should be a pretext for this gathering it was not just because I was flattered but more because of my esteem for the York Centre for Medieval Studies, starting with my affection for Elizabeth Salter, and appreciation of this series of biennial conferences Derek Pearsall has chaired here since 1981 on medieval manuscripts and Middle English literature, though not expressly or exclusively confined to the latter. Arising from my scruples, however, I am glad that I persuaded Alastair to widen the proposed theme of this conference from his original notion of devotional literature to the whole range of Religious Texts and their Transmission, and that the programme is in consequence quite capacious. After all, the majorities of medieval literatures and of surviving manuscripts are religious in the widest modern sense. When I chose to restrict my doctoral thesis (1953)[1] to certain later Middle English texts I styled them theological (I think now misleadingly), in order to avoid the more professional medieval sense of religious (meaning a life by a rule), though that was in fact a good deal of what it referred to, and I did so only after surveying a much larger field. As I mentioned in my essay in the volume of studies presented to George Russell,[2] I had originally intended, following an undergraduate dissertation, to work on Langland, and so I look forward to two papers here on *Piers Plowman*. In my thesis I discussed the transmission of the *Ancrene Riwle* and, despite a number of important discoveries and publications since, it seems to me that it has still not had the amount of attention it deserves, so it is good to see Dr Millett's paper on the programme. In my Lyell lectures at Oxford in 1967 on 'Some English Scribes and Scriptoria of the Later Middle Ages' I broached some of the questions about Wycliffite manuscripts which Professor Hudson has gone a long way in exploring subsequently; the catch-title of her paper is particularly apposite in that I have spent much of my career tending the books and memory of Martin Joseph Routh, whose obiter dictum she is quoting.[3] And Dr Fletcher is to handle a nexus of Wycliffite copying which I have long hoped to see unravelled. If I do not specify the other speakers and papers I am sure they will understand it

---

[1] 'A survey of the origins and circulation of theological writings in English in the 14th, 15th and early 16th centuries, with special consideration of the part of the clergy therein', Cambridge Ph.D. dissertation 2301-2, 1954.

[2] G. Kratzmann and J. Simpson (eds.), *Medieval English Religious and Ethical Literature* (Cambridge, 1986), pp. 35–48.

[3] 'You will find it a very good practice always to verify your references, Sir': J. W. Burgon, *Lives of Twelve Good Men* I (London, 1888), p. 73.

is not for lack of interest but because I cannot claim myself to have ventured much or anything in public on their subjects and I hope to learn all the more from them. One of their topics evokes a recent regretted loss to our studies, Rossell Hope Robbins, whose thesis (1937) was one of my earliest guides, to which I was sent by H. S. Bennett, my first research supervisor, whose exemplary conscientiousness in that task (relinquished after a year, perhaps in despair, and ill repaid, I fear, in a review of the first volume of his nonetheless useful *English Books and Readers*), I have come to see as what too few students get or, like me, value sufficiently when they do.

To the papers of the first York conference, published in 1983,[4] I added a Retrospect and Prospect, the still valid remarks of which I shall mostly not repeat here. Since then, and even more since my King's College, London, Special Lectures in Palaeography (1965) on 'Later Middle English Manuscripts', in which I surveyed the then state of our studies, many religious texts have appeared in print, generally with considerable improvements in editorial presentation, especially their treatment of the manuscripts and early editions, yet not all as good as they ought to have been; and there are still major gaps, no doubt because of the sheer size of the tasks and because what is now expected of editors can occupy nearly the whole of a career, and in the outcome often more than one: notably the C-text of *Piers Plowman*, books I and II of the *Scale of Perfection*, the *Speculum Vite* and a new edition of the *Prick of Conscience*. In addition to the original and supplementary output of the Early English Text Society, Professor Görlach's and Dr Pickering's Middle English Texts have now produced a substantial row of well-done works and Dr James Hogg's several Salzburg series a number of more varying quality, while it is usually possible to obtain one-off copies of unpublished theses, some of which one would still like to see in print, such as the *Abbey* and *Charter of the Abbey of the Holy Ghost*. In respect of facsimiles, monographs, symposia and Festschriften we are of course greatly indebted to the enterprise of Derek Brewer and Richard Barber, which I hope has not been entirely unprofitable to them.

There have been great advances in the bibliography of Middle English texts, manuscripts, editions and studies, through the revised Wells/Hartung *Manual*, Jolliffe, Revell, the *Index of Printed Middle English Prose*, and a growing list of separate *IMEP* handlists, while Ringler has extended the indexing of verse and Richard Hamer is indexing the manuscripts cited in Brown and Robbins and Cutler for *English Manuscript Studies*, with new locations for some which have wandered. Although the specifically Middle English 'Work in Progress' lists formerly published in *PMLA* and *Neuphilologische Mitteilungen* have lapsed, we have new ones for smaller areas such as Sermons, and while there is always the chance of inadvertent clash of projects (from which a fruitful collaboration can sometimes, if too rarely, be wrung), there is not the same excuse as once there was for ignorance of the material and sources. I am sorry to say that over the years I have come across not a few students whose supervisors have encouraged them to enter lines of research with only a hazy notion of what was involved, and even now I see some hasty seizing of what looked at first sight like unoccupied

---

[4] D. Pearsall (ed.), *Manuscripts and Readers in Fifteenth-Century England* (Cambridge, 1983), pp. 142–6.

texts and topics, with consequent disappointments. Multiple handling of the same things can however sometimes have benefits for knowledge.

I should like to repeat what I have said elsewhere, that we cannot do very well to study English texts and manuscripts in isolation from those in other languages and from other countries and I think there are increasing signs of that being realised. We must be aware of tools like Bloomfield's *Incipits*, Walther's *Carmina and Proverbia*, Rézeau's and Sinclair's additions to Sonet, and the indexes of the Institut de Recherche et d'Histoire des Textes (now partly available elsewhere in microfiches and an on-line data base), and we must hope for the completion soon of Professor Ruth Dean's revision of Vising's Anglo-Norman bibliography.

The previous York conference was to celebrate the *Linguistic Atlas of Late Mediaeval English* (1986), the third-of-a-century's thinking and work for which has already transformed the geographical dimension of our knowledge and offers continual prospects for relocation of particular manuscripts and texts. One warning I had already to give people wanting permission to consult or quote my thesis was not to rely too much on its suppositions about the dialect or region of origin of a manuscript, derived then from less thorough sources or guessed from a sampling of inadequate evidence. Another was not to have too much faith in my dating of manuscripts then, impaired as it was by shortness of experience and want of comparative criteria. Not that I would forswear all my early judgements but I should like to revise them in the light of subsequent knowledge and improvements in later medieval palaeography and codicology, which do not however, I think, yet match those in dialectology. Malcolm Parkes's *English Cursive Book Hands* (1969) presented the outlines of a fresh morphology, terminology and chronology for some of the scripts we may meet but, I will venture to say with him here, I fear it has proved too compressed for many users to understand thoroughly and apply accurately; like the works of Aristotle, Peter Lombard, or Isaac Newton it calls for a succession of glossators, commentators and *vulgarisateurs*. Unfortunately or otherwise the well-intended if in details arguable attempt of the late Anthony Petti[5] to marry several terminologies for more elementary use does not seem to have had much influence, while some scholars who ought to know better have unconsciously or wilfully reversed the Parkesian nomenclature of anglicana and secretary, and other writers have merely muddled them.

We still have too few demonstrable criteria for dating. It is not good enough for us to carry our personal ones in our heads and occasionally let some out in assessments we are asked for. You may have noticed how when Doyle and Parkes are both quoted (in reciprocal ignorance or not) the one tends to go for an earlier and the other a later option, whether from clashes of criteria or of temperaments. That may be cautionary for the enquirer. The publication of the volumes of dated and datable manuscript codices in the British Library, Oxford and Cambridge has put a lot more evidence at everyone's disposal,[6] and there are more to come, yet all of patchy incidence and liable to misinterpretation. What

---

[5] *English Literary Hands from Chaucer to Dryden* (London, 1977); cf. *The Library*, 5th series, 33 (1978): 343–9.
[6] By A. G. Watson, British Library, 1979, and Oxford, 1984; by P. Robinson, Cambridge, 1988.

we also need are albums of dated and datable specimens from medieval documents of various parts of the British Isles, systematically selected to show the coming in and going out of certain styles and features of writing, such as at present we have to search for, often in vain, in many miscellaneous collections of facsimiles. They might also show us if there really are distinct regional styles in the thirteenth, fourteenth and fifteenth centuries or rather, as I suspect, chiefly professional or educational ones.

I do not apologise for saying so much about palaeography, since it is, in the broad British sense, a main means by which a number of us here have worked. Palaeography in the narrower sense of studying the details of the development of handwriting is, beyond the elementary stages, like philology of the stricter sort, a somewhat special interest which not many people can be expected to follow. At the best it needs a gift of visual observation and memory, which can be fostered but which some enthusiasts for manuscripts seem wholly to lack. To identify reliably the hands of individual scribes or schools is not always as easy as some novices seem to suppose, though they may just be lucky. It is very rewarding if it yields a habitation and a name, or potentially productive if it only connects two or more as yet anonymous unlocated manuscripts. Any such recognition or argument must be confirmed by graphic analysis, sufficient comparison of contemporaries and a contextual hypothesis. There can rarely be any *proof* that two or more individuals' hands are *distinguishable* when we know that many are not, it is a question of relative likelihood, with regard to the characteristics of the writing and circumstantial factors. In the last resort we can only point and persuade in the manner of the literary critic, as proclaimed by my master F. R. Leavis (to whom York paid the respect Cambridge failed in, and the fund in whose honour subsidised the publication of the papers of our first conference): 'these are the details I see, combined in these ways, leading to my judgments. Aren't they like that? Isn't that more likely to be true than any alternative?'

Understandably it has been in codicology, the archaeology of the book, the wider reaches of palaeography, that most people have done useful work, on a small or large scale, in some cases, such as the Thornton manuscripts, collaborative in effect if not in conception. At the simplest an account of a single manuscript can be a valuable exercise for a student so long as he or she has been competently taught or is capable of intelligent imitation. If it is good enough to be published, it will go to augment the growing body of descriptions complementary to the often inadequate ones in even the better printed catalogues. Unfortunately not all the published complete facsimiles of the more important manuscripts (the flow of which has now somewhat diminished) have comprehensive introductions, but they serve to provoke and facilitate examination, and editions now commonly include fuller accounts of all the manuscripts and not infrequently photographic specimens of more than one. The development of exact paper studies has been increasingly brought to bear on both the dating and the make-up of books, for which there is large scope in our field, especially if the notion of a repertory of archivally dated or datable occurrences of medieval watermarks in England, Wales and Ireland could be implemented, along with Professor R. J. Lyall's for Scotland. Dr Kathleen Scott's Survey of Illuminated Manuscripts from 1385, now not long from publication, I hope, will tell us much about the books she includes and offer guidance on many others.

The fresh classification and nomenclature of initial and border decoration she is also developing ought to reveal new affinities and artists as well as a chronology improving on Margaret Rickert's, and so afford us new possibilities of connecting manuscripts with each other and to places and episodes of production.

Binding history is another area of recent advances and prospects which could affect us: how many of you know that a census of medieval western bindings in Britain and Ireland has started, and are you able to say how many of the books you have handled retain all or some of their early covers and how that affects their contents and utilisation? A number of you will know of the History of the Book in Britain project, of which two volumes will cover the periods we have been concerned with. For the second, from 1400 to 1557, a sample data bank of evidence of ownership, prices, decoration and binding is being compiled by Dr M. L. Ford, of the Warburg Institute, a task in which other scholars contributions are invited.

So far I have been talking chiefly about the manuscripts which are the focus of our conferences, and our methods of studying them, but I want to say a little more about our interest in their contents, from which most of us start and with which many of us end. A month or two ago, in the course of newspaper discussions about changes in English teaching in schools, a lecturer at the University of East Anglia was quoted as saying that children could not be expected to understand Chaucer or Milton. I think that a very depressing reflection of the state of English studies, if only in some places or mentalities, at university as well as school level today. Indeed it makes me angry at the contempt it shows for people's abilities from an early age to learn and benefit from different ways of speaking and thinking than their own, and from finding out about the antecedents of their own. My fellows and I in a Liverpool day school fifty years ago got immense enjoyment and enlightenment from studying compulsory untranslated Chaucer, to the extent of making our own parodies, and I do not believe that children today, despite all the unchallenged competition of contemporary commercial culture, and the consequent decline of reading, are not capable of doing as well for themselves, and, *a fortiori*, our undergraduates.

Obviously Catholics of my generation and somewhat later had considerable advantages of initial sympathy with and comprehension of both the essentials and accidentals of medieval religion, familiarity with Latin in worship and even further knowledge of that language and its literature. The actual, if not inevitable, results of the Second Vatican Council have gravely reduced that lead, while the parallel changes of general education in the English-speaking world are no doubt making it more difficult to find students inclined or equipped with a Christian and old-fashioned linguistic training to venture into Middle (let alone Old) English, but I am sure it is not impossible to help them to it, and I hope I do not need to preach to the present audience not to be defeatist. You do however need to be ready to stand up against arrogance in your academic colleagues and administrative superiors. I wish I were in a position to do so still. I had two undergraduates sent to me recently who wanted to study early Middle English manuscript texts on microfilm and who told me, very sadly, that by a new syllabus they were only able to do them as Language, not also as Literature! I suppose they are lucky to have had either option. The process may not have gone as far in other countries as in this, from what I know, but if so it is paradoxical that our inheritance should be so dependent on foreigners' interest in and cultivation of it.[7]

It is encouraging how many are present here, and how many we know of, who combine interests in the texts and manuscripts, but sometimes I am depressed when I have to read, even in work on those subjects, passages of what at the best may be only lip-service, though I fear sometimes addiction, to today's gurus and jargons of fashionable literary or historical theory, and where, if there are fresh ideas, they could be stated more simply, while often there is only a maze or morass of verbiage, scholastic in the bad sense. I am appalled to see undergraduates being encouraged to waste their time and minds in the same sorts of pursuit. As a disciple of Leavis I have no patience with substitutes for thoughtful and sensitive response to the words on the page and what they should mean for both medieval and modern audiences. What I deplore is something very different from the pragmatic history of criticism and of critical theory, which Leavis did value and illuminate in his teaching, and which Alastair Minnis has made himself an authority on.

Other unhappy, but older and more excusable tendencies of publications in our field, are, for one, the multiplication of virtually equivalent books and articles on literary texts and themes, and, for another, in manuscript studies the expansion to article length of observations which could have been well fitted into a page or two of *Notes and Queries*, another periodical or even a footnote. My heart sinks whenever I see a good topic spoilt by waste or haste, and I do suspect that manuscripts are thought by some to be an easy game and endless quarry, when the texts themselves have been conspicuously over-handled.

Within the field of religious literature itself there is probably more justification for the proliferation of commentaries on *Piers Plowman* than on most other works, involving as it does exploration, beyond purely vernacular sources, of a peculiarly cryptic and crucial set of texts; the manuscripts themselves have not for long enough begun to be looked at closely and an album of photographs of them is a desideratum. Of other big thirteenth and fourteenth-century English poems the manuscripts of the *South English Legendary* and the *Prick of Conscience* have had exemplary surveys by Manfred Görlach for the one and Angus McIntosh and Bob Lewis for the other, both lacking photographs. I hope the survey of Gower's manuscripts by Jeremy Griffiths, Kate Harris and Derek Pearsall will have a specimen of each hand, like Root's for *Troilus*, and of course we need the same for the *Canterbury Tales*.

Another religious area of flourishing publication is that covered by the oxymoronically-named *Mystics Quarterly*, where the motivation is to a smaller extent purely academic, although a fair amount of what it contains and reports is scholarly. I cannot begrudge the spiritual assistance or psychological fascination which many writers and readers get from repetitive versions and discussions of the *Cloud of Unknowing*, Walter Hilton, and Julian of Norwich, so long as they are not unfaithful to the authors' original meaning and contexts. Hilton's many

---

[7] For other views by two friends see T. A. Birrell, 'English as a foreign literature and the decline of philology', *English Studies*, 70 (1989): 581–6; S. Wenzel, 'Reflections on (new) philology', *Speculum*, 65 (1990): 11–18.

and Julian's few manuscripts have had quite a lot of attention, but Richard Rolle's longer list much less than it calls for, since Hope Emily Allen's monumental study.[8] Many anonymous English and Latin ascetical, devotional and catechetical texts are however benefitting from strongly manuscript-related investigations; sermons too, with the essential European dimension, promoted by the International Medieval Sermon Study Society, its conferences and newsletter. The New Wycliffe Society seems to be dormant, and the mass of Wycliffite material has been engaged by comparatively few minds but those to good effect. A codicological survey of all copies of the Wycliffite biblical translations, the most numerous class of our manuscripts, well on its way to completion, is one of the (one hopes temporary) casualties of the shortage of academic employment available on either side of the Atlantic at the present time. That is a trouble I remarked on in the Retrospect and Prospect to our first conference ten years ago, and if it is not to get worse it does depend partly on you, as I said earlier with regard to school and university courses, not to be content merely to hoe your own furrows or share the produce solely with your fellow-labourers.

---

[6] I was thinking of his Latin works; Sarah Ogilvie-Thomson has done a lot for the English epistles and verses.

MOUVANCE AND THE MEDIEVAL AUTHOR: RE-EDITING *ANCRENE WISSE*

Bella Millett

For some years now I have been working, in collaboration with George Jack of the University of St Andrews, on a project inherited from our former supervisor, Eric Dobson: a critical edition of the Middle English guide for recluses, *Ancrene Wisse*.[1] This work survives in seventeen medieval manuscripts or manuscript fragments, ranging in date from the early thirteenth to the late fifteenth century, and the manuscript versions – which include two separate translations into French and one into Latin – often differ considerably from one another. The labour of editing has been much reduced by the existence of diplomatic or semi-diplomatic editions of most of the English manuscripts, and of the French and Latin translations, published by the Early English Text Society '*in usum editorum philologorumque*';[2] and the only unedited English text, in the Vernon manuscript, is now available in an excellent photographic facsimile.[3] But it could be argued that the very existence of these editions makes a critical edition unnecessary. What is the point of using authentically medieval versions of *Ancrene Wisse* to construct a purely hypothetical text based on editorial assumptions about the author's original intentions? Over the past century, there has been an increasing tendency among writers on textual criticism to challenge the validity of this approach to medieval vernacular works. A long-standing objection has been the difficulty of establishing authorial intentions with any certainty; more recently, and more radically, it has been argued that the aim of reconstructing the 'author's original' is not only hopeless but misconceived, since it is based on a misunderstanding of the nature of the work itself.[4]

---

[1] I have not followed the traditional distinction between the titles *Ancrene Wisse* (for the version in Cambridge, Corpus Christi College, MS 402) and *Ancrene Riwle* (for all other versions); it has no medieval authority (*Ancrene Riwle* is an editorial title) and I share Dobson's view that it is 'arbitrary and misleading' (see E. J. Dobson, *The Origins of 'Ancrene Wisse'* [Oxford, 1976], pp. 51–3).

[2] The phrase is Dobson's, echoing Housman; see E. J. Dobson (ed.), *The English Text of the Ancrene Riwle*, edited from London, British Library, MS Cotton Cleopatra C. vi, EETS OS 267 (London, 1972), p. xix.

[3] *The Vernon Manuscript: A Facsimile of Bodleian Library, Oxford, MS Eng. Poet. a. 1*, introduced by A. I. Doyle (Cambridge, 1987). There is also an uncompleted transcription (Part 1 and the beginning of Part 2) by Kikuo Miyabe (died 1981), 'The Vernon Manuscript of the *Ancrene Riwle*', *Poetica: An International Journal of Linguistic-Literary Studies*, 7 (1979): 80–107; 13 (1982): 1–14. (I am grateful to Roger Dahood for this reference.)

[4] There is a basic historical survey, with further references, in Alfred Foulet and Mary Blakely Speer, *On Editing Old French Texts* (Lawrence, 1979), pp. 1–39, usefully supplemented by Mary Blakely Speer, 'Wrestling with Change: Old French Textual Criticism and *Mouvance*', *Olifant*, 7 (1980): 311–26; and a more searching account, linking developments in textual criticism with the broader intellectual movements of the time, in Bernard Cerquiglini's stylish polemic, *Éloge de la*

The first of these objections was most fully articulated by Joseph Bédier, who from his 1913 edition of *Lai de l'Ombre* onwards maintained that the stemmatic method of textual criticism was too open to unconscious manipulation by the editor, anxious to maintain freedom of judgement by the construction of 'bifid stemmata', to have any scientific reliability. In his view, the best editorial policy for medieval vernacular texts was to concentrate on the existing *formes du texte* rather than trying to reconstruct their hypothetical archetype. The editor should follow the archæologist's maxim, 'Il faut conserver le plus possible, réparer le moins possible, ne restaurer à aucun prix'[5], choosing a good manuscript and editing it from a position of extreme conservatism, 'un énergique vouloir, porté jusqu'au parti pris, d'ouvrir aux scribes le plus large crédit et de ne toucher au texte d'un manuscrit que l'on imprime qu'en cas d'extrême et presque évidente nécessité'.[6] The widespread acceptance of Bédier's views meant that by 1939 Eugène Vinaver felt able (although, as it turned out, prematurely) to announce the death of the critical edition:

> Recent studies in textual criticism mark the end of an age-long tradition. The ingenious technique of editing evolved by the great masters of the nineteenth century has become as obsolete as Newton's physics, and the work of generations of critics has lost a good deal of its value. It is no longer possible to classify manuscripts on the basis of 'common errors'; genealogical 'stemmata' have fallen into discredit, and with them has vanished our faith in composite critical texts.[7]

Picking up and developing Bédier's analogy between textual criticism and archaeology, he argued that the editor should not presume to alter any manuscript readings which were not demonstrably scribal errors:

> Historians of art, who have over textual critics the advantage of dealing with more tangible material, have long realised that to 'restore' does not mean to reconstruct an object in its entirety, but to clear it as far as possible of adventitious and foreign matter. A textual critic . . . should approach his task in much the same spirit as if he were an archæologist anxious to preserve every shade of colour that can possibly be authentic in a dilapidated mural painting, every detail of the sculptor's design in a broken statue, every stone in a battered building that may conceivably belong to the original structure.[8]

---

variante: Histoire critique de la philologie (Paris, 1989). On the implications of these developments for other areas of medieval literature, see A. G. Rigg (ed.), *Editing Medieval Texts, English, French, and Latin, Written in England* (New York and London, 1977), and the papers by Lee Patterson, 'The Logic of Textual Criticism and the Way of Genius: The Kane-Donaldson *Piers Plowman* in Historical Perspective', and Derek Pearsall, 'Editing Medieval Texts: Some Developments and Some Problems', in Jerome J. McGann (ed.), *Textual Criticism and Literary Interpretation* (Chicago and London, 1985), pp. 55–91, 92–106.

[5] Joseph Bédier (ed.), *Le Lai de l'Ombre par Jean Renart*, SATF (Paris, 1913), p. xlv.

[6] Joseph Bédier,'La Tradition manuscrite du *Lai de l'Ombre*: réflexions sur l'art d'éditer les anciens textes', *Romania*, 54 (1928): 356.

[7] Eugène Vinaver, 'Principles of Textual Emendation', in *Studies in French Language and Mediæval Literature presented to Professor Mildred K. Pope* (Manchester, 1939), p. 351.

[8] Vinaver, 'Principles of Textual Emendation', p. 367.

There is no doubt that in practice the construction of stemmata for medieval texts depends heavily on the editor's judgement of what constitutes a 'shared error'; that Dobson's stemma for *Ancrene Wisse*,[9] while I have found no reason to challenge it for those parts of the text I have edited,[10] is (as Eric Stanley pointed out[11]) an example of the 'bifid stemmata' which Bédier distrusted; and that, even if Dobson's stemma is sound, the nature of the manuscript transmission of *Ancrene Wisse* means that it cannot necessarily be relied on to establish the text. As Dobson himself emphasised, the textual tradition of *Ancrene Wisse* is complicated by frequent cross-collation of manuscripts, and by revisions and additions either entered in the manuscripts themselves or separately circulated: 'one can plot the main lines of descent and the normal affiliations, but one can certainly not predict the behaviour even of closely related manuscripts'.[12] For all these reasons, any critical text of *Ancrene Wisse* must inevitably be based to a large extent on the exercise of editorial judgement, which Bédier dismissed as no more, ultimately, than a matter of personal taste – 'la chose la plus faillible du monde et la plus précaire'.[13] Would it be more prudent, as Bédier recommends, to limit oneself to the conservative editing of a particular scribal version, accepting the scribe's reading wherever possible? George Rigg has warned us of the need for a proper editorial modesty: 'A scribe of 1250 surely knew more about a text written in 1200 than I do'.[14] The point is worth making; but much depends on both the difficulty of the text and the ability of the scribe. In the case of the Pepys manuscript of *Ancrene Wisse* (to take an extreme example) the scribe's invention of a brand-new Biblical character, Fatt, reflects not only his habitually high tolerance for nonsensical readings but an ignorance both of Scripture and of the earlier stages of his own language (the name comes from a misunderstanding of the obsolescent *rechels-fatt*, 'censer') which would not be shared by a competent modern editor.[15] And editorial emendation based on probabilities rather than certainties is not necessarily an act of cultural vandalism. The Bédierist analogy between archaeology and textual criticism is misleading; the textual critic emending a text is not in quite the same position as an archaeologist restoring an artefact. If you are restoring a work of art which is

---

[9] See E. J. Dobson, 'The Affiliations of the Manuscripts of *Ancrene Wisse*', in *English and Medieval Studies Presented to J. R. R. Tolkien*, ed. Norman Davis and C. L. Wrenn (London, 1962), pp. 128–63, and his later discussion in *The Origins of Ancrene Wisse* (Oxford, 1976), pp. 286–311, which includes a revised and simplified version of his original stemma (p. 287).

[10] Parts 5, 7, and 8 (only the third of which was used by Dobson in his trial collation).

[11] See E. G. Stanley, review of *English and Medieval Studies presented to J. R. R. Tolkien*, ed. Davis and Wrenn, in *Archiv*, 201 (1965): 130–1.

[12] Dobson, 'The Affiliations of the Manuscripts of *Ancrene Wisse*', p. 148.

[13] Bédier (ed.), *Lai de l'Ombre*, p. xliv.

[14] 'Medieval Latin', in Rigg (ed.), *Editing Medieval Texts*, p. 121.

[15] See A. Zettersten (ed.), *The English Text of the Ancrene Riwle*, edited from Cambridge, Magdalene College, MS Pepys 2498, EETS OS 274 (London, 1976), p. 144. The problem here is not caused by the chronological gap between the composition of *Ancrene Wisse* and the date of the MS (late fourteenth century); the passage the scribe is misunderstanding is not part of the original text, and was probably added by a late-fourteenth-century reviser (see Eric Colledge, '*The Recluse*: A Lollard Interpolated Version of the *Ancren Riwle*', *RES* 15 [1939]: 1–15, 129–45). For a defence of editorial vs. scribal expertise, see George Kane, 'Conjectural Emendation' (1969), rpt. in Christopher Kleinhenz (ed.), *Medieval Manuscripts and Textual Criticism* (Chapel Hill, N. Carolina, 1976), p. 220.

also a unique physical object (like the ceiling of the Sistine Chapel, to take a recent and controversial example), then any modification you make runs the risk of damaging or destroying the work itself (are you removing a layer of grime, or Michelangelo's original shading?). Critical editions, on the other hand, leave their material intact; rather than destroying the evidence, they simply add to the series of *formes du texte* already in existence. The chronological and cultural gap between modern editor and medieval author may mean that it is difficult to reconstruct authorial intentions, but there seems no reason why we should not make the attempt, as long as we regard the reconstructed text as (in Mary Speer's words) 'not . . . a historical certainty, but an editorial hypothesis open to revision'.[16]

Over the last twenty years, however, a more radical objection has been raised to the critical edition: that in trying to produce a single definitive text it misunderstands an important characteristic of much medieval literature, what Paul Zumthor, in his *Essai de poétique médiévale* of 1972, christened *mouvance* – its essential textual instability or fluidity. Developing further ideas already present in Bédier's work,[17] Zumthor argued that for many medieval works, particularly in the vernacular, a critical edition was inappropriate, since any attempt to reconstruct 'une source prototypique' failed to take into account the way the work was seen in its own time.[18] He noted that the transmission of medieval works often involved extensive textual variation, and that this suggested a rather different concept of the nature of the work, not as a single, completed entity but as something more fluid and open-ended, constantly adapted as it travelled through space and time. Zumthor defined the medieval work in this sense as something dynamic rather than static: the *oeuvre* is the collectivity of its different manifestations, its successive *états du texte*. 'Dans une grande mesure, pour le philologue moderne, l'édition critique d'un texte médiéval est une hypothèse de travail, rendue nécessaire par la différence des cultures qui nous interdit de percevoir le texte de la manière dont il le fut de son temps'.[19] More recently Bernard Cerquiglini, in his *Éloge de la variante* (1989), has similarly criticised the editors of medieval vernacular works for treating them as if they were texts in the modern sense, fixed at the point of publication and remaining the intellectual property of the author, rather than acknowledging their 'variance essentielle': 'L'oeuvre littéraire, au Moyen Age, est une variable . . . Qu'une main fut première, parfois, sans doute, importe moins que cette incessante récriture d'une oeuvre qui appartient à celui qui, de nouveau, la dispose et lui donne forme'.[20] Editors have been preoccupied with the loss of 'une authenticité perdue', the hypothetical perfection of the completed work as it left the author's hands, rather than coming to terms with the 'authenticité

---

[16] Mary Speer, 'Wrestling with Change', p. 312.

[17] See Bédier, 'La Tradition manuscrite du *Lai de l'Ombre*', pp. 353–5, on the special conditions of transmission of Old French literary works, and on the possibility of both authorial and scribal revision leading to distinct ''états' du texte', almost equally 'cohérentes et harmonieuses' and requiring separate editing.

[18] Paul Zumthor, *Essai de poétique médiévale* (Paris, 1972), p. 70.

[19] Zumthor, *Essai de poétique médiévale*, p. 72.

[20] Cerquiglini, *Éloge de la variante*, p. 57.

généralisée' of medieval vernacular works which might be revised and rewritten indefinitely, both by their original authors and by others.

The problem of *mouvance* needs to be taken seriously by any editor contemplating a critical edition of *Ancrene Wisse*. Both Zumthor and Cerquiglini are mainly concerned in their discussions with the Old French literature of entertainment – *chansons de geste*, romances, lyrics, and fabliaux – and not everything they say applies to *Ancrene Wisse*, which is a very different type of work. But there is no doubt that the textual history of *Ancrene Wisse* also reflects, in its own way, the effects of *mouvance*. The editor is not dealing with a single, static original increasingly corrupted by mechanical scribal errors (although these errors certainly occur); *Ancrene Wisse* was continuously and deliberately reworked, over a period of nearly three centuries, by a succession of adaptors, translators, and what Derek Pearsall has called 'participatory scribes'. Its Middle English was modified and modernized as it travelled through space and time, and it was translated into two other languages; it was abridged or expanded; its content was adapted, sometimes quite radically, for different audiences; and even its basic structure changed, as sections were dropped, extracted for separate use, or incorporated into other works altogether. As Ian Doyle concluded in his study of its dissemination, '[the] social changes of ownership and the geographical movement of copies and versions of the *Riwle*, as well as the adaptations of it, throughout its history, between one sex and the other, one class and another, one region and another, and back again, manifest its exceptionally dynamic character'.[21]

The key to the textual instability of *Ancrene Wisse* lies in its functionality. In spite of its high literary quality, it is essentially a work of practical religious instruction; and two factors, its genre and its intended audience, combined from the beginning to give it a built-in potential for *mouvance*, both in the short term and over a longer period.

The short-term instability is implicit in the first and final sections of the work, the 'Outer Rule' of daily prayers and observances. As the author himself points out in the final section, Part 8, these provisions do not constitute a Rule which all recluses are expected to follow; they are simply guidelines, which may be modified according to individual needs and circumstances.[22] The 'Outer Rule' is concerned not with matters of principle but with the everyday routine of its users; and its closest resemblances are with the customaries of the new religious orders of the period, the manuals of detailed regulations designed to supplement the more general Rule followed by the order.[23] Dobson has pointed out that *Ancrene Wisse* shows the influence of one of these customaries, the statutes of the Premonstratensian canons, both in its overall structure and in some direct

---

[21] A. I. Doyle, 'A Survey of the origins and circulation of theological writings in English in the fourteenth, fifteenth and early sixteenth centuries with special consideration of the part of the clergy therein' (Cambridge Ph.D. dissertation 2301–2302, 1954), i.234.

[22] Cambridge, Corpus Christi College, MS 402, fol.111r/11–20 in J. R. R. Tolkien (ed.), *The English Text of the Ancrene Riwle: Ancrene Wisse*, edited from Cambridge, Corpus Christi College, MS 402, EETS OS 249 (London, 1962), p. 210.

[23] On the development of the distinction between Rules and customaries from the mid eleventh century onwards, see *Guigues Iᵉʳ, Prieur de Chartreuse: Coutumes de Chartreuse*, ed. par un Chartreux, Sources Chrétiennes 313 (Paris, 1984), pp. 17–21.

verbal borrowings.[24] Customaries were by their nature *oeuvres mouvantes*, in a state of continuous textual evolution; the Premonstratensian statutes are a case in point. Between the 1130s and the 1230s they went through three major codifications, and there are a number of secondary versions surviving, which include interim revisions and additions.[25] The 'customary' element in *Ancrene Wisse* seems to have followed a similar pattern of development, affecting particularly the detailed regulations for the recluses' daily life in Part 8; there is a partial revision in the Cleopatra manuscript of *Ancrene Wisse* by a slightly later hand, that of Dobson's 'Scribe B',[26] and a more thorough and systematic overhaul in the revised version of the work which lies behind the Corpus manuscript.

The central part of *Ancrene Wisse*, the 'Inner Rule' which governs the heart rather than the daily life, might reasonably be expected to be more resistant to alteration. The author emphasises that this, unlike the Outer Rule, is permanent and stable; it applies to everyone, and its provisions do not change.[27] But here too there is a built-in potential for textual instability, and one which increases in the long term. It lies in the gap between the very specific audience for whom *Ancrene Wisse* was originally composed – three well-born sisters, laywomen who had renounced the world to become recluses – and the much wider audience which would be capable of benefiting from its spiritual content. It is this adaptability which guaranteed both the extended life of *Ancrene Wisse* and its long-term textual instability, as it was continuously modified to suit new and different audiences. At an early stage it was adapted for a larger group of recluses; and it was later reworked for nuns, for male religious, for a mixed general audience including both religious and laity, and for a lay audience.

There is evidence, too, that the author of *Ancrene Wisse* accepted both the short-term and the long-term instability of his work, and that he actively collaborated in the process of textual change. It is clear from the internal evidence of the text that from the very beginning he expected his work to be used by more people than the three sisters who had requested it (one reason for this may have been, as the evidence is beginning to suggest, that he was a Dominican friar and so professionally concerned with the spiritual instruction of a variety of audiences[28]). He refers to other recluses who might use it, and the long section on confession is written not just for recluses but for a general audience, 'alle men iliche'.[29] When the numbers of its original audience of recluses increased, and their circumstances changed, he seems to have been prepared to modify his text, particularly but not only the more provisional 'Outer Rule', to suit the new

---

[24] Dobson, *The Origins of 'Ancrene Wisse'*, p. 109; see also the following note.

[25] See A. H. Thomas, 'Une version des statuts de Prémontré au début du xiiie siècle', *Analecta Praemonstratensia*, 55 (1979): 153–70; this article, describing a version of the statutes identified in 1977 in Glasgow, Mitchell Library, MS 308892, confirms Dobson's hypothesis that *Ancrene Wisse* was influenced by a version of the statutes intermediate between the second and third codification.

[26] See Dobson (ed.), *The English Text of the Ancrene Wisse* (Cleopatra MS), pp. ix–xi.

[27] Cambridge, Corpus Christi College, MS 402, fols. 1v/12–2r/20 in Tolkien (ed.), *The English Text of the Ancrene Riwle: Ancrene Wisse*, pp. 7–8.

[28] See Bella Millett, 'The Origins of *Ancrene Wisse*: New Answers, New Questions', *Medium Ævum*, 61 (1992): 206–28.

[29] See Bella Millett, 'The Audience of the Saints' Lives of the Katherine Group', *Reading Medieval Studies*, 16 (1990): 139–42.

situation; both the 'Scribe B' revisions in the Cleopatra manuscript and the more comprehensive revisions behind the Corpus manuscript are probably authorial,[30] as are some other revisions entered in the manuscripts in the early stages of textual transmission.[31] Dobson's analysis of the 'Scribe B' alterations in the Cleopatra manuscript shows that while the author was clearly unhappy with the 'negligence and rape' of the Cleopatra scribe, correcting even minor details of punctuation and spelling, his corrections are essentially pragmatic, 'often designed to restore the sense (or occasionally an acceptable sense that varies from the original sense), not the original wording; sometimes indeed the principle governing his correction seems to be to restore sense by the slightest change possible.'[32] He does not correct the Cleopatra text systematically from an earlier and better manuscript but works freehand, revising as well as correcting; he seems less concerned with the textual integrity of his work than with its functionality at that particular point in time, how far it is intelligible to the reader and fits the needs of its current audience.

Ancrene Wisse, then, seems to have undergone a process of continuous adaptation and evolution, begun by the author himself and carried on by his successors; and the critical editor has to find some way of handling this problem. The usual method of critical editors confronted with a work that survives in more than one version is to select one particular version, and edit that; but in the case of *Ancrene Wisse*, on what grounds should the version be selected?

Dobson chose, as the basis for his critical edition, the revised version of *Ancrene Wisse* found in the Corpus manuscript, and in many ways it would be hard to dissent from his judgement. Among the *Ancrene Wisse* manuscripts, it is in a class of its own. It fits admirably Kane and Donaldson's definition of 'the ideal basic manuscript or copy-text' as 'the one which first provides the closest dialectal and chronological approximation to the [author's] language, and then second, most accurately reflects his original in substantive readings.'[33] Its dialect is close to that of the 'Scribe B' annotations in the Cleopatra manuscript, which may be in the author's own hand.[34] While it is not without faults – the scribe has a tendency to omissions caused by eyeskip, and occasionally he seems to have fits of distraction, leading to small clusters of errors – it offers on the whole an exceptionally good text, requiring very little emendation; and since it seems to go back to an annotated form of the author's original draft,[35] for much of the time it is our most reliable witness not only for the revised version but for the original text as well.

However, the choice of the Corpus version as the basis for a critical edition still involves some problems. Dobson believed that the Corpus manuscript, as 'a close copy of the author's own final and definitive revision of his work',[36] had a particular authority. But this does not necessarily follow; it may have been by

---

[30] See Dobson (ed.), *The English Text of the Ancrene Riwle* (Cleopatra MS), pp. xciii–cxxv.

[31] See footnote 49 below; and Dobson, *Origins of 'Ancrene Wisse'*, pp. 259–71.

[32] Dobson (ed.), *The English Text of the Ancrene Wisse* (Cleopatra MS), p. xcvii.

[33] George Kane and E. Talbot Donaldson (eds.), *Piers Plowman: The B Version* (London, 1975), p. 214.

[34] See Dobson (ed.), *The English Text of the Ancrene Wisse* (Cleopatra MS), pp. cxxvi–cxl.

[35] See note 10 above.

[36] Dobson, 'The Affiliations of the Manuscripts of *Ancrene Wisse*', p. 163.

chance rather than design that the author's revisions in the Corpus version were 'final', and they seem to have been 'definitive' only in a limited sense. The textual tradition of *Ancrene Wisse* has much in common with that of the monastic customaries on which it draws. For these works, continuous textual evolution is the norm. The early development of the Premonstratensian statutes, which is relatively well-documented, shows a recurring pattern, which in theory could continue indefinitely: each codification is followed by a series of intermediate versions, with piecemeal amendments which eventually accumulate to the point where a further codification becomes necessary. In this cycle, each codification is equally 'definitive' in its turn; but its authority is only temporary. It is probable that the author of *Ancrene Wisse* saw his own work in the same way; in the Corpus revision of Part 8, he not only retains but reiterates his original emphasis on the provisional quality of the 'Outer Rule',[37] and we cannot assume that the finality of the alterations in the Corpus version was anything more than a historical accident. There is one significant respect, however, in which the textual tradition of *Ancrene Wisse* differs from that of the monastic customaries. The Premonstratensians, with their tight central organization, were able to ensure that new codifications superseded old ones; but it looks as if the author of *Ancrene Wisse*, whose recluses were not organized within a formal institutional structure, was not in a position to do this. While the revised version behind Corpus is occasionally reflected in later manuscripts, the Corpus manuscript is its only surviving full-length representative; all other versions are descended from the original work. The Corpus version appears to have remained peripheral to the mainstream textual tradition, and so to have been in practice, if not in intention, less 'definitive' than the original version.

There is also the problem that the coherence in structure and content that one might expect from the 'final and definitive' version of a work is lacking in the Corpus revision. If we are to identify evidence for what what Derek Pearsall calls a 'definitive textual moment'[38] in the textual tradition of *Ancrene Wisse*, we have to look further back, to the author's valedictory words in the original version of Part 8, where he tells his audience of recluses that they had better make good use of his work, since he has spent so much time on it; 'Me were leouere, Godd hit wite, do me toward Rome þen for te biginnen hit eft for te donne.'[39] The nature of his later revisions suggests that he meant what he said. His characteristic method of revising seems to have been by piecemeal and rather unsystematic alterations, either entered in the manuscripts themselves or (in the case of longer additions) circulated on separate sheets, and the version underlying the Corpus manuscript, although it represents a more thorough

---

[37] See Cambridge, Corpus Christi College, MS 402, fols. 111r/11–20 (retained from the original version) and 115r/15–21 (first added by 'Scribe B' in the Cleopatra manuscript (see Dobson [ed.], *The English Text of the Ancrene Riwle* [Cleopatra MS], pp. 308–9), then incorporated with minor modifications in the Corpus version), Tolkien (ed.), *The English Text of the Ancrene Riwle: Ancrene Wisse*, pp. 210, 217-8.

[38] Pearsall, 'Editing Medieval Texts', p. 100.

[39] Cambridge, Corpus Christi College, MS 402, fol. 117v/3-4, Tolkien (ed.), *The English Text of the Ancrene Riwle: Ancrene Wisse*, p. 221; also found, with minor variants, in the Cleopatra, Nero, and Titus manuscripts, and in the two French translations.

overhaul of his work, seems to have used the same method.[40] One result of this is that the Corpus version is sometimes rather *less* satisfactory in sense and style than the original version; inconsistencies between the original text and the revisions are not always removed, and sometimes the alterations distort the syntax or (if they are substantial) push a whole argument out of shape.[41] Another is that the Corpus version remains textually multi-layered; in some places it has to be read not as a single, unified utterance but as a dialogue. This comes out most clearly in the most heavily revised part, the instructions to the recluses in Part 8. J. A. W. Bennett's reading of Part 8 in *Middle English Literature* (1986) illustrates the problems of treating it as a unified piece of writing. Bennett, basing his reading on the Corpus version but making no distinction between the earlier and later strata of the text, sees it as a revelation of the author's character: 'He is rich in reasonableness and saving common sense, never niggling over details.'[42] But some of the passages he cites as evidence for this – like the author's statement that he would rather his recluses bore a hard word patiently than a hard hair-shirt, and his warning that dirt was never pleasing to God – were only added in the Corpus version;[43] and the overall pattern of the revisions in this part suggests that Bennett's 'flat' reading is an oversimplification. The general tendency of the Part 8 revisions is to temper the asceticism recommended in the original version;[44] this means that a number of passages which may seem at first sight to demonstrate the author's 'reasonableness and saving common sense' are in fact qualifications of the greater austerity of his original advice. And while the change of emphasis between the two versions may reflect a mellowing in the author's spiritual outlook (in which case Bennett's judgement would be justified at any rate for the Corpus version), the nature of the revisions suggests that it was at least partly determined by external factors – the excessive austerities practised by some over-enthusiastic recluses and the changed circumstances of a larger community. If we are to make full sense of the Corpus version of Part 8, we need to read it in terms of its textual history, as a modification of an existing text rather than as a self-contained literary unity.

For all these reasons, a critical edition of the Corpus version of *Ancrene Wisse*, whatever its practical advantages for the editor, cannot on its own offer a 'definitive' text of the work, or even (since the other surviving Middle English

[40] See Dobson, 'The Affiliations of the Manuscripts of *Ancrene Wisse*', pp. 152–63.

[41] For an example of surviving inconsistency, see Cambridge, Corpus Christi College, MS 402, fol. 31v/15–16 (an undeleted reference to the original three sisters); and of syntactical clumsiness, the additions in the sentence on haircutting and bloodletting, fols. 114v/26–115r/2 (themselves a tidying-up of a still more unwieldy 'Scribe B' alteration to the Cleopatra manuscript, fol. 195r/2–4, *The English Text of the Ancrene Riwle* [Cleopatra MS], ed. Dobson, p. 310). Cases of lopsided argument include the deletion after *blisse*, Corpus fol. 51v/1, of a passage on the circumstances of the original three sisters (which takes with it the author's discussion of 'soft' as opposed to 'hard' exterior temptations) and the addition on family visits, Corpus fols. 114r/22–114v/2. See Tolkien (ed.), *The English Text of the Ancrene Riwle: Ancrene Wisse*, pp. 62, 217, 99, 216.

[42] J. A. W. Bennett, *Middle English Literature*, ed. and completed by Douglas Gray, The Oxford History of English Literature, 1.2 (Oxford, 1986), pp. 270–1.

[43] Cambridge, Corpus Christi College, MS 402, fols. 113v/17–18 ('ah eauer . . . here'), 115r/13–15 ('ant ower . . . licwurðe'), Tolkien (ed.), *The English Text of the Ancrene Riwle: Ancrene Wisse*, pp. 214–5, 217.

[44] For a brief overview of these revisions, see Bella Millett and Jocelyn Wogan-Browne (eds.), *Medieval English Prose for Women* (Oxford, 1990), p. xxxiv.

versions belong to a different branch of the textual tradition) a genuinely representative one. If the reader is to understand the Corpus version fully, or see clearly how it relates to other versions of *Ancrene Wisse*, the edited text needs to be placed within the broader context of the overall development of the work. The availability of editions of all the surviving *états du texte* of *Ancrene Wisse* goes some way towards dealing with this problem, but does not solve it completely. Editions of individual manuscript versions are, as Cerquiglini complains, 'seulement des instantanés',[45] snapshots freezing a single point of textual development rather than representing the process of that development. The editor has also to find some way to represent *mouvance*, indicating the relationships between the different *états du texte*.

I had originally intended to use the *apparatus criticus* for this purpose, particularly since the existence of diplomatic editions of the manuscripts meant that it could be highly selective in the variants cited; but there are both theoretical and practical objections to using an *apparatus criticus* in this way. Cerquiglini, developing a view already found in Bédier,[46] has argued forcefully that the *apparatus criticus* misrepresents the nature of variation in the medieval work; metaphorically as well as literally, it marginalises textual variants, giving a misleading centrality to the version of the text selected for editing by relegating deliberate variations and scribal errors alike to the confined space – somewhere between rubbish-tip and dungeon – at the foot of the page. It is also an inefficient means of handling variation over more extended grammatical units than the word or phrase; if a sentence in a particular manuscript, for instance, contains two separate but related variants from the edited text which together significantly alter its meaning, the variants will normally be extracted from the sentence, separately entered in the *apparatus criticus*, and probably distanced still further from each other by unrelated variants from other manuscripts, so that it is impossible for the reader to pick up their significance at a glance.[47]

What the alternative method should be, however, is not an easy question to answer. Cerquiglini's view is that no printed edition can offer an adequate reflection of the way in which the variant versions of a medieval work are related to each other; he concludes that the solution lies in information technology. If we exploit the possibilities offered by hypertext software, the computer screen, 'dialogique et multidimensionnel', can be used to present multiple versions of a text simultaneously, while at the same time allowing the reader to trace the links between the different versions. 'Dans l'espace illimité que la technologie offre aujourd'hui à l'inscription, il convient de suspendre la constellation changeante de l'écrit médiévale . . .'.[48]

But editions of this kind require more resources, human, technological, and financial, than any editor of *Ancrene Wisse* is likely to command; and if the

---

[45] Cerquiglini, *Éloge de la variante*, p. 101.
[46] See note 50 below.
[47] Cerquiglini, *Éloge de la variante*, pp. 105–116 (see also Millett, review of *The Pilgrimage of the Life of the Manhode*, ed. Avril Henry, *Medium Ævum*, 57 [1988]: 314–5).
[48] Cerquiglini, *Éloge de la variante*, p. 114. For an example of the hypertext edition in practice, see Patrick W. Conner, 'The *Beowulf* Workstation: One Model of Computer-Assisted Literary Pedagogy', *Literary and Linguistic Computing*, 6 (1991): 50–8 (I am grateful to the Oxford University Computing Centre for introducing me to this edition).

problem of *mouvance* is to be handled with old technology rather than new, we have to begin by limiting the amount of material to be dealt with. Since there is already a full record of the textual development of *Ancrene Wisse* – or, at any rate, the raw materials for that record – accessible in the printed texts of the different versions, it is not essential to incorporate all this information in the critical edition. There is a good case, however, for incorporating as a separate body of material, and in a form full enough to be easily intelligible, all those early variants which are possibly or probably authorial,[49] rather than leaving them (as Bédier puts it in a memorably repulsive image) 'bizarre, shapeless, and deformed . . . swarming like maggots in the depths of an *apparatus criticus*'.[50] It could be objected that this concentration on authorial variants in itself works against the nature of the medieval text; there has been an increasing tendency in twentieth-century writings on textual criticism to shift textual authority away from the author, either reassessing or (for certain types of text) denying altogether the significance of the distinction between the original authors and their successors in the line of transmission. But the fact remains that even the *oeuvre mouvante*, as Zumthor says, must ultimately lose its initial coherence and disintegrate under the the the pressures of time and transmission:

> Le texte est le produit d'une opération d'encodage, pratiquée à partir de l'intégrité structurelle et culturelle d'un état de langue. Un élément intentionnel y a été introduit, qui a pour fonction d'orienter le décodage: mais rien ne résiste plus mal à la durée que cet effet. Dans le meilleur des cas, les décodages successifs actualisent les potentialités toujours nouvelles du texte. Mais nous retrouvons ici le facteur temps: la capacité d'étirement du texte a des limites, au-delà desquelles tout craque, et il n'y a plus de communication possible.[51]

This kind of disintegration can be seen in the late-fourteenth-century Pepys manuscript of *Ancrene Wisse*, where Lollard interpolations praising the active rather than the contemplative life pull against the argument of the original, and cumulative scribal errors have made the text at some points unintelligible.[52] *Mouvance* must be, sooner or later, also a process of deterioration; and the greater the learning and literary skill of the original author, the earlier and steeper the decline is likely to be. While the later versions of *Ancrene Wisse* have considerable interest of their own, it makes sense with limited resources to concentrate on the development of the text in the author's own lifetime, over the period when it was still held together, to a greater or lesser extent, by its original *élément intentionnel*. How far the complexities of this development can be

---

[49] On this class of variants and the case for their common authorship, see E. J. Dobson, 'The Date and Composition of *Ancrene Wisse*' (1966), rpt. in J. A. Burrow (ed.), *Middle English Literature: British Academy Gollancz Lectures* (Oxford, 1989), pp. 106–115.

[50] Bédier is discussing the possibility of authorial variants: 'Les variantes de nos anciens textes! Pauvres choses bizarre, informes, difformes, quant on les regarde grouiller comme des larves au fond d'un appareil critique, mais qui, si souvent, prennent du sens et du charme à l'instant où on les replace dans leur contexte, à l'instant où, de variantes, elles redeviennent leçons'. 'La Tradition manuscrite du *Lai de l'Ombre*', p. 353.

[51] Zumthor, *Essai de poétique médiévale*, p. 11.

[52] See Colledge, '*The Recluse*', note 15 above.

presented in an immediately intelligible way remains to be seen – the combination of typographical variation and footnotes used by some editors of monastic customaries provides a possible model.[53] But there is no doubt that one of the main tasks facing an editor of *Ancrene Wisse* is to find a way of representing its 'dynamic character' on the printed page.

---

[53] E.g. the edition of the early Dominican constitutions in *De oudste Constituties van de Dominicanen: voorgeschiedenis, tekst, bronnen, ontstaan en ontwikkeling (1215-37)*, ed. A. H. Thomas, Bibliothèque de la Revue d'Histoire Ecclésiastique, 42 (Louvain, 1965).

THE OUTSPOKEN *SOUTH ENGLISH LEGENDARY* POET

O. S. Pickering

I

Widespread evidence of textual revision has always been one of the fascinating aspects of the late thirteenth-century *South English Legendary (SEL)* collection. It is a feature of many individual poems of both *sanctorale* and *temporale* – broadly, lives of saints and lives of Christ – and holds the key to understanding the relationships between them. The multiplicity of extant manuscripts, preserving poems in different stages of development, provides ample raw material for detailed study of the phenomenon. The rewriting of existing verse is at times so striking that it is clear that a poet other than the original author was responsible. The mixture of styles within the *SEL* corpus suggests in any case that more than one writer was active.

Work on the collection was transformed in 1974 by the publication of Manfred Görlach's *The Textual Tradition of the South English Legendary*,[1] in which he pointed to unambiguous evidence of revision in some twenty saints' lives, and posited a general development from what he called the 'Z' version, compiled in Worcestershire possibly in the 1270s, to the 'A' version, compiled in Gloucestershire possibly in the 1280s.[2] It has subsequently become clearer (as Professor Görlach always acknowledged was likely) that the development into 'A' was the result of more than one rewriting.[3] The task of disentangling the contribution of different poets is, however, immense, because of the scores of manuscripts and thousands of lines of verse involved. It might also not be thought worth it, given the pedestrian nature of much of the *SEL*, were it not for evidence, throughout the collection, of the presence of a more than usually competent writer.

Recent work on the *temporale* narratives has demonstrated the following relationships between the major poems of this group:

---

[1] Leeds Texts and Monographs, n.s. 6 (Leeds, 1974).

[2] The 'A' version is broadly represented by Charlotte D'Evelyn and Anna J. Mill (eds.), *The South English Legendary*, 3 vols, EETS 235, 236, 244 (London, 1956-59), which prints the text from Cambridge, Corpus Christi College, MS 145 and London, British Library, MS Harley 2277. Carl Horstmann (ed.), *The Early South-English Legendary*, EETS OS 87 (London, 1887), is an edition of the earliest *SEL* manuscript, Oxford, Bodleian Library, MS Laud 108, which partially preserves 'Z' texts.

[3] See O. S. Pickering, 'The Expository *Temporale* Poems of the *South English Legendary*', *Leeds Studies in English*, n.s. 10 (1978): 1-17, and Thomas R. Liszka, 'The First "A" Redaction of the *South English Legendary*: Information from the "Prologue"', *Modern Philology*, 82 (1985): 407-13.

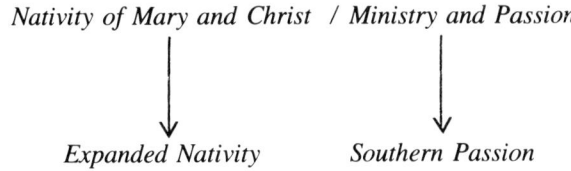

Nativity of Mary and Christ / Ministry and Passion

Expanded Nativity   *Southern Passion*

It is likely that the *Ministry and Passion* (*MP*) was written as a sequel to the *Nativity of Mary and Christ* (*NMC*), but the latter circulated independently, and the two poems were revised separately into the *Expanded Nativity* (*EN*) and the *Southern Passion* (*SP*).[4] *NMC* and *MP*, at least, were almost certainly written to stand outside the *SEL* cycle, and were perhaps composed independently of it. *SP*, in contrast, was probably written to fill a place within the *SEL*, and it became the standard Passion poem of the collection.

It seems certain that the same writer was responsible for both *EN* and *SP*. The two poems are, in content, closer to the gospels than are *NMC* and *MP*, and the reviser achieves this both by fresh gospel translation and by cleverly adapting lines and phrases from the earlier compositions for his own purposes.[5] *EN* and *SP* also have in common instances where the poet speaks in a more personal voice with considerable intensity, seemingly because his feelings are strongly engaged. Two examples from each poem may be given here. The first of those from *EN* asks how it was that the ox and ass knelt down before the Christ child, and then answers its own question:

> Now was þis a wonder dede . and aȝe kunde inow;
> Vor wel ichot þat oxen kunne . bet now drawe ate plow,
> And asses bere sackes . and corn aboute to bringe,
> Þan to make meri gleo . and knele bi fore a kinge . . .
> How couþen heo here legges bowen . & here knen so to wende,
> To knele bifore a king? . who made hem so hende?
> Now weren hit wonder gleomen to, . who brouȝte hem such mod?
> Ac whan we habbeþ al ido, . þat child ibore was god.
> (*EN* 331–34, 337–40)

The second example from *EN* is from slightly further on in the poem, where the writer strongly criticises those who maintain that St Anastasia could have been present at the birth of Christ:

> Þe lesinge of mani foles . telleþ of seint anastase,
> Þat heo scholde wiþ oure ledi beo; . hit nis bote þe mase:

[4] For editions of *NMC* and *MP*, see O. S. Pickering (ed.), *The South English Nativity of Mary and Christ*, Middle English Texts, 1 (Heidelberg, 1975), and *The South English Ministry and Passion*, Middle English Texts, 16 (Heidelberg, 1984). For *SP*, see B. D. Brown (ed.), *The Southern Passion*, EETS 169 (London, 1927), and for *EN*, Carl Horstmann (ed.), *Altenglische Legenden* (Paderborn, 1875), pp. 81–109, from which editions I quote. For general information, see O. S. Pickering, 'The *Temporale* Narratives of the *South English Legendary*', *Anglia*, 91 (1973): 425–55.
[5] See O. S. Pickering, 'Three *South English Legendary* Nativity Poems', *Leeds Studies in English*, n.s. 8 (1975): 105–19, and 'The *Southern Passion* and the *Ministry and Passion*: The Work of a Middle English Reviser', *Leeds Studies in English*, n.s. 15 (1984): 33–56.

Vor heo ne seiȝ neuer oure ledi her, . vor to hundred ȝer bifore
And more, ar heo come an erþe . oure lord was ibore.
Som wrecche bifond þis lesinge . wiþ onriȝte,
Vor as muche as me makeþ of hire munde . a midewinter niȝte.

                                                        (*EN* 355–60)

In the first example from *SP* the writer contrasts Judas's plain dealing with the Jews with the over-pricing practised by medieval merchants, but still concludes bitterly that he was a *luþer chapman*:

Goed chep þe shrewe him grauntede . þat him so solde;
He ne axede nouȝt a ferþing more . þan þe gywes him tolde.
He ne lowede him nouȝt to deore . as þis chapmen wolleþ echon
Þing þat is dreoreworþ . ak he axede ham anon
'What wolleþ ȝe for him ȝiue' . as who seiþ 'beode ȝe
And as goed chep ich wolle him ȝiue . as ȝe wolleþ bydde me'.
Now luþer þrift vp-on his heued . Amen seggeþ alle,
For luþer chapman he was . and al-so him is byfalle.

                                                        (*SP* 779–86)

The second example is from the end of *SP*'s outspoken defence of women from slanderous attack; 146 lines long in the complete version, it occurs immediately after Christ's post-resurrection appearance to Mary Magdalene, Mary being taken as a model of love and faithfulness:[6]

And whanne we habbeþ alle isede, God ȝeue hem alle chame
Þat withoute enchesoun seyþ wommen eny blame.
For more myldehede ne goodnesse in non erþelyche beste nys,
Ne more mylce ne treunesse þan in good womm[a]n is.
Ȝe seiþ Mary Magdalene oure lord ȝhe souȝt alone
Þo þe apostlis þat wit hym were lete hym lygge echone.
Wheyþer was here a [pert]ere loue? Seggeþ þat ȝe ne lyȝe!
Was þer eny stabelere þan [was] þis holy Marye?   (*SP* 1983–90)

In these extracts we see the poet ranging from gentle tenderness to strong invective, the latter a result of his uncompromising attitude to flawed or wicked behaviour – he does not suffer gladly either fools or villains, who in consequence are mocked scornfully or condemned outright. Particular aspects of his style are the direct, colloquial way in which he addresses his audience, frequently supplying or anticipating their reactions; lively illustrations from contemporary life, often including direct speech; expressions of wonder, and of imaginative sympathy with individuals (or, as in the first example, animals); and repeated, often exclamatory, rhetorical questioning. He also possesses the ability to round off a passage with a striking, summarising line, and to escape the limits of the couplet by constructing longer or shorter units of sense. Certain phrases recur as a further mark of individual style; we may compare 'Ac whan

---

[6] This second quotation from *SP* is from O. S. Pickering, 'The "Defence of Women" from the *Southern Passion*: A New Edition', in Klaus P. Jankofsky (ed.), *The South English Legendary: A Critical Assessment* (Tübingen, 1992), pp. 154–76 (p. 172). The line numbers from Brown's edition are however given here for ease of comparison.

we habbeþ al ido', from line 4 of the first example, with 'And whanne we habbeþ alle isede', from line 1 of the fourth.[7]

This poet's manner of writing in *EN* and *SP* is so marked that it would be surprising if it were not identifiable elsewhere in the *SEL* collection, assuming he had a hand in it. Further examples will demonstrate that he was in fact more widely involved, but something may first be said about 'normal' *SEL* verse style.

Critics over the years, notably Theodor Wolpers, have drawn attention to the simplicity and transparency (arising from devotional and homiletic impulses) of much of the writing in the saints' lives, and to its success in communicating emotion; the style has more recently been characterised by Gregory Sadlek as 'basically light and childlike', and as giving an 'impression of primitive lucidity'.[8] There have also been a number of publications demonstrating that the *SEL* contains a considerable amount of effective dialogue.[9] We may take as a rewarding example of these studies a new article by Anne Thompson which analyses the narrative style of the life of Mary Magdalene.[10] Thompson shows convincingly that the author is good at conveying the feelings of the protagonists (partly through attention to detail) and good at involving our feelings as readers. She remarks (p. 23) on 'the skill with which narrative and dialogue, direct and indirect speech are mingled', and quotes one particular passage of dialogue between the king and queen in the story, which may be reproduced here as typical:

> To is wif he wend anon, 'dame, Ichelle,' he sede,
> 'In alle manere to Peter wende, he ssel me bet rede.'
> 'Certes, sire,' quaþ þis wif, 'þou ne sselt noȝt fram me wende
> Þat inelle þe siwy uot wiþ uot, sende wat God me sende.'
> 'Dame,' quaþ þe oþer, 'þou spext folie, þi red is wel wilde,
> Þou miȝtest adrenche in þe se, noste þou ert mid childe?'
> Þis gode wife fel to hure louerdes fet, wepinge wel sore,
> 'Ichelle,' heo sede, 'wiþ þe wende þeȝ i necome aȝe namore.'
>
> (129–36)

This extract is undoubtedly successful in combining narrative and speech economically – it is not claimed that the reviser who is the subject of this paper is

---

[7] The quality of writing in *SP* has been remarked on by earlier commentators, notably by Brown in the Introduction to her edition (pp. xv–xvi) and by Derek Pearsall, *Old English and Middle English Poetry* (London, 1977), pp. 105–06.

[8] Theodor Wolpers, *Die englische Heiligenlegende des Mittelalters* (Tübingen, 1964), pp. 209–58; Gregory M. Sadlek, 'Three Basic Questions in Literary Studies of the *South English Legendary*' (unpublished Ph.D. dissertation, Northern Illinois University, 1983), pp. 221, 242, when analysing the life of Vincent. Wolpers, p. 215, also notices what is in effect the outspoken poet's style, but does not suggest that such passages are the work of a separate writer.

[9] For example, Klaus Jankofsky, 'Entertainment, Edification and Popular Education in the *South English Legendary*', *Journal of Popular Culture*, 11 (1977): 706–17, and 'Personalized Didacticism: The Interplay of Narrator and Subject Matter in the *South English Legendary*', *Texas A & I University Studies*, 10 (1977): 69–77, in both of which he also stresses what he calls the *SEL*'s pervasive tone of compassion; and Karen Bjelland, 'Defining the *South English Legendary* as a Form of Drama', *Comparative Drama*, 22 (1988): 227–43.

[10] Anne B. Thompson, 'Narrative Art in the *South English Legendary*', *Journal of English and Germanic Philology*, 90 (1991): 20–30. Her quotations from the poem are from D'Evelyn and Mill, *South English Legendary*, but with altered punctuation.

the only *SEL* poet capable of writing well – but the language is noticeably plain, without any expressive variety. Thompson (p. 29) praises 'the simple, almost spare quality of the redactor's diction . . . with its emphasis on nouns and verbs and its lack of rich or varied descriptive terms' as enhancing 'the expressive qualities of the narrative'. Effective it may be, but the point to be made here is that the words and phrases used are ones which occur again and again throughout the bulk of the saints' lives. Unlike the language employed by the author of *EN* and *SP* when his feelings are aroused, they are not special in themselves.[11]

The sentences in the above passage from *Mary Magdalene* also keep carefully within the couplet framework, as is largely the case with a passage of pure narrative also quoted by Thompson (p. 24):

> Þo hi come ver in þe se gret tempest þer com
> And hi dradde forto adrenche, gret del ech to oþer nom.
> Þis gode wif was sore adrad þat for angwise & fere
> Child heo hadde in þe se wel ar hure time were,
> And for defaute of womman help þat non nei hure nere
> And [for] gret angwise and drede heo deide riȝt þere.   (145–50)

Such writing has a leisureliness characterised not only by the length of line and, as Thompson remarks (p. 28), 'the need to find only one rhyme for each couplet (i.e. no midrhyme)', but by the expectation of a syntactic pause each time the second line of a couplet comes round. *SEL* couplets, as Sadlek comments when discussing the style of the 'Prologue' or 'Banna Sanctorum', are usually complete units of thought.[12]

Strikingly different is the following passage of narrative, taken once again, though at random, from *SP*:

> A man was while an hosebonde . þat sette a gret vyne,
> And by-wallede hit aboute . and suþþe atte fyne
> He dalf þeron and arerede . al a tour amydde,
> And hurede him eorþ-tylyers . and so þat hit bytydde
> Þat he wente a pilgrinage . and þo þe tyme was ney
> Of þe frut to gadery . of hynen he him by-sey,
> And sende to þo eorþ-tylyers . þat frut to vnderfonge.
> Þe eorþ-tylyers þis hinen nome . and some in pyne stronge
> Hi bete and some slowe . and wiþ stones heuede þerto.
> Þe lord sende ȝut mo hynen . and me dude ham also.
>   (*SP* 233–42)

Even though the poet is not here speaking in his 'personal' voice, but translating from the gospel, it is clear that the verse moves in a much more fluid way than is normal in the *SEL* saints' lives, overflowing the couplet boundaries with ease. It is the work of a writer who is quite happy to stop one idea part-way through a couplet and begin at once on a different one.

---

[11] Sadlek, 'Three Basic Questions', also stresses the *SEL*'s typical plainness of style and repetition of core vocabulary (see, for example, pp. 178, 243–44, and 277).

[12] Sadlek, p. 181. The appropriateness of the slow-moving septenary couplet for the clarity of style and devotional-didactic purpose of the *SEL* is remarked on by Wolpers, *Die englische Heiligenlegende*, p. 214.

In order to illustrate this further we may return again to his lengthy defence of women. In all manuscripts except one this passage is basically 92 lines long, which is how it was published by Beatrice Brown in her EETS edition of *SP*. But in one manuscript, Oxford, Bodleian Library, MS Bodley 779, there are an extra 54 lines which occur as five separate blocks within the standard text. Brown printed these lines in her Notes (pp. 99–100), evidently believing them not to be original, and indeed Bodley 779 is a 15th-century manuscript written well over a hundred years after the date of composition of the piece. There is, however, no doubt that these 54 lines are part of the poet's original composition, partly because they are at times integral to his closely-reasoned argument but also because they are in his habitually unrestrained verse style. There is ample evidence, but a single example must suffice.[13]

The passage in question consists of six lines of the standard text (*SP* 1953–58) followed by eighteen of the 'extra' lines, which are here italicised. The poet is asking whether men or women are more lecherous: the answer is men, which he illustrates at length by explicit comparison of the sexual behaviour of male and female animals:

> If lecherie is so leþir dede, and so leþir to do,
> As þe gospel vs seyþ and þe bok, and oure lord sulf þerto,
> Wheyþer is þenne more to blame þat þe dede deþ so,
> Oþer þilke þat ne deþ here nouȝt ac soffreþ þat me here do?   4
> Wel ȝe wete þat þe man hit is þat þe dede deþ:
> Whoso seyþ þat nere nouȝt ryȝt, he lyȝth þorwȝout his teþ
> – *Bot he be al toþles, as God ȝeue þat he were!*
> *Þe kynde ek of alle oþer bestis vs wolle ȝit soþ lere*   8
> *Þat þe goodnesse of women is more of [worþ] inouȝ,*
> *And þe clennesse also, [þan] of men, and þat me hem blameþ wit*
> *wouȝ:*
> *ȝe seþ wel chip and roþerin and houndis ȝit þerto,*
> *Hennis and ges and ek hors and ech maner beste also,*   12
> *Þat þe ȝhe best halt here stille as non soche þyng nere,*
> *Alle in pes but as hit falleþ in here tyme of þe ȝere;*
> *And ȝut somme of hem, but ȝif hy be in good lese ido,*
> *From soche þyng stille beþ ȝere and oþer to.*   16
> *How þenkeþ ȝou of þe he bestis? Fareþ h[y] alle so?*
> *Nay, forsoþe, nouȝt mony, ȝif hy mowe come þerto,*
> *Ac beþ alle euere ȝare when h[y] mowe here make fynde,*
> *Boþe somer and winter ek; þer bleueþ fewe behynde.*   20
> *And ȝif hy habbeþ son a smel at þen tounnis ende*
> *Of folye of here make, ȝit hy wolleþ þedir wende,*
> *And so synful beþ in here dede þat chame hit is to þenche;*
> *Here mou folis neme ensaumple and here leþir wordis quenche!* 24

The poet begins the comparison at l. 8, half-way through a couplet, after an extra piece of invective (l. 7) that wittily continues the mention of teeth in the

---

[13] The matter of the 'additional' lines is fully discussed and illustrated in O. S. Pickering, 'The "Defence of Women" ', from where the quotation is again taken (see pp. 160–61, 169–70).

preceding line. There can be no doubt that the 'additional' passage is original, as a different writer interpolating the animals comparison would naturally have begun with a new couplet following immediately on l. 6. Lines 1–4, 11–16, in particular, illustrate the long, discursive sentences that come naturally to this poet, but 8–10, 18–20, 21–23 demonstrate equally his disregard of couplet boundaries.

II

The examples of the 'outspoken' poet's work so far discussed have all come from the *temporale* narratives of the *SEL*, predominantly *SP*. The remainder of this paper will show that the same style of writing can be found elsewhere in the collection. It will have become apparent that the poet is at his most characteristic when commenting, expounding or 'preaching', and it is in certain expository sections of the *sanctorale* that his voice most clearly reappears.

We may look first at two passages from *All Souls Day*, which is largely about purgatory, preparation for death, and the fate of the soul. Throughout the legend the explanatory writing overflows couplet boundaries as need arises, making the outspoken poet's authorship at once a possibility, but the vocabulary used is generally plain. It is the illustrative anecdotes from contemporary life that reveal his presence, for (as in *SP*) it is the opportunity to denounce real specimens of sin and folly that move his verse on to a different level. In this mode he fiercely exposes the dangers of going to a bad priest for confession and penance:[14]

> 3wat, hou is hit þanne of Ianekin . and of robinet þe wilde,
> Of annot and of Malekin . þat wollez habbe þene preost so
>   milde,
> And huy seggez, 'þilke preost is to hard . god schilde us fram is
>   lothþ;
> Go we to sire Gilbert þe preost . he nis neuere wrothþ,
> He wollez schriue us nessche i-nou3 . and ore sunnes al
>   for-3yue'.
> Bi god, 3wane huy habbez al ido . hom huy gothþ vnschriue;
> For heore penaunce schal beo so luyte . þat sire Gilbert and huy
>   also
> Schullen gon a-deuelewey . bote god nime 3eme heom to.
>
>   (49–56)

It is noteworthy that the phrase '3wane huy habbez al ido' in l. 6 occurs in very similar form ('Ac whan we habbeþ al ido') in l. 340 of *EN*, quoted earlier.

---

[14] Quotations in the remainder of the paper are normally from D'Evelyn and Mill, *South English Legendary*, but the first two passages from *All Souls* are quoted from Horstmann, *Early South-English Legendary*, pp. 421–22, 430 (where they are ll. 45–52 and 339–46), because of corruption in the text printed in the former edition. A lesser degree of corruption occurs in other of the quotations from D'Evelyn and Mill, but no attempt at emendation has been made here.

Sir Gilbert crops up again later in *All Souls* as an example of a priest who has said mass while in a state of sin:[15]

> Ake þei þe Masse ne beo þe worse . þe preost, bi mi swere,
> Þat hire singuth in dedlich sunne . a-corie it schal ful deore!
> For ʒwane sire Gileberd i-massed hath . his lif he wole so diʒhte
> Atþe tauerne to beon a-day . and bi is quene bi nyʒhte;
> He seith, ʒwane Men cleopiez him preost . 'sittez stille, mine
>   guode i-fere,
> Þe preost hanguez at churche . and ich am nouþe here'.
> His cope oþur is surplis . þe preost he seith it isse;
> Ake his cope schal bi-leue at hom . ʒwane he schal to helle, i-
>   wisse!   (342–49)

Similar colloquial or conversational comment, drawing in the audience either directly (by addressing them) or indirectly (by force of language), occurs at ll. 123–26, 190–94, 304–05 and 374–79 of *All Souls*. But much of the legend comprises tales – *narraciones* – told in a straightforwardly plain style, and it has therefore to be considered that the poet merely revised a pre-existing composition, retaining its narrative elements. However, we cannot rule out that a writer of such demonstrable versatility was capable of adopting the 'normal' *SEL* style if he wished, particularly for simple didactic purposes. Illustrative tales are of course found alongside exposition and invective in prose sermons, and ll. 187–94, which move from story to characteristic address in mid-couplet (189–90), support the theory that the outspoken poet wrote the whole legend. The tale is of a clerk attacked by thieves who is rescued by dead bodies which rise from their graves and beat off the assailants:

> Aboute þis þeoues hi come echon . & gonne hem to dryue
> To here put hi wende siþþe aʒe . þe clerk hamward blyue
> & þus his beden were iʒulde . þat he bad er ofte
> Ich am siker aweiward þe þeoues . ne makede here pas noʒt
>   softe
> For ich wot non of ʒou nescholde . hem habbe so sore agaste
> A wonder bataille hit was on . hadde hit longe ilaste
> For ich wene þer nis no champioun . þat hadde þer ibeo
> Þat nadde sone ynome his red . hamward forto fleo   (187–94)

Our poet's hand is again clearly evident in *Michael*, which is only partially a saint's life. The first of its three sections, recounting tales of Michael's guardianship of Mt Gargano, is mainly narrative in what is apparently the usual style, but there are two distinctive passages of amused, almost gloating comment on the fate of 'bad' characters. After the story of a miraculous arrow which turns back against its archer, we find:

---

[15] Brown, *Southern Passion*, pp. c–ci, quotes both of the Sir Gilbert passages as examples of *SEL* denunciations of less than perfect priests, and compares a short passage in *SP* itself (175–78) criticising avaricious clergy. She does not mention the much more strongly worded *SP* 2249–54 on the consequences at Doomsday for priests (like Sir Gilbert here) who through their own deficiency cause other men to fall into sin; the passage is discussed in Pickering, 'The *Southern Passion* and the *Ministry and Passion*', pp. 48–49.

Nou was þat a wonder arwe . and wonder wei he soȝte
I ne kepte noȝt leorni so to ssete . ne such arwe þat me broȝte
A wonder ssere wind he was on . wonder wat he þoȝte
Ac euere he þat him sset . me þincþ þe game aboȝte   (23–26)

The expression of wonder is typical of this poet – we may compare 'Now was þis a wonder dede' from the first extract from *EN* quoted earlier – but here it's a sardonic wonder that makes fun of the man who suffered by debunking him ironically, bringing the whole miracle down to earth with a splash of realism. Soon afterwards we find reference to another 'game' after Michael and his angels have helped defeat the Saracens: the latter, says the poet, would have done better to have stayed at home picking their toes:

A wonder game hi pleide þer . þat miȝte segge hor fo
Hom hadde betere be[o] atom . and ipiked hore two   (67–68)

Michael part II also commences with miraculous narrative, and again we find a characteristic comment (noticeably beginning in mid-couplet) following the story of a woman and her new-born child who were saved from the sea:

For Gode þer nis non of ȝou . þat hure couþe habbe iwest so
    wel
Ne so iued hure ne hure child . þat necostnede worþ a strau
For þei he[o] hadde viss & drinke inou . ȝe witeþ wel it was rau
And to fleote so in þe grete se . wonder þat heo nas ded
Sein Michel was a god wardein . wanne we habbeþ al ised
                                        (150–54)

As often, this passage encompasses wonder, sympathy, down-to-earth realism, an address to the audience (involving them by contrasting their abilities unfavourably, as in *All Souls* 191), and once more the phrase 'wanne we habbeþ al ised'.

The real subject of *Michael* II is Lucifer and the devils of hell, a subject with which the poet does not find it hard to get involved. His account of the fall of Lucifer is marked by strikingly unusual imagery and vocabulary:

Fram þe hexte stude þat is . wiþ one swenge he com
To þe lowest iwis . a wonder wei he nom
No wonder wat was him . wi uerde þe ssrewe so
He pleide mid þe valling torn . to wel he couþe it do
Iambeleue he com swenge . into helle gronde
A murgore in he hadde er . þat worse þere he fonde
A wonder sweng me þincþ he made . is biȝete was wel lute
Acorsi he may eueremo . is misfaringe prute   (173–80)

Lucifer 'swings' down into hell; *valling torn* apparently refers to a fall at wrestling; *Iambeleue* 'headfirst' is from Old French *jambes levees*.[16] And once again we see the evil characters described in terms of losing at games, and as being better off if they hadn't done what they did.

---

[16] See *Middle English Dictionary, falling* ppl., 2(f), and *jaumb-leve* n., (b).

The remainder of *Michael* II can be attributed without difficulty to our poet, comprising, as it does, strongly-written homily enlivened with graphic illustrations and his idiosyncratic colloquialisms. Devils are said to visit wicked men in their sleep ('Hi of liggeþ as an heui stok . as hi wolde a man astoffe / Þat he ne ssel wawy fot ne hond . ne vnneþe enes poffe', 233–34); the devil himself is compared in detail to a guard-dog who will bite those who come near him; and there is in particular a long and expert exposition of the devil's five fingers, with which he entices men to sin in different ways ('Þe deuel stont & fawe wolde . hente him bi þe polle / Wiþ liteman is leste finger . he ginþ him ferst to t[o]lle', 323–24).[17] The whole of *Michael* II could profitably be analysed in detail as an example of combined poetic and homiletic skill.

The third part of *Michael* is different again, being the relatively well-known scientific treatise which leaves the subject of Michael altogether, and discourses in great detail and with impressive knowledge on the subjects of cosmology, the world, weather, the elements and humours, the development of the human foetus, and the relationship of the body and the soul. It appears to have enjoyed a popularity separate from that of the *SEL*, as it occurs out of context in a range of non-*SEL* manuscripts.[18] Once again it is highly likely that our poet was responsible. The treatise is consistently strongly argued, and interestingly written, but it continues for some four hundred lines. There is the feeling that the poet, taking the opportunity to instruct an audience at length on matters that interest him, gets somewhat carried away on his flow of words. It has recently been well argued that the subject-matter of *Michael* III is not inappropriate for the saint in question, and that the tripartite legend possesses, if not unity, at least thematic coherence;[19] but *Michael* III is a digression from the saint's life in the same way that the long defence of women is a digression from *SP*'s narrative of Christ's resurrection.

Much of *Michael* III is patiently explanatory in style, but the audience is kept involved (e.g. 497–98, 593), and there are typical exclamations and occasional personal touches. Thus when the poet explains the origin of hoar-frost:

> He cleueþ in hegges al aboute . and in weodes also
> And ichot in my uortop . he haþ ofte ido   (623–24)

The most striking passage stylistically is 717–28, which describe in great detail the undignified position of the foetus in the womb, comparing it to a hare lying bent in its form and proceeding as a result to warn against human pride:

> Al round it liþ in þe wombe . and ibud as an hare
> Wanne he in forme liþ . for is in is somdel nare
> And ibud þe legges beoþ . it nolde noȝt elles veie
> Þe helen atte bottocs . þe knen in eiþer eiȝe

---

[17] This episode is discussed and praised in Gregory M. Sadlek, 'The Image of the Devils's Five Fingers in the *South English Legendary*'s "St Michael" and in Chaucer's Parson's Tale', in Jankofsky (ed.), *The South English Legendary: A Critical Assessment*, pp. 49–64.

[18] See Görlach, *Textual Tradition*, p. 288 (n. 278), and Thomas R. Liszka, 'MS Laud Misc. 108 and the Early History of the *South English Legendary*', *Manuscripta*, 33 (1989): 75–91 (p. 86, n. 17).

[19] Gregory M. Sadlek, 'The Archangel and the Cosmos: The Inner Logic of the *South English Legendary*'s "St Michael" ', *Studies in Philology*, 85 (1988): 177–91.

> Þat heued ibuyd adonward . þe armes ek wiþinne
> Þe elbowes toward þe ssere . þe vestes to þe chinne
> Al i[b]ud him is þe rug . so þat nei rount it is
> Man ware of comþ al þi prute . for þer nis non iwis
> Þou makest þe so hei her . and to man nelt abowe
> Loke hou croked þou were þere . & to wan þou miȝt þe powe
> Þou nemiȝtest noȝt holde up þin heued . ne enes vndo þin eiȝe
> Wannene com it suþþe to bere . þin heued so heie

Such a precise account of the relative position of a baby's limbs in the womb would suggest specialist knowledge on the part of the author.

An examination of *All Souls* and *Michael* has clearly revealed the outspoken poet's presence in these two predominantly expository and homiletic *sanctorale* legends. Before we turn to consider his possible part in the narrative saints' lives it can be shown that his hand is also distinguishable in certain of the *temporale* poems that expound the feasts and fasts of the church year.

Of these *Rogationtide* is one likely candidate, being full of couplet enjambement and sermon-like distinctions; there is also an anecdotal explanation of the custom of blessing people when they sneeze,[20] and a typically testy dismissal ('And noȝt as seiþ many fol', 9) of those who have the wrong idea about why one fasts at the time of year in question. But it is in the much longer *Lent* that our poet's voice is particularly audible. It has been suggested that the extant text is composite, with the lively section on fasting and confession (the bulk of the item) representing an intrusion after the 'dry technical' ll. 1–40 which explain how the length of Lent is calculated.[21] The style certainly appears to change at l. 41, and there soon follows a vivid passage on gluttons – who should be fasting – breaking wind uncomfortably from all parts of their body:

> Hi goþ up and doun and bolkeþ . wiþ wel dreori chere
> Hi nolleþ ete a mossel more . bote hore mawe amti were
> Hi bolkeþ and bloweþ aboue . ac ine segge noȝt elles ware
> Hi poffeþ and meneþ hore stomak . þat mot nede vuel vare
>
> (51–54)

When the fast-breaker tries to excuse himself, says the poet, he can give only 'A balled [i.e. "threadbare"] reson' (68) – an evocative and unusual phrase found also in *SP*'s defence of women passage.[22] The section on shrift continues in similar style, with tell-tale lines such as 'And wanne ȝe seoþ reson wy . ne wiþ seggeþ me noȝt' (151), and memorable comparisons of a residue of sin, left over after confession, with a hen's nest egg (163–72), and of those who forget about

---

[20] Most of this passage is omitted from the 'A' tradition as a result of archetypal homoeoteleuton (see Görlach, *Textual Tradition*, p. 162), and so is not included in the version of *Rogationtide* printed in D'Evelyn and Mill, *South English Legendary*. For the text, printed from Cambridge, St John's College, MS B.6, fol. 83ᵛ, see Pickering, 'The Expository *Temporale* Poems', p. 8.

[21] Görlach, *Textual Tradition*, p. 156.

[22] In a line unique to MS Bodley 779, and so not printed as part of the main text in Brown, *Southern Passion*. See Pickering, 'The "Defence of Women" ', where it occurs in l. 133 of the full text there printed.

fasting as soon as Easter comes with a bloodhound who loses his sense of smell in springtime:[23]

> Ac hi vareþ as deþ þe blod hond . at bigynnynge of þe ȝere
> Þe smul hap wel of euerich best . of hare & ek of dure
> Ac wanne þe hauþorn bigynneþ to blowe . al it is forlore
> For swotnesse of þulke flour . þe smul þat was biuore
> Þei lesyn þanne al here smel . & here cours ecchon
> & þe hunte sitt at hom . hym lest not to felde gon
> So it farith be suyche men . þat al here þouȝt don ȝeue
> For to smelle oure lordis grace . qwan þei ben wel schryue
> But anon as lente is don . þat is here soulys bote
> Þei etyn flesch wol hertylyche . þe smak is ful sote

III

The question of the outspoken poet's involvement in the narrative saints' lives is a difficult one, which can only be touched on here. Much more research is needed to resolve the matter. On the one hand there is extensive evidence for his presence, as the following characteristic couplets will testify:

> For it was god inou to him . wiþinne & eke aboue
> Wat segge ȝe segge ich soþ . ne lieþ noȝt for is loue
>
> > *(Juliana* 135–36)
>
> Nou was þis a sori couple . and also him mote biualle
> And luþer þrift uppon hore heued . amen seggeþ alle
>
> > *(John the Baptist* 21–22)
>
> Nou an alle deuelwey . and ne come he neuere aȝen
> Wy sitte ȝe so stille . wi ne segge ȝe amen
>
> > *(Peter* 391–92)
>
> Ȝe ȝolle mote he eueremo . & uuel him mote bitide
> Þe ssrewe fond is macche þo . ichot he ssolde abide
>
> > *(James the Great* 363–64)
>
> A ȝe ȝe wel was þat . such gleo ich wolde ihure
> An hard puf him was blowe aȝen . to teche him pleie wiþ fure
>
> > *(Matthew* 137–38)
>
> Nou wo worþe is pol so wis . & sorwe him come to
> Ichot þer nys non of ȝou . þat couþe aposy so
>
> > *(Andrew* 213–14)

---

[23] Lines 5–10 of this passage are quoted from St John's College, MS B.6, fol. 81ᵛ, as some thirty lines of *Lent*, including these, are omitted from the version of the poem printed in D'Evelyn and Mill, *South English Legendary*; all are very likely the work of the outspoken poet. See Görlach, *Textual Tradition*, p. 156, and Pickering, 'The Expository *Temporale* Poems', pp. 7–8. Lines 1–4 of the passage are ll. 113–16 in D'Evelyn and Mill.

Nou vuele iþeo þat him haþ . such lesing ibroȝt
ȝe mowe iseo hou me lieþ . on wymmen for noȝt

(Clement 67–8)

It may be noted that the last-quoted couplet displays the same attitude as *SP* towards the unjust treatment of women.

Similar couplets or longer passages can be found in, for example, *Scholastica, Chad, Benedict, Alphege, Theophilus, Alban, Swithun, Margaret, Jerome, The Eleven Thousand Virgins, Lucy,* and *Anastasia.* The problem of the extent of our poet's involvement arises from the frequent isolation of such exclamations and asides in the midst of sober, straightforward story-telling in apparently normal *SEL* mode. Has the poet, acting as a reviser, simply inserted his comments into existing legends, or did he in many cases compose the surrounding narrative in the traditional style, as was suggested for the *narraciones* in *All Souls*? In the following passage from *Swithun* plain story and 'outspoken' comment alternate, exemplifying the problem particularly well:

A day as þis werkmen . aboute þis worke stode   55
And þe contreiemen to chepinge . come mid muchele gode
Mid a bagge uol of eiren . a womman þer com
A mason sone þis womman . inis folie nom
And biclupte hure in ribaudie . as foles doþ ȝute ofte
And brak hure eiren nei echone . he ne handlede hure noȝt
    softe   60
Þo þe womman hure harm ysei . reulich he[o] gan bygynne
For he[o] is hadde igadered longe . som seluer to wynne
He[o] weop and made deol inou . and cride also anhey
Sein Switthin com þo þer uorþ . and þis deol isey
Of þis womman he hadde reuþe . he nom up his hond anon   65
And blessede þe eiren tobroke . and hi bicom hole echon
Ase sonde as hi euere were . hi bicome attelaste
Glad was þo þis sely womman . & þonkede him wel faste
Miȝte eirmangars fare nou so . þe baldeloker hi miȝte
Hup[p]e ouer diches ware hi wolde . & boþe wraxli & fiȝte   70

Lines 61–68, in particular, use phrasing and vocabulary found throughout the *SEL*, while the *foles* of 59b, the ironical understatement of 60b, and the extravagant fantasy of 69–70 immediately identify the outspoken poet. The final couplet might be a later addition, not being structurally connected, but 59–60 are so closely bound up with the foregoing lines, completing the sentence begun in 58, that this passage would seem to be the work of a single writer.

We are assisted somewhat by the existence of different manuscript traditions, that is to say, not all of the lines to be attributed to our poet are found in all manuscripts. On the face of it this would seem to add weight to the theory that isolated comments surrounded by 'ordinary' narrative are likely to represent a reviser's interpolations. The split between the 'Z' and 'A' traditions of the *SEL*, identified by Manfred Görlach, can often be equated with the textual differences between MS Laud 108 (=L) and MSS Cambridge, Corpus Christi College 145 and London, British Library, Harley 2277, the manuscripts used for the two main *SEL* editions.[24] Görlach more precisely associates L with a tradition 'L', deriving partly from 'Z' and partly from 'A'; from 'L' in turn derive traditions 'G' and 'F', of which prominent representatives are the Vernon manuscript (Oxford, Bodleian Library, MS English Poetry a.1, =V) and London, Lambeth Palace Library, MS 223 (=G).[25]

Of the seven couplets quoted above, *Juliana* 135–36 are not in GV (the legend is omitted from L); *John* 21–22 are not in LV (the legend is omitted from G); *Peter* 391–92 are not in GV which diverge from the main 'A' tradition after l. 195 (the legend is not in L); *James* 363–64 are not in LGV;[26] *Matthew* 137–38 are not in LGV; *Andrew* 213–14 are not in GV (the legend is omitted from L); and *Clement* 67–68 are not in LG (lines 1–326 are lost in V). On this evidence there appears to be a strong possibility that the outspoken poet interpolated his comments into existing compositions.

The matter is in fact more complex. *John* 65–66 – a curse – are not in LV, but this couplet merely concludes a strongly-written passage on Salome which they *do* have. *Alban* has a markedly unrestrained sequence (85–90) on the gruesome fate that befell the saint's executioner, of which LGV possess the first four lines –

> Ac þe tormentour þat smot of . seint Albones heued
> He nedorste noȝt ȝilpe þerof muche . him were betere habbe
>   bileued
> For þo he smot of is heued . riȝt in þulke stonde
> Is eiȝne folle out of is heued . & þer wiþ he fel to gronde

– but not the final two:

> Is biȝete was wel lite þer . it fel doun al byhinde
> He miȝte segge wanne he comþ hom . war her comþ þe blynde

Jerome, not present in L, has a passage that brings together several of the outspoken poet's features of style with which we have become familiar (sympathy with animals, imagined direct speech, a challenge to the audience, expression of wonder, questioning), but the second half (73–76) is not in GV:

> Þe lion bigan to vauni þo . as wo seiþ ichelle vawe
> Fram daie to daie as ȝoure [asse] . ȝoure wode hom drawe
> Boþe on rugge & on carte . bocsomliche inou
> Mildore þanne þe asse dude . hare wode hom he drou
> And naþeles it bicom him vuele . such mester to do
> Ich wene þere nis non of ȝou . þat him ssolde bringe þerto
> A wonder cartare he was on . ware were is wilde pas
> Wanne we habbeþ al itold . a uair miracle þer was (69–76)

---

[24] See note 2 above.
[25] See Görlach, *Textual Tradition*, pp. 51–60, and the chart of affiliations on p. 304. I am indebted to Görlach's analysis of the texts of the different legends for what follows, which is, necessarily, a simplification of the total manuscript evidence. The inclusion or omission of individual lines in the numerous different manuscripts of the *SEL* is an extremely complex matter, as Görlach shows.
[26] Görlach, p. 183, accidentally fails to note the omission from MSS GV.

In these three examples it is comment rather than narrative that is absent from the control manuscripts, but it does not seem likely that the comment was added later by a different writer. In the case of *Lent* it is GV and other manuscripts representing the presumed earlier tradition that preserve the fullest text – preserving in effect more of the work of the outspoken poet – and the 'A' tradition that has what seems to be an abridgement.[27] Similarly, the full text of *SP*'s defence of women exists (as was said) in only a single manuscript, Bodley 779; and *SP* as a whole more often than not survives in shortened rather than complete form.[28] The reason for such abridgement may well have been that later redactors or scribes wished to tone down, or reduce the extent of, the poet's asides, digressions, and general 'outspokenness', and this may also explain some of the differences in the textual transmission of the saints' lives; it may be that curses and personal comments are at times being excised rather than interpolated.

In this connection it may be noted that *All Souls* and *Michael*, full-scale legends that I attributed with some confidence to the outspoken poet, occur in MSS LG and LGV respectively, and not merely in manuscripts of the 'A' tradition. In both cases L possesses texts equivalent to those in 'A', whereas G is noticeably divergent.[29] Its *All Souls* begins quite differently; thereafter a number of typically outspoken lines are omitted, including the distinctive 304–05 (not quoted earlier) –

> Away mi child saiþ þe dame . þat snyueleþ bi þe wowe
> Bi Crist heo auȝte þonki God . þat nom hit for his owe

– and ll. 344–49 (but not 342–43) of the second 'Sir Gilbert' passage. Of the quotations given earlier from *Michael*, G completely lacks 23–26, 67–68 and 623–24; leaves out 151–54 after a different version of 150; leaves out 175–78 while preserving 173–74, 179–80; omits not only 323–24 but the whole passage on the devil's fingers; and retains 233–34 and 717–28. The balance of the evidence here is that G contains abridged versions of *All Souls* and *Michael* rather than texts free of later interpolation.

It is in fact likely that our poet treated different *sanctorale* subjects in different ways. More work is needed, but when *SEL* style is thoroughly investigated it may prove to be the case that on some occasions he left existing legends scarcely altered whereas on others he composed virtually from scratch. Certainly the strength and variety of writing in (for example) *Alban*, *John the Baptist*, and *Peter* (not to mention *Michael* and *All Souls*) suggest that the poet was primarily responsible for the extant texts.

Meanwhile it can be shown that he was an active reviser of *sanctorale* legends (in the same way that he revised *MP* into *SP*, and *NMC* into *EN*), although the evidence is not extensive because the presumed 'Z' layer of the *SEL* survives only partially, if at all, in manuscripts like L and G. As has become obvious, there is plentiful minor variation between different texts of the same legend,

---

[27] See note 22 above. MS L contains none of the expository *temporale* poems.
[28] See Brown, *Southern Passion*, pp. xvii–xxx, summarized in Pickering, 'The *Temporale* Narratives', pp. 444–45.
[29] As before, I am indebted to Görlach, *Textual Tradition*, for the details that follow.

much of which may be said to represent revision in the sense of being deliberate; but there are comparatively few legends of which two different versions survive, particularly in the second half of the calendar year.[30]

Two rewarding examples, however, are *Dunstan* and *Bridget*, of which the revised versions contain clear examples of our poet's style. *Dunstan* is the more straightforward case. Görlach (p. 168) records that the 'A' redactor 'added the dates of Dunstan's birth and death in 21–24, 203–4, the episode of the temptation in the smithy 59–92, and replaced [the original 41–48, as in L] by a completely new passage on the antiquity of Glastonbury, 45–58'. Whereas the additions are self-contained (which potentially opens their status to dispute), it is evident that the last change is the work of a reviser. L says wrongly (and vaguely) that Dunstan founded Glastonbury Abbey. The 'A' version is clearly concerned to put things right, and spends six lines establishing very precisely – in effect contradicting the other – that the abbey existed 453 years earlier, before the time of either St Patrick or St Augustine. The smithy episode, in which the devil comes to Dunstan in woman's form, is a typically skilful anecdote in the outspoken poet's liveliest style. At the climax the saint applies red-hot tongs to the devil's nose, so that:

> He ȝal & hupte & drou aȝen . & made grislich bere
> He nolde for al is biȝete . þat he hadde icome þere
> Wiþ is tonge he strok is nose . & twengde him euere sore
> Forte it was wiþinne niȝte . þat he ne miȝte ise[o] namore
> Þe sshrewe was glad & bliþe inou . þo he was out of is honde
> And flei & gradde bi þe lift . þat me hurde into al þe londe
> Out wat haþ þis calwe ido . wat haþ þis calwe ido
> In þe contreie me hurde wide . hou þe ssrewe gradde so
> As god þe ssrewe hadde ibe[o] . habbe ysnut atom is nose
> He ne hiȝede namore þuder ward . to tile him of þe pose
>
> (83–92)

Bridget is rewritten much more extensively, L's 58 lines being expanded to 270. Görlach (p. 142) describes the 'A' redactor's procedure in some detail, and his analysis need not be repeated here. Most of the new material is narrative of a generally ordinary *SEL* kind; given that our poet's hand is clearly apparent elsewhere in the rewritten legend, as will be seen, this is presumably good evidence that he could indeed turn his hand to basic *SEL* style when necessary (unless, of course, there was a stage of intermediate narrative revision, which cannot wholly be ruled out).[31] Otherwise, various short miracles from L's text are re-used at appropriate points, and the way in which the first of these is adapted is, as Görlach points out, evidence that a reviser is at work. It is the characteristic couplets (161–62, 171–72) inserted after each of the first two

---

[30] Görlach. *Textual Tradition*, does not list these legends as such, but for references see pp. 11 and 52–54.

[31] Görlach, pp. 169, 142, shows that the reviser consulted fresh, presumably Latin, sources, for the new material he inserted into *Dunstan* and *Bridget*. It may be that there is a link (for this writer) between the activity of translation and the use of a plain, unadventurous style. It is certainly the case that the conscientious gospel translations included in *EN* and *SP* are normally stylistically unexceptional.

miracles that reveal the poet in his 'outspoken' mode; in each case the effect is somewhat to devalue the miracle by suggesting that it could be repeated for everyday benefit. Thus after Bridget has been enabled to hang her wet clothes to dry on a sunbeam:

> Me þingþ he[o] ne dorste carie noȝt . perche forto finde
> Wanne he[o] wolde hure cloþes honge . & þe sonne ssinde
>
> (171–72)

In the second main block of added story (173–252) the poet's presence is perhaps betrayed by a single complex sentence stretching over six lines (203–08). Not long afterwards there is a characteristic comment on Bridget's willingness to lose an eye rather than marry:

> Wel leouer hure was to leose hure eiȝe . ȝe parde boþe to
> Þanne to be[o] iwedded wif . folie forto do
> Were wymmen ivare nouþe so . wo so wolde ȝeorne crie
> As wel we mowe segge nay . wat halt it to lye   (235–38)

L's text has only four lines on Bridget's refusal to marry. As Görlach comments (p. 142) about the 'A' version, 'the stress is much more on the details, which often serve for sensation rather than piety'. From the accumulated evidence we now have about our poet's contributions to the *SEL*, there is little doubt that he is a sensationalist.

Manfred Görlach (p. 141) says that *Bridget* is 'the best example of the "A" redaction in the *SEL* corpus'. This paper has refrained from identifying the outspoken poet as *the* 'A' reviser, but it has become clear that he must, at least, have played a major part in fashioning the *SEL* that has come down to us.[32] It has been shown that he was active in both *temporale* and *sanctorale* portions, and now that the most striking features of his style have been recognised it may become possible to trace him at work in less obvious places. Certainly the full extent of his activity is still very unclear, particularly the degree to which he involved himself in composing *sanctorale* narrative. He is most naturally a preacher, and his principal talents appear to be those of a lecturer, homilist, anecdotalist, and social and ecclesiastical critic. As this is a York occasion it may be appropriate to conclude with four lines from *Chad* in which he castigates modern archbishops (including the Archbishop of York) for going everywhere on horseback, for fear, he says, of stubbing their toes:

> Þe erche bissop of Euerwik . ne kepte noȝt nou go
> To prechi aboute inis vet . ne anoþer noþemo
> Hi rideþ up hore palfrei . leste hi sperne hore to
> Bote richesse & worles prute . deþ Holi Churche wo   (25–28)

---

[32] The evidence of abridgement in the 'A' text of *Lent*, and the archetypal homoeoteleuton in the 'A' *Rogationtide*, suggest that he was working at a stage before the version represented by the Corpus Christi and Harley manuscripts printed in D'Evelyn and Mill, *South English Legendary*.

THE APPLE'S MESSAGE: SOME POST-CONQUEST HAGIOGRAPHIC ACCOUNTS OF TEXTUAL TRANSMISSION*

Jocelyn Wogan-Browne

What is a text and how is it transmitted? Vernacular saints' Lives are often thought of as the edifying productions of clerics translating from Latin for illiterate lay people. This producer-centred model is in part the one promoted by hagiographic texts themselves in their creation of clerical narrator figures, officiants with privileged access to Latinity and the past who, with humble (but indispensable) utility, mediate saints' lives to less literate estates. So Wace, for instance, in his Life of Nicholas:

> A ces qui n'unt lectres aprises
> Ne lur ententes n'i ont mises,
> Devient li clerc mustrer la lei,
> Parler des seinz . . . .[1]

> [To those who have have not learnt Latin, nor have given their attention to it, clerks must expound the faith, speak about the saints]

This influential model privileges clerisy and literacy: transmission of the authoritative truths of Latin and of the past is the business of the suitably-equipped professional. Similarly, in the Anglo-Norman 'Ypocras' texts, a transmission story for medical writing imitates important *topoi* of hagiographic transmission: Hippocrates is said to have had himself buried with his book 'ou estoit escrit la nature de tut le cors et secretz . . . a son chif en sepulcre ou il gist'.[2] Augustus Caesar passes before the tomb and commands it to be opened for treasure. The book is sent to Caesar who commits it to his own doctor, whose reading of it constitutes a French text of this 'liber Ypocratis'.[3] High textual authority and a professionally qualified relation to the text constitute the transmission here – the doctor is to the medical text as the officiating cleric

* I am grateful to Renate Blumenfeld-Kosinski for generously making available to me her excellent study of Caesarean birth, to Alan Fletcher, Anne Savage and Sebastian Sutcliffe for interest and for shared information and to Alastair Minnis for patient editing.
[1] Einar Ronsjö (ed.), *La vie de saint Nicolas par Wace*, (Lund and Copenhagen, 1942), ll. 1–4, discussed by Karl Uitti in 'The Clerkly Narrator Figure in Old French Hagiography and Romance', *Medioevo Romanzo*, 2 (1975): 394–408.
[2] This prologue occurs in Cambridge, Trinity College, MS 0.2.5 and elsewhere; see P. Meyer, 'Les manuscrits français de Cambridge', *Romania*, 32 (1903): p. 99.
[3] On medieval Hippocratic texts see Pearl Kibre, '*Hippocrates latinus*: Repertorium of Hippocratic Writings in the Latin Middle Ages', *Traditio*, 38 (1982): 165–92, esp. pp. 167–68.

translator is to the saint's *vita*, unlocking the authority and power of the past through his professional mystery.[4]

Yet this model is of course not the whole truth, though such professional agendas need to be remembered in considering vernacular transmission. The hagiographic text's nature and functions can also be viewed in terms of the demands and needs of its audiences. The historical circumstances of hagiographic production, dissemination, and use, are, not surprisingly, more complex and less one-directional than the model of transmission as from literate to illiterate, cleric to lay, suggests.[5] Here I shall be concerned with some examples from post-Conquest saints' Lives' own accounts of transmission to their textual communities; with hagiological valorization of seeing, wearing, touching, carrying and eating as modes of textual transmission; and with the interplay between various modes of transmission and users of hagiographic texts.

However important clerical agendas may be in the post-Conquest hagiographic corpus as a whole, even very bookish saints' Lives show the co-presence of the literate and the oral (which, following Stock, I will take as including visual and personal testimony).[6] Text is not their only mode nor does it occupy an exclusively privileged place in the hierarchy of witness. An example is the interplay between vision and text in two Anglo-Norman re-workings of Aelred's life of Edward the Confessor, a late twelfth-century one by an anonymous nun of Barking, and one from St Albans by Matthew Paris, up to seventy years later, between 1236 and 1245.[7] Both these Lives, like their source, give a great deal of attention to vision and its textualization, appropriately so in the Life of a saint

---

[4] Compare the famous St Alban's story in which a vellum text in the ancient British tongue is discovered in a wall in a box of relics: it is translated by an old British priest and transcribed by the monks under Abbot Eadmer's direction into the permanent, time-defying form of Latin. As soon as the translation is completed, the vernacular text irreparably crumbles into dust (see [Walsingham's edition of] Matthew Paris' *Gesta Abbatum Monasterii Sancti Albani*, ed. H. T. Riley, Rolls Series, [London, 1867–69], i.26–27). In the one case, Latin is required as a preserving language, in the other French as a disseminating language, but the transmission is managed by a professional or group of professionals in each case.

[5] See further the important article by John Frankis, 'The Social Context of Vernacular Manuscripts', in P. Coss and S. D. Lloyd (eds.), *Thirteenth Century England I: Proceedings of the Newcastle-upon-Tyne Conference* (Woodbridge, 1986), pp. 175–84. Some vernacular saints' Lives were written in Anglo-Norman [*not* Latin] by monks and canons for use in male communities (see M. Dominica Legge, *Anglo-Norman in the Cloisters* [Edinburgh, 1950]), some by women (who though they might read, be Latinate, and have scribal skills, are by definition not clerics); see further J. Wogan-Browne, ' "Clers u lai, muïne u dame": Women and Anglo-Norman Hagiography', in Carol Meale (ed.), *Women and Literature in Britain, 1150–1500* (Cambridge, 1993), pp. 61–85.

[6] Brian Stock, *The Implications of Literacy: Written Language and Models of Interpretation in the Eleventh and Twelfth Centuries* (Princeton, 1983), Introduction and ch. I. Increased attention to hagiography as not only what is produced but what is received has recently begun to produce study of hagiography as an 'oral-literate' genre. See Evelyn Burge Vitz, 'Vie, légende, littérature: traditions orales et écrites dans les histoires des saints', *Poétique* 72 (1987): 387–402; also her 'From the Oral to the Written in Medieval and Renaissance Saints' Lives', in Renate Blumenfeld-Kosinski and Timea Szell (eds.), *Images of Sainthood in Medieval Europe*, (Ithaca and London, 1991), pp. 97–114.

[7] Osten Södergård (ed.), *La vie d'Edouard le confesseur: poème anglo-normand du XIIe siècle* (Uppsala, 1948); Kathryn Young-Wallace (ed.), *La Estoire de Seint Aedward le Rei*, ANTS 41 (London, 1983), henceforth cited by line numbers in the text and distinguished as 'Barking' and 'Paris' when necessary. Pending completion of the Corpus Christianorum edition of Aelred's works, see *PL* 195.737–90 for Aelred's Life of the saint.

particularly associated with cures of blindness. Edward himself is a source of visions, prophetically seeing the downfall of a Danish leader (Barking, ll. 1537–1630; Paris, ll. 1305–68), a shift of position on the part of the Seven Sleepers of Ephesus (4039–4132; 3383–3452), and on his death-bed a visionary tree which is shifted from its roots but which flowers again (4827–48 and 4913–5006; 3766–3858). Access to Edward, once he is known as a miracle-worker, is also controlled through vision: those seeking cures must narrate the dreams which have inspired them to request contact with the saint to Edward's chamberlain (3311–44; 2730–70). Edward's own eucharistic vision, observed by Earl Leofric, creates a text relic: on return to Worcester, the earl has his confessor write up the vision and lock the document away with some relics until after Edward's death, when both the miracle and the king's modesty become known (2961–3074; 2514–97).

The most extended visionary incident concerns Edward's absolution from a vow of pilgrimage if peace from Danish attacks can be secured (Barking, ll. 1641–2264; Paris, ll. 1407–1890). Both Lives give a close translation of Aelred's Latin text of Pope Leo's letter to Edward (itself the same text as that incorporated in Edward's founding charter for Westminster Abbey).[8] A saintly king's decision not to go on pilgrimage needs weighty authority to be presented as an indication of great virtue. If it is to be seen as the quotation of a source, the incorporation of the letter's text in the narrative appears to place great weight on text as documentation (though one might also say that it moves the letter rather in the direction of prosopopeia, of being an object that speaks, particularly when, as in the Barking life, 'lur brief fud parlit', l. 2225). However the really authoritative underpinning of events here comes not from the pope and his text but from the visionary appearance of the pope's predecessor, St Peter, to a hermit.[9] The hermit is living in a hole in the ground near Worcester (in order to escape the temptations of the world). In a long, directly-reported speech of St Peter's, the hermit is instructed to convey to Edward the saint's approbation both of the king's conduct and of the pope's absolution from the pilgrimage vow, an absolution, says St Peter, which Edward's messengers are even at that moment bearing towards England. In the Barking Life, the hermit now has to arrange to have the vision written down to get it sent to the king: the expediency and efficiency of vision compared with the laborious physicality of documentation is striking in this earlier vernacular life:

> Quant saint Piere ço dit li out,
> Si s'en ala, si cum li plout.
> Le produmme pas n'en tarja,
> Un escrivain [Aelred, *notario*] tost apela,
> Ki tut li ad mis en ecrit
> Ço qu'il enceis oï e vit.

---

[8] Barking, ll. 2019–2102; Paris, ll. 1656–1722; Aelred, *PL* 195.752: and see Dugdale, *Monasticon Anglicanum*, ed. J. Caley, H. Ellis, B. Bandinel (London, 1846), i.293–94.

[9] On the status of hermits in the high Middle Ages see Henrietta Leyser, *Hermits and the New Monasticism: A Study of Religious Communities in Western Europe 1000–1150* (London, 1984); Henry Mayr-Harting, 'Functions of a Twelfth-Century Recluse: St. Wulfric of Haselbury', *History*, 60 (1975): 337–52.

> Puis l'ad al messagier livré,
> Ki al rei Edward l'ad porté.   (Barking, 2213–20)

> [When St Peter had said this to him, he went away as it
> pleased him. The good man did not delay: he quickly called
> a scrivener who put into writing for him what he had heard
> and seen. Then he handed it over to the messenger who
> carried it to King Edward.]

Through God's will, the hermit's letter and the pope's become available in
Edward's court at the same time. In the Barking version, the hermit's messenger
arrives at court just when the Roman messengers' letter is being read out
(2221–28). In Matthew Paris' version, Edward receives the hermit's text first,
reads it privately and waits to see whether the pope's letter will accord with it
(1837–48). Here as so often vision is the originary authority for a text (above
and beyond even the scribal and bureaucratic capacities of the papal court). The
authenticating feature of the story is not its documentability (there is little stress
on the precise terms of the papal letter), but the divine management of time and
space in the rhyming events of the messengers' and the hermit's communica-
tions. For, as both vernacular lives point out, how did the reclusive hermit
staying underground near Worcester know what they had been doing in Rome if
not through God?

> Kar cument savreit le produme
> Ço qu'il aveient fait a Rume,
> Ki pres de Wirecestre esteit
> E suz tere tuz tens maneit . . .
> Se il par Deu ço ne seüst?
>   (Barking, 2243–49: cf. Paris, 1865–76)

The text of the papal letter is given in both Lives less because it is a text than
because it is a physically compatible relic of a vision. Here, in a sort of multi-
media chirograph, vision and text are part of a transaction which involves text,
but is more than text. In Matthew Paris' thirteenth-century account there is an
increased concern with the formal organization of the text ('fist escrivre en
parchemin/De chef en chef la matire', 1832–33) compared with the twelfth-
century Barking Life ('Un escrivain . . . tut li ad mis en escrit', 2216–17).
Nevertheless, what is of principal concern in the account is the way in which
these documentary, textual and testamentary processes witness to God's shaping
of events. Hermit and pope, Worcester and Rome: the very halves of the world
cohere in Matthew Paris' comment that there was no doubt but that God and St
Peter had sent the messages, since one came from the east and one from the west
(1857–64). Documents have increased importance and are a source of
fascination in themselves, but are still, in a society where more people see or
handle them than decode them, objects.[10] In these Edward Lives, writing – and
reading – are not so much privileged modes of textuality, as they are means,

---

[10] Although not specifically concerned with hagiography, Michael Clanchy's classic study, *From
Memory to Written Record: England 1066–1307* (London, 1979), is suggestive for this genre as for
many others: see esp. ch. 8, 'Hearing and Seeing'.

among others, of embodying contact with the saint's life. Literacy could be seen here, as Brian Stock has argued, as ancilliary to a reality primarily conceived in 'physical, personal and verbal terms'.[11]

When a text is in question in saints' Lives, it is often not only its existence as a text, but also its ability to function as a species of contact relic that is significant. Some assumptions of hagiographic writing germane to its liturgical uses provide a theoretical underpinning in which hagiographic texts, in all their material components – parchment, script, images –, can be seen as presenting (rather than re-presenting) the saint. J. W. Earle has discussed the usefulness of the early medieval concept of the *imago* and its extension to hagiography as well as to images and icons.[12] In *lectiones horae* and *lectio divina*, Earle argues, hagiographic material is typological and ritual. Every image made with the hands- churches, pictures and stories of the saints – is related to its prototype in the way a historical *figura* is related to its fulfillment: God makes the invisible visible in images. Christ is the prototype of this relation, bringing together visible human nature and invisible divine nature, and the saints in turn are Christ-like *imagines*. Like the icon and like most ritual art, the hagiographic *vita* does not just record but embodies sacred history; it 'participates in the eternal truth which it represents (or rather 'presents'), and, like Scripture . . . embodies that truth in a . . . super-literary [and typological] way'.[13] The relation between *vita* and saint is a relationship between an *imago* and its prototype.

The operation of iconic principles in the production and transmission of hagiographic texts need not exclude textual modes more familiar to us (whereby writing operates as a signifying system rather than as a form of contact with an *imago* and in which particular textual representations participate in an intertextual system independent of the individual book). Nor are specific social and political inflections towards actual and inscribed audiences of texts excluded. Typological principles of construction can co-exist with (for instance), the socialization implicit in hagiography's provision of role-models, or the legitimation of economic and social ends for text-producers and audiences. By iconic principles, however, textuality embraces the un-Latinate and the illiterate.[14] For us, then, the presence of typological and iconic principles can usefully 'un-privilege' writing, realigning the written text of a Life as one among other forms of contact with spiritual power available to users of the *vita*, and repositioning writing as a system with tactile as well as semiotic values, a medium in which the image reproduces itself.

That these principles apply not only to the production but to the reception of the hagiographic text can be illustrated from the case of St Margaret of Antioch.

---

[11] *Implications of Literacy*, p. 59. Stock sees such conceptions as particularly characteristic of the eleventh and twelfth centuries, but they also apply in large part to pre-Conquest culture (see Rosamund McKitterick [ed.], *The Uses of Literacy in Early Medieval Europe* [Cambridge, 1991] for a critique and accounts of the earlier period).

[12] 'Typology and Iconographic Style in Early Medieval Hagiography', *Studies in the Literary Imagination*, 8 (1975): 15–46.

[13] 'Typology and Iconographic Style', p. 35.

[14] See Stock, *Implications of Literacy*, pp. 7–10 for further discussion of textuality in this sense. For extended study of non-literate relations with sacred texts and images, see further Margaret R. Miles, *Image as Insight: Visual Understanding in Western Christianity and Secular Culture* (Boston, 1985).

Lives of this saint survive in many different versions in English, French and Latin.[15] In most cases each version includes, in the saint's final prayers, explicit statements envisaging the transmission of the life, as in this example from the Katherine Group *Margarete*:

> Ich bidde ant biseche þe, þet art mi weole ant wunne, þet hwa se eauer boc writ of mi liflade, oðer biʒet hit iwriten, oðer halt hit ant haueð oftest on honde, oðer hwa se hit eauer redeð oðer þene redere liðeliche lusteð, wealdent of heouene, wurðe ham alle sone hare sunnen forʒeuene. Hwa se on mi nome makeð chapele oðer chirche, oðer findeð in ham liht oðer lampe, þe leome ʒef him, Lauerd, ant ʒette him, of heouene. I þet hus þer wummon pineð o childe, sone se ha munneð mi nome ant mi pine, Lauerd, hihendliche help hire ant her hire bene; ne i þe hus ne beo iboren na mislimet bearn, nowðer halt ne houeret, nowðer dumbe ne deaf ne ideruet of deofle. Ant hwa se eauer mi nome munegeð wiþ muðe, luueliche Lauerd, et te leaste dom ales him from deaðe.[16]

> [I beg and beseech you, [God], who are my bliss and joy, that whoever writes a book on my life, or acquires it when written, or whoever has it most often in hand, or whoever reads it aloud or with good will listens to the reader, may all have their sins forgiven at once, ruler of heaven. Whoever builds a chapel or church in my name, or provides for it any light or lamp, give him and grant him, Lord, the light of heaven. In the house where a woman is lying in labour, as soon as she recalls my name and my passion, Lord, make haste to help her and listen to her prayer, and may no deformed child be born in that house, neither lame nor hunchbacked, neither dumb nor deaf nor afflicted by the Devil. And whoever calls on my name aloud, gracious Lord, at the Last Judgement save him from death.]

Here it is immediately apparent that conceptual distinctions customary to literacy are not being observed. Rather than carrying any sort of originary authority, writing a book on the life of the saint is functionally equivalent with acquiring, holding, reciting or hearing Margaret's Life. The verb 'writ' is itself ambiguous here: 'writen' in the Katherine Group texts often means to write in the sense of copying rather than composing.[17] All the text-based modes of relation with Margaret's life are here in any case on a par with making or illuminating a building, with seeking the saint's help in the production of healthy children, and with invoking her intercession for salvation. Book, church, household, and the bed of childbirth and death are all contexts in which contact with the power of the saint can be efficacious.

[15] For Latin Lives, see BHL *Novum Supplementum* nos. 5303–10; English Lives are listed by Charlotte D'Evelyn and F. A. Foster, 'Saints Legends', in *A Manual of the Writings in Middle English 1050–1500*, ed. Albert E. Hartung, rev. ed. J. Burke Severs (Hamden, Conn., 1970), ii.606–8; French Lives by Paul Meyer, 'Légendes hagiographiques en français', *Histoire Littéraire de la France*, Académie des Inscriptions et Belles Lettres (Paris, 1906), xxxiii.328–458. For details of Anglo-Norman Lives see note 24 below.

[16] Bella Millett and Jocelyn Wogan-Browne (ed. and tr.), *Medieval English Prose for Women* (Oxford, 1990, repr. 1992), p. 78/18–30. Hereafter quotations are referenced by page and line number in the text.

[17] Millett and Wogan-Browne, p. 162, note to 140/16, and p. 163, note to 148/26–7.

St Margaret's model of a textual community well illustrates Stock's distinction between literacy and textuality and his claim that early medieval cultures are not *il*literate but *non*-literate.[18] The modes of transmission envisaged in the saint's prayers are not hierarchically arranged to co-ordinate socio-economic status and degrees of literacy: building a church in the saint's name, for instance, though listed in the second group of activities, implies socio-economic resources beyond even those of having a text of the Life copied. While it might be argued that the attention here given to non-literate participation in the textual community of the saint is a *faute de mieux* concession to an illiterate audience, the modes of transmission here envisaged are equally well accounted for by the iconic principles of hagiography as a genre and the differently-positioned status of literacy in a non-literate society. Although one audience for whom this particular version of Margaret's life was adapted and copied was almost certainly a community of literate well-born anchoresses, accustomed to reading aloud from their 'English boke of Seinte Margarete',[19] the text which was re-worked for them also invokes a wider audience, referring initially to married and widowed as well as virgin listeners and finally, in the prayer quoted above, to pregnant women.[20]

Heaven itself authenticates the various modes of transmission in Margaret's prayer. An authoritative dove comes down to answer her, and evisages further illiterate (or better, non-literate) contacts with her:

> . . . ant muche mare is iȝeuen to þeo þe munieð þi nome, ant iȝettet moni þing þet nu nis nawt imuneget. Ant hwer se eauer þi bodi oðer ei of þine ban beon, oðer boc of þi pine, cume þe sunfule mon ant legge his muð þerupon, Ich salui him his sunnen; ne ne schal nan unwiht wunien in þe wanes þer þi martyrdom is iwriten inne, ant alle of þe hus schulen gleadien i Godes grið ant i gastelich luue. Ant alle þe þe biddeð, to ȝarkin Ich ȝetti ham of hare bruchen bote (p. 80/4–11).

> [. . . and much more is given to those who commemorate your name, and many things granted which have not been mentioned here. And wherever your body may be, or any of your bones, or a book on your passion, if a sinful man comes and touches it with his lips, I will heal his sins for him; and no devil will remain within the walls where a written account of your martyrdom is kept, and everyone in the house will rejoice in the peace of God and in spiritual love. And as for all those who pray to you, I am ready to grant them remission of their sins.]

According to the dove, oral contact with the saint's body, bones or book constitutes access, as does keeping a text of Margaret's Life in one's house. If writing a book is listed first in the saint's prayers, the dove's sequence is body–bones–book: the burial-place, relics and the text of the Life are all on a continuum as parts of the saint's material identity.

---

[18] *Implications of Literacy*, p. 7.
[19] J. R. Tolkien (ed.), *The English Text of the Ancrene Riwle: Ancrene Wisse*, EETS OS 249 (London, 1961), fol. 66a/19.
[20] Millett and Wogan-Browne, p. 44/24–5 and cf. p. 78/25 quoted above, p. 44.

That a corpus and a text might be identifiable, a body a text as much as texts a corpus, is not a modern juggling of terms, but a medieval assimilation: the equation of a document from heaven and Christ's incarnate body is perhaps most startlingly made in Truth's pardon in *Piers Plowman*, but has many analogues in heavenly letters and charters of Christ and in cartographic conventions as well as in hagiological thought.[21] The body as a witnessing text is a datum of represented hagiographic torture and dismemberment, as its disseminability is of hagiological relics. Bodies are partible and yet whole (so that Margaret's whole body is thought of as present at her burial site, but her bones in dissociation from that site can still be seen as carrying the power of the whole body): texts are partible, but when they too are a form of relic, their fragments, like their material components, retain the meaning and force of the whole text. Body-centred modes of participation in textual communities are so validated a form of relation that clerical narrators seek them, authenticating themselves by contact with the corpse as well as with the corpus of documentation on the saint. In *Margarete* the narrator Theotimus is initially a collector of the documents of Margaret's passion (p. 44/22–3). At the end of the narrative, even though the scene when narrated shows only women witnesses (p. 58/6–8), he claims also to have been one of those who fed the saint during her time in the dungeon (p. 82/29–30) and to have brought the saint's body back to her grandmother's house (p. 82/27–8).[22]

Margaret is especially, though not exclusively, associated with women in childbirth: women should, according to Wace in his Life of her, 'love her very much and praise God for her'.[23] In Anglo-Norman as in English versions of

---

[21] See M. C. Spalding, *The Middle English Charters of Christ*, Bryn Mawr College Monographs xv (Bryn Mawr, 1914). The vernacular Christ-charters are late medieval but have an ancestry in the Sunday letter (see W. R. Jones, 'The Heavenly Letter in Medieval England', *Medievalia et Humanistica*, 6 [1975]: 163–78), and in the use of Christ's body as the material on which the world is inscribed for reading in *mappae mundi* of the Ebsdorf type (see David Woodward, 'Reality, Symbolism, Space and Time in Medieval World Maps', *Annals of the Association of American Geographers*, 75 [1985], 510–21). To the example of the heavenly letter as text-relic in the *South English Legendary* Kenelm Life discussed by Earle ('Typology and Iconographic Style', pp. 25–8) could be added a group of documents sometimes classed as 'fragments' from saints' lives, but which may have functioned as complete text relics: e.g. London, British Library, MS Harley 912, an Anglo-Norman account of the heavenly letter naming to St. Giles an unmentionable (and hence unabsolvable) sin committed by Charlemagne (ed. Louis Brandin, 'Un fragment de la *Vie de saint Gilles*', *Romania*, 33 [1904]: 94–98); an Anglo-Norman account of the miraculous transmission of Edward the Confessor's ring between the saint and John the Evangelist (Cambridge, University Library, MS Additional 3392. C, fol. 137ᵛ, ed. H. J. Chaytor in *Miscellany of Studies in Romance Languages and Literatures Presented to Leon Kastner*, ed. Mary Williams and James A. de Rothschild [Cambridge, 1932], pp. 124–27). For a wide-ranging survey primarily concerned with later Middle English examples, see Margaret Aston, *Lollards and Reformers: Images and Literacy in Late Medieval Religion* (London, 1984), ch. 4, 'Devotional Literacy' (I am grateful to Alan Fletcher, of University College, Dublin, for this reference).

[22] This inconsistency could be due to carelessness on the part of the vernacular writer, but it would be a carelessness shared with the Latin text which also alters Theotimus' role in this way; see F. M. Mack (ed.), *Seinte Marherete: þe Meiden ant Martyr*, EETS OS 193 (London, 1934; repr. with corrections 1958), pp. 128/12–14 and 141/35–142/8). On increased valorization of the body as participating in the sacred from the early thirteenth century on, see Caroline Bynum, 'The Female Body and Religious Practice in the later Middle Ages', in her *Fragmentation and Redemption: Essays on Gender and the Human Body in Medieval Religion* (New York, 1991), esp. pp. 222–38.

[23] 'Dames la devent mult amer/E pur li Damnedé loër', Hans-Erich Keller (ed.), *Wace: La vie de sainte Marguérite; édition, avec introduction et glossaire par Hans-Erich Keller, commentaire*

Margaret's Life, the saint prays that any house containing a copy of her passion may have no deformed children born in it, and more specifically, in many cases, that if a woman in labour calls on her or 'face mun martire devant luy recont*er*' (Cambridge, University Library, MS Ee. 6. 11, fol. 9ʳ, l. 27) she may be delivered alive of a live and healthy child.[24] The initially puzzling association of this virgin martyr with pregnancy is partly clarified by medieval illustrations (more frequent in continental than in insular texts): the dragon is often shown twisted on its back with the saint emerging (something in the manner of medieval illustrations of Caesarean births) from the midst of its body.[25] Association with the pearl ('margarita') such as is prominent in Jacobus de Voragine's influential late thirteenth-century *Legenda Aurea* version of Margaret's Life will have enriched the association, since pearls were believed to help stop excessive bleeding.[26]

In the version of Paris, Bibliothèque nationale, MS fr. 1555 (Version 'G'), the saint prays in further detail for the relief of pregnant women. She intercedes for the woman who crosses herself with a book 'ou ma vie sera' (l. 537), or looks inside such a book or has the book placed on her body ('dessus li metra le livre', l. 539). For women commemorating Margaret in churches dedicated to her, the saint asks that when they have prayed to her and heard her life, their children

---

des enluminures du ms. Troyes 1905, Beihefte zur Zeitschrift für romanische Philologie, Band 229 (Tübingen, 1990), p. 115, ll. 735-6.

[24] Anglo-Norman versions: (I) Wace, ed. Keller; (II) F. Spencer, *La vie de sainte Marguerite* (Leipzig, 1889) [Cambridge, University Library MS Ee. 6. ii]; (III) K. Reichl, 'An Anglo-Norman Legend of Saint Margaret', *Romania*, 96 (1975): 53-66 [London, British Library, MS Additional 38664: the 'Edwardes MS']; (IV) F. Spencer 'The Legend of St. Margaret', *MLN* 5 (1890): 213-21 [York, Cathedral Chapter Library, MS 16. K. 13]; (V) Joly, *La vie de seinte Marguerite*, pp. 83-98 [Paris, Bibliothèque Nationale, MS fr. 19525]; (VI) P. Meyer, 'Notice du MS Sloane 1611 du Musée Britannique' *Romania*, 40 (1911): 541-58; (VII) M. Amelia Klenke, (ed.), *Three Saints' Lives by Nicholas Bozon*, Franciscan Institute Publications History Series I (St Bonaventure, N.Y., 1947). For a translation of the best-known continental version, and for summaries of other Anglo-Norman and continental versions, see now Brigitte Cazelles, *The Lady as Saint: A Collection of French Hagiographic Romances of the Thirteenth Century* (Philadelphia, 1991), pp. 216-37. Versions II-VII survive in Anglo-Norman manuscripts, or in continental copies of Anglo-Norman texts; version I, though extant in continental manuscripts, may be counted as Anglo-French, since it is by an author with strong connections with the Anglo-Norman court. In Margaret's final prayers, a copy of her passion is envisaged as ensuring healthy lineage (Versions I, VII), as is a reading of it (II, V); calling on the saint by the woman in labour will help safe delivery (I, III, IV), as will faith on the part of the pregnant woman (VI). Other early Middle English versions: Charlotte D'Evelyn and Anna J. Mill (eds.), *South English Legendary*, I EETS OS 235 (London, 1956), p. 301/283-288 (invocation of saint or hearing of life by pregnant women); quatrains ed. C. Horstmann, *Altenglische Legenden, N.F.* (Heilbronn, 1881), p. 497/281-4 (prayer for women); Auchinleck, Horstmann, p. 234/366-8 (prayer for women in labour who invoke the saint); Couplets, Horstmann, p. 240/545-241/551. Horstmann's editions are convenient, rather than totally reliable, but specific prayers for women are clearly present in these texts.

[25] See Stones, 'Le ms. Troyes 1905, le recueil et ses enluminures', in Keller (ed.), *Wace: La vie de sainte Marguerite*, pp. 185-333 (esp. figs. 76, 77, 80); Lillian Randall, *Images in the Margins of Gothic Manuscripts* (Berkeley, 1966), figs. 620, 621; L. Réau, *L'iconographie de l'art chrétien* III, *Iconographie des saints*, 2e partie, G-O (Paris, 1958), pp. 877-82. On Caesarean births, see Renate Blumenfeld-Kosinski, *Not of Woman Born: Representations of Caesarean Birth in Medieval and Renaissance Culture* (Ithaca and London, 1990), esp. chs. 1 and 2.

[26] Aristide Joly (ed.), *La vie de sainte Marguerite* (Paris, 1879), p. 29. See also Blumenfeld-Kosinski, *Not of Woman Born*, pp. 7-8 for a rich late medieval example of a childbirth prayer to Margaret.

will be preserved whole, uncrippled and mentally sound from conception to birth.[27] This continental French version of Margaret's Life is extant in over a hundred manuscripts from the later middle ages up to the sixteenth century, and it continued to be published in the eighteenth and nineteenth centuries.[28] Some rare continental survivals show that this text of the saint's life was indeed transmitted as a healing text-relic, worn or placed on the bodies of pregnant women. A late thirteenth-century text of Margaret's Life in amulet form has been known since the 1920s, while in the most recent study, Carolus-Barré describes a mid fifteenth-century amulet-text of Version G discovered in 1977.[29] It is foldable into 25 little squares, each with cut corners forming lozenges. Accompanying this amulet or 'bref' in its modern casing is the fragment of a ribbon 'ayant servi sans aucun doute à attacher antérieurement le parchemin une fois plié.'[30] In addition to *brefs* which could be folded up and worn as amulets, some Margaret Lives are extant in the form of scrolls (which may have been worn as girdles).[31]

Though there seem to be extant no such insular Margaret texts, this does not mean that such practices were unknown in insular culture, for there is a high likelihood of such texts becoming worn away through use. The word *bref* survives in Middle English in the same sense as the French bref: 'yf a woman

---

27
          Que dame qui soit empreignie,
          Puis qu'ele sera seignie
          Du livre ou ma vie sera
          Ou dedens regarde aura
          Ou dessus li metra le livre
          Sans peril soit quite et delivre.
          Et dame qui moi servira
          En Eglise qu'elle saura
          Qu'en mon propre nom soit fondée,
          Si tost come elle aura finée
          Sa proiere et son oroison,
          Et oie ma passion,
          Que ja ses fruis ne soit peris,
          Puis quil sera engenouis
          Et concheus dedens son cors;
          Mais anchois que il isse hors,
          De tous ses membres soit membrés,
          Ne tors ne soit, ne afolez.

Ed. Joly, *La vie de seinte Marguerite*, p. 114, ll. 541–552; excerpted and tr. Cazelles, *Lady as Saint*, pp. 217–28.
28 Meyer, 'Légendes hagiographiques', p. 363, no.7.
29 Louis Carolus-Barré, 'Un nouveau parchemin amulette et la légende de sainte Marguerite patronne des femmes en couches', *Comptes rendus de l'Académie des Inscriptions et Belles Lettres* (1979): 256–75.
30 Carolus-Barré, p. 261.
31 Two such fifteenth-century French scrolls in the Wellcome Library collections are respectively 2550 x 110 and 60 x 55mm. in dimension, and one of them has an eighteenth-century title 'Ceinture de Sainte Marguerite [pour] les femmes Grosses'. For descriptions, see N. R. Ker, *Medieval Manuscripts in British Libraries*, I (Oxford, 1969), pp. 400–1. Fifteenth-century midwives are reported asking the brother of a woman in childbirth 'Por Dieu, lisez la vie sainte Margarite sur votre seur, et au plaisir Dieu elle enfantera.' (Yves Chauvin, [ed.], *Livre des Miracles de Sainte-Catherine-de-Fierbois (1375-1470)*, Archives Historiques du Poitou 60, Société des archives historiques du Poitou, Poitiers, 1976, p. 42: I am grateful to Sebastian Sutcliffe, St John's College, Oxford, for this reference).

trawayle of chyld, [and] a prest or a clerk . . . rede þis breve ouer here hewede'.[32] There is also a fifteenth-century English scroll with prayers to the infant martyr Quiricus and his mother Jutta extant as London, Wellcome Library, MS 632, with inscriptions explaining its obstetric and other uses. This scroll combines the impeccable provenance of the heavenly letter transmission-story with the protective power of invocations. One inscription declares the scroll to be 'oure lady seynt mary sengter [cincture]': another explains that the scroll was sent from an angel to pope Leo in Rome, and promises that 'who so beryth thys mesure uppon hym wyth trewe fayth and good devocyon' will not be 'slayne in battel nor by no devull be combryd . . . nor wyth no soden deth be smyttyn nor dye wythowte howsyll and shryft nor byfore no juge wrongefuly dampned nor . . . perysshed wyth ffyer nor water nor blastys ne wyndys on water ne on lond shal not grew hym . . . .' While such a girdle might seem even better suited to helping Sir Gawain against the Green Knight than to a pregnant woman, it is also promised that if a woman in travail 'gyrdes thys mesure abowte hyr wombe . . . she shall be safe delyvyrd wythowte parelle and the cylde shall have crystendome and the mother puryfycatyon'.[33]

In the post-Conquest period, practices analagous to the use of text-amulets are documentable among the Anglo-Norman medical collections recently made systematically available in Tony Hunt's monumental volume.[34] Holy names are invoked via inscription on scraps of parchment tied to the bodies of pregnant women, or are carved on apples for their ingestion. In London, British Library, MS Sloane 3564, for instance, a charm for women in childbirth recommends the following:

> Escrivez en une poume, si li donez a manger: 'De virga virgine ubi oritur radix Jesse. Anna peperit Mariam, Maria salvatorem. In nomine domini Jesu Cristi, infans, exi foras, sive sis masculus sive femina. Pater Noster et Ave Maria et Credo. In nomine Patris etc. Sicut vere credimus quod beata Maria peperit infantem, unum verum deum et hominem. Item et tu, ancilla Cristi, pare infantem. In nomine Patris etc.'[35]

Another charm in the same manuscript prescribes writing a similar invocation 'in parchemyn' and tying it 'entour le destre flank de la femme . . . et tantot istera l'enfant vif u mort'.[36]

---

[32] MED s.v. bref, 3a; cited from Stockholm, Royal Library, Med. MS X. 90 (*olim* Med. Misc. MS XIV), edited by Gottfried Müller, *Aus Mittelenglischen Medizintexten* (Leipzig, 1929), p. 60, ll. 29–30.

[33] See the description in S. A. J. Moorat, *Catalogue of Western Manuscripts in Medicine and Science in the Wellcome Historical Medical Library, vol. I, MSS Written Before 1650 AD* (London, 1962), pp. 491–93. 'Mesure' in the sense used here is not entered in the MED. under *mesure* n., but scroll-like lengths of ribbon sometimes appear in *sachets accoucheurs* and are noted as measuring dimensions of holy figures, as with the 1.79m. ribbon labelled as 'Longhezza di Nostro Signore Giesu christo' in the Auvergne survival described by Carolus-Barré, 'Un nouveau parchemin amulette', p. 257.

[34] Tony Hunt, *Popular Medicine in Thirteenth Century England: Introduction and Texts* (Cambridge, 1990).

[35] Hunt, p. 361, n.135. There is a similar Latin charm among the later English prescriptions in Stockholm, Royal Library, MS X.90: Müller, p. 131, ll. 3–6.

[36] Hunt, p. 92, no. 46.

Though these practices are often assumed to be 'popular' medicine, they are so in the sense of being in demand, rather than being limited to lower classes. Royal French women used St Margaret text-amulets in childbirth, insular women of good birth were the *destinataires* of Margaret Lives.[37] The eating of a text-apple by a pregnant woman may not have been clearly categorizable as part of a separable realm of 'popular culture' when clerical practices valorize not only the figurative ingestion of the Word by *ruminatio* – 'la manducation de la parole'[38] – but by oral contact with relics (St Hugh of Lincoln, for instance, is famously shown in the contemporary late twelfth-century life by Adam of Eynsham as biting off fragments of Mary Magdalen's arm at Fécamp: reverently kissing and gazing upon the relic – 'sacratissimum os ori et oculis suis reurenter applicuit' – and then using first his incisors and then his molars).[39]

Hearing, touching, wearing, consuming saints' Lives are, as I have argued, practices embracable within, and even the logical consequence of, hagiography's ritual and typological structural principles. But the textual history of the Margaret legend suggests that hagiographic endorsement of such audience relations is also the product of interaction between hagiographic producers and consumers. Before the twelfth century, versions of Margaret's Life envisage writing or buying a text of the life, building or lighting a church, invoking Margaret's name and thereby having a house free of maimed or deformed offspring, a devotional use which is either not gender-specific or related to general concern for the production of adequate heirs.[40] All early vernacular versions, Anglo-Saxon, Anglo-Norman and Early Middle English, derive from the 'Mombritius' version of Margaret's Latin *passio* in which the concluding promissory prayers and programme of cult development are outlined by the saint as follows:

> . . . ut si quis librum geste mee legerit, aut meam audierit passionem, ex illa hora deleantur peccata eius. [Et quisquis lumen fecerit in basilica mea de suo labore, non imputentur peccata eorum.] Et quicumque in iudicio terribili fuerit inuentus, et nominis mei memor fuerit, liberes eum a tormento. Et adhuc qui legerit aut tulerit libellum passionis huius, huic peccata ex illa hora non imponantur; quia caro et sanguis sumus, et semper peccamus, nullomodo cessantes. Et qui fecerit basilicam in nomine meo,

---

[37] For royal French women, see Joly, *La vie sainte Marguerite*, p. 29: for some examples of English versions of Margaret's Life with gentry audiences, see, in addition to the early Middle English *Margarete* discussed above (pp. 44–6), the Life by Bokenham (ed. M. Serjeantson, *Bokenham's Legendys of Hooly Wummen*, EETS OS 206 [London, 1938], pp. 7–38; (see also Bokenham's Life of St Anne), and Lydgate's *Margarete*, with its envoi to 'Noble princesses and ladyes of estate, /And gentilwomen lower of degre' as well as to 'all wymmmen that haue necessite' (ed. Horstmann, *Altenglische Legenden, N.F.*, p. 453, ll. 520–24).

[38] For clerical interest in this idea, see Jesse Gellrich, *The Idea of the Book in the Middle Ages: Language Theory, Mythology, and Fiction* (Ithaca and London, 1985), p. 22 and frontispiece.

[39] D. L. Douie and D. H. Farmer (eds.), *Magna Vita Sancti Hugonis: The Life of St. Hugh of Lincoln* (Oxford, 1985), ii.168 (and cf. pp. 152–4).

[40] Cf., e.g., the saint's prayers and the heavenly replies in G. Herzfeld (ed.), *The Old English Martyrology*, EETS OS 116 (London, 1900), p. 116/6–11, 12–16; Cambridge, Corpus Christi College, MS 303, ed. B. Assmann, *Angelsächsische Homilien und Heiligenleben* (Kassel, 1889), xv.179/314–25, 331–37); London, British Library, MS Cotton Tiberius A.III, ed. O. Cockayne, *Narratiunculae Anglice Conscriptae* (London, 1861), pp. 47/7–20, 47/26–48/5.

aut scripserit passionem meam, aut emerit eam de iusto labore, repleatur Spiritu Sancto; et in domo eius non nascatur infans claudus, cecus, nec mutus, neque a spiritu temptatur immundo; et quod petierit indulge illi.[41]

The first life explicitly to mention pregnant women invoking the saint is Wace's life of *c.* 1135: after this, though independently of Wace, most twelfth- and thirteenth-century versions in English and Anglo-Norman specify pregnant women in the saint's textual community.[42]

There exists a further version of the Latin *passio*, discovered by Elizabeth Francis when editing Wace's *Vie de seinte Marguerite*, and called by her the 'Caligula' version after one of its principal manuscripts.[43] This life, close to, but with significant differences from, the Mombritius life, includes explicit mention of pregnant women: 'Iterum si in domo me invocans mulier pregnans in partu laboraverit, ab imminente eripe eam periculo, infansque quoque ex utero fusus lumine potiatur seculi huius, absque suorum aliquo detrimento membrorum'.[44] This Latin life exists in twelfth- and thirteenth-century English and French manuscripts, as does the Mombritius life, but unlike that version, does not have an early tradition.[45] We may therefore have here an example of vernacular applications of the saint's life feeding back into its Latin tradition, the Caligula version supplementing the Mombritius one through priests' and clerics' associations with and awareness of the customs of, pregnant women. (The fact that some vernacular versions use a Caligula source is not incompatible with the Caligula version's having received its initial impetus from awareness of female obstetric practice.)[46]

In considering who requires copies, who makes them and what is done with them, unexamined gender and class models can constrict or give misleading direction to the implications of the evidence. In the case of pregnant women or women in childbirth as text-users, the audience component of the textual community at least seems securely gendered, but without specific evidence of identity, confident assumptions about other participants in the transmission process cannot be made. One text of a Life of St Margaret, a thirteenth-century Anglo-Norman version, is to be found in London, British Library, MS Sloane 1611, together with two Anglo-French medical treatises, the *Régime du corps* (translated from Aldobrando of Siena) and a collection of 'Ypocras' remedies.[47] The Margaret Life is not inserted, but copied into the

---

[41] Ed. Mack, *Seinte Marherete*, p. 140/2–16.

[42] See note 24 above.

[43] E. A. Francis, 'A Hitherto Unprinted Version of the *Passio Sanctae Margaritae* with Some Observations on Vernacular Derivatives', *PMLA* 42 (1927): 87–105.

[44] Francis, p. 103.

[45] Francis, p. 87–88.

[46] Anglo-Norman versions I, III, IV and the English versions in Mirk's *Festial* and Barbour's *Legendary* use a Caligula source (see d'Evelyn and Foster, 'Saints' Legends', for editions); of the Anglo-Norman versions (V,II,VI) which use the Mombritius *passio*, II and VI explicitly mention pregnant women as well as healthy children; Bozon (Version VII, late thirteenth/early fourteenth century) uses the *Legenda Aurea* version (itself a reworking of Mombritius) which mentions women in labour. See further note 24 above.

[47] In his edition (see note 24 above, Version VI), Meyer argues that the copyist was northern French, but working in England and copying Anglo-French medical texts and the Anglo-Norman Life of the saint (pp. 534–35, 539).

manuscript as part of its compilation. On fol. 147[r] there are recipes and invocations for women in labour similar to those quoted above (p. 49).[48] On fol. 147[v] the Life of Margaret begins, suggesting that this Life was needed by users of the medical treatises in the manuscript. Under a subsection of the Ypocras collection, 'De la nature de lait' (fol. 136[v]–fol. 137[r]), a later hand has added a small marital *curriculum vitae* of the Virgin's mother, detailing St Anne's three husbands, and the three daughters she had by them: by Joachim, the virgin Mary, 'la qele enfaunta Jhesu del seinte esperite'; by Cleophas, Mary, who in turn gives birth to James, Josephus, Simon and Jude, and by Salome, Mary ('de qi ele enfaunta Marie qui fust mariee a Zebedee la qele enfaunta Jakes le graindre e Johan leuangelist'). This holy female genealogy, with its repeated emphasis on giving birth (not on begetting) was widespread in the later Middle Ages and suggests use of the manuscript in an obstetric context: perhaps it was added in the margins of this medical treatise as a copytext for apples or parchment scraps.[49] Though the Margaret text in this manuscript is not in amulet form, it may have served a similar function, perhaps being read to pregnant women approaching their term or in childbirth.

Such readers might be male physicians, but until the later thirteenth century's medicalization of birth, were more likely to be midwives or other women. As Blumenfeld-Kosinski and Green have shown, vernacular and Latin medical texts cannot be seen as inhabiting two separate spheres of learned and popular: in the professionalization of medicine doctors did not long leave the vital and profitable area of obstetrics to midwives alone, but neither were midwives or other women attendant on lyings-in without knowledge, or, in some cases, without literacy.[50] In this context, the presence of the vernacular is ambiguous evidence: does it testify to pragmatic access to textuality on the part of female users, or does it show the extent to which professional medical formalizations of female obstetric practices have captured the birthing chamber and now offer vernacular access as a sign of their own power to concede it? It is precisely in the late twelfth and thirteenth centuries that transmission stories authorizing clerical textuality burgeon, both in hagiography and medicine (two discourses arguably brought still closer together in gynaecological matters by the development of the Feast of the Conception in insular Marian devotion) and from the later thirteenth century that the marginalization of midwives in the medicalization of birth becomes

---

[48] 'A feme qui travaille d'enfant, liès a son ventre cest escrit: Maria peperit Christum. + .Elizabet Johannem. + .Selina Remigium. + .Sator. + .Arepo. + .Tenet. + .opera. + .ritas. Ou donés lui a boivere ditandre, si enfantera sans peril. Ou escrisés la paternostre en un mazelin au fons (in the bottom of a [wooden] cup) et lavés a vin et a iaue benoite, si enfantera sans dolor et sans peril; ou donés li a boivre ysope a iaue chaude, si enfantera, tout soit li enfant mors ou porris', fol. 147[r]. For this and other gynaecological prescriptions see Meyer, p.538.

[49] On St Anne and her holy lineage, see Francesca Sautman, 'Saint Anne in Folk Tradition' Late Medieval France' and Pamela Sheingorn, 'Appropriating the Holy Kinship: Gender and Family History', respectively pp. 69–94 and pp. 169–198 in Kathleen Ashley and Pamela Sheingorn (eds.), *Interpreting Cultural Symbols: Saint Anne in Late Medieval Society* (Athens and London, 1990).

[50] Monica Green, 'Women's Medical Practice and Health Care in Medieval Europe', *Signs: Journal of Women in Culture and Society*, 14 (1989): 434–73, esp. pp. 461–73; Blumenfeld-Kosinski, *Not of Woman Born*, esp. p.102.

visible.[51] It is thus by no means clear that we should assume *either* that Margaret amulet-texts hung only at the belts of pregnant women and midwives rather than doctors, *or* that they were not copied by female practitioners. The very 'grammaire choquante' of which the editor of the Margaret Life in MS Sloane 1611 complains ('*Il* [sic] devait tout juste savoir le français de *Stratford atte Bowe*') suggests limited formal training and hence perhaps that the copyist of this manuscript may be female.[52] On the other hand, though the early modern context for one of the surviving French Margaret *brefs* or amulets is that of the *sachet accoucheur*, the texts therein may have been part of the physician's or priest's equipment as much as that of the midwife. (Small portable 'brefs' of charts and tables for prognostication were worn at the waist for ready consultation by medieval physicians).[53]

The mimetic principle whereby Margaret's emergence from the dragon's body prefigures and eases that of the child from the woman in labour may be thought not to indicate much care or concern for women's bodies, except perhaps as the source of reproduction. If not actual hell-mouths, female bodies are consigned by this congruence to the role of expendable dragons. On the other hand, Margaret herself triumphs and redirects the meaning of her pain and suffering in her legend. Within culturally endemic depreciation of the female body, the promise Margaret's Life held for so many audiences must have been of significant comfort. In such need as often has attended European childbirth, prayers for wholeness and survival are not meaningless.[54] It is a sobering thought that, apart from a few chance remains, an entire world of hagiographic textual practice centred on the important audience constituted by pregnant women has virtually disappeared, in part because of the very urgency of that audience's need for transmission of the saint's life in a particularly perishable form. The social contexts and cultural principles of hagiographic transmission by physical contact do, however, seem here to mesh sufficiently with other types of textual survivals and to have left enough traces of interaction between clerics, women and physicians to serve as a reminder that the transmission of textuality is a wider activity than the transmission of texts as such.

---

[51] See Blumenfeld-Kosinski, *Not of Woman Born*, ch. 3, 'The Marginalization of Women in Obstetrics', esp. pp. 95–6, 102, 109–110. The marginalization of actual women in attending on birth is not incompatible with the developing cult of holy motherhood. Of this latter, Wace's mid-twelfth century *Conception Notre-Dame* and *Histoire des Trois Maries et Assomption Nostre Dame*, important early Anglo-French vernacular accounts of holy maternity, are one indication (ed. V. Luzarche, *La vie de la vierge Marie de maître Wace* [Tours, 1859]). Mary Clayton argues strongly for the development of the feast of the Conception of the Blessed Virgin not as an eighth-century English innovation, but a post-Conquest development: 'Feasts of the Virgin in the Liturgy of the Anglo-Saxon Church', *Anglo-Saxon England*, 13 (1984): 209–33.

[52] Meyer, 'Notice du Ms. Sloane 1611', pp. 539, 535.

[53] On portable physicians' texts in England, see R. H. Robbins, 'Medical Manuscripts in Middle English', *Speculum*, 45 (1970): 393–415, pp. 396–7.

[54] Early modern evidence testifies, unsurprisingly, to great apprehensiveness on the part of women in advanced pregnancy; see Adrian Wilson, 'The Ceremony of Childbirth and its Interpretation' in Valerie Fildes (ed.), *Women as Mothers in Pre-Industrial England: Essays in Memory of Dorothy MacLaren* (London, 1990), pp. 68–107.

TWO MIDDLE ENGLISH PENITENTIAL LYRICS: SOUND AND SCANSION

Thomas G. Duncan

The phrase 'from script to print', used as the title of a well-known book by H. J. Chaytor,[1] defines the span of transmission from the author's manuscript to the modern printed page. But with poetry, and especially with lyric poetry, the operative span is rather wider, and perhaps more appropriately to be defined as 'from sound to sound', that is, from the sound, sung or spoken, that a medieval lyricist had in mind for his poem, to that distant echo that its representation in modern print may allow today's reader. Any attempt to arrive at some notion of what the original sound may have been depends crucially on some understanding of metre; and any attempt to convey that sound to the modern reader raises the issue of an appropriate modern presentation. The aim of this paper is to reopen the question of metre in Middle English lyrics, a fundamental problem in any consideration of the transmission of these texts, and to illustrate some of the points raised by a close examination of two well-known penitential lyrics, 'Mirie it is while sumer ilast' and 'Lord, thou clepedest me'.[2]

Discussions of the metre of Middle English lyrics have seldom passed beyond generalities. In his edition of *The Harley Lyrics*, G. L. Brook distinguishes two kinds of metre. The first is the type most common in the Harley Lyrics, where Brook claims 'unstressed syllables alternate fairly evenly as in Modern English versification';[3] the second is the line 'descended from the Old English alliterative line with two stressed syllables and a variable number of unstressed syllables in each half',[4] a type common in political and satirical poems, but less common in lyrics. Brook barely moves beyond this rudimentary distinction, which, in any case, he ignores in his account of the length of lines, which are described solely in terms of stress. 'The number of stresses in a line,' we are

---

[1] *From Script to Print: An Introduction to Medieval Literature* (Cambridge, 1945).
[2] The penitential nature of 'Mirie it is' is made clear by David L. Jeffrey in his *The Early English Lyric and Franciscan Spirituality* (Lincoln and London, 1975), pp. 12–15. Although 'at first glance a reader might, quite naturally, think of it as a secular poem . . . in this poem the realm of natural experience is actually charged with implication for another and increasingly immanent kingdom.' (p. 13) This emerges from the final two lines:
> And ich wid wel michel wrong
> Soregh and murne and fast.
The crucial final word *fast* is not now visible in the manuscript, Bodleian Library, MS. Rawlinson G.22, f.1ᵛ, but is unanimously adopted by modern editors as the required reading. In the three verbs of the last line Jeffrey sees an anticipation of 'the three traditional steps involved in what Chaucer's Parson called "verray repentance" – true repentance: *contrition* ("soregh"), *confession* (suggested by "murne"), and *satisfaction*, involving penitential action ("fast")' (p. 14).
[3] G. L. Brook (ed.), *The Harley Lyrics* (Manchester, 1956, Fourth Edition, 1968), p. 18.
[4] *The Harley Lyrics*, p. 18.

55

told, 'varies from two to seven'; but: 'it is not uncommon to find a line containing fewer stresses than we should expect . . . Some of these lines may be corrupt, but it is unlikely that all of them are, and it is better to regard the occasional substitution of a three-stress for a four-stress line as a form of licence to avoid monotony'.[5] And with the phrase 'a form of licence to avoid monotony', further analysis of the detail of Middle English lyric metre is abandoned.

In his Cambridge Inaugural Lecture, 'The Old Sound and the New', Professor John Stevens quoted two short Middle English lyrics in illustration of his view that

> to a degree which has not been true again of poetry until this century, a medieval poet worked with units of speech and made up his poems out of spoken phrases.[6]

The claim that the rhythm of Middle English verse is that of 'very speech itself'[7] is important; it differs significantly from the more usual view, namely, that 'most Middle English lyric verse is based on stress-rhythm'.[8] Presumably, however, Middle English poets conceived of poetic form as something more than simply 'units of speech'. Stevens recognises this: he speaks of 'the constraints and artifices of poetry',[9] but without, however, any further indication as to what these constraints might be in the case of the Middle English lyric.

A much more precise and exact account of lyric metre was attempted by E. J. Dobson in the volume of medieval English songs which he edited jointly with F. Ll. Harrison. Dobson drew a distinction between Middle English 'literary' lyrics in which, he claimed, poets were 'accustomed to count stresses rather than syllables and [were] indifferent to the order of stressed and unstressed syllables',[10] and songs, where 'the music . . . may require perfect or near-perfect metrical regularity, in syllable-count and in rhythm'.[11] However, if by 'the music' we are to understand the actual musical notation of the surviving manuscripts, this evidence may be held to support a greater flexibility in songs than Dobson was willing to allow in two important respects.[12]

The first concerns a feature as common in lyrics as in other Middle English verse, namely, the variation of lines beginning with a weak syllable and lines beginning with a stressed syllable, so-called 'headless' lines. The musical notation found in the manuscripts supports this as an acceptable variant in the songs by virtue of allowing for an optional leading-in note. Thus, in the carol 'Als I lay on Yoolis night' (*Medieval English Songs*, No. 20), the first lines of the sixteen stanzas vary: eight are 'headless', having seven syllables; the other eight have eight syllables. The music, given as usual with the words of the first

---

5 *The Harley Lyrics*, p. 18.
6 John Stevens, *The Old Sound and the New: An inaugural lecture* (Cambridge, 1982), p. 7.
7 *Old Sound and the New*, p. 7.
8 R. D. Stevick (ed.), *One Hundred Middle English Lyrics* (Indianapolis, 1964), p. xxvii.
9 *Old Sound and the New*, p. 8.
10 E. J. Dobson and F. Ll. Harrison (eds.), *Medieval English Songs* (London, 1979), p. 167.
11 *Medieval English Songs*, p. 32.
12 See Thomas G. Duncan, in *Medium Ævum*, 50 (1981): 338–41 (review of Dobson and Harrison, *Medieval English Songs*), where other points are discussed.

stanza only, fits the seven-syllable first line of stanza i. However, comparison with the burden, which has an eight-syllable first line and music to match, shows exactly how an extra leading-in note would have been supplied for the stanzas with eight-syllable first lines, since the first full bars of the music for the first line of the burden and for the first line of the full stanza are identical. Had this principle been recognised in the case of 'On hir is mi lif ilong' (*Medieval English Songs*, No. 6b), there would have been no need, against what Dobson admits to be 'the balance of the literary evidence',[13] to emend the eight-syllable first lines of stanzas i, ii and v to match the seven-syllable first lines of stanzas ii and iv of this lyric. Likewise, Bukofzer's transcription[14] of the music of 'Man mai longe lives weene' (*Medieval English Songs*, No. 6a) demonstrates how the actual surviving musical notation can, by the overlapping of lines within one musical phrase, accommodate eight syllables in lines two and four of the first stanza, which Dobson, in his quest for strict regularity, reduced to seven syllables each.[15] It would indeed be odd if a medieval singer had found any difficulty in dealing with the kind of variation which an average congregation takes in its stride when accommodating such lines as 'O come, all ye faithful' and 'Sing choirs of angels' to the same tune.

The second point concerns the matching of rhythm and word stress. Here too there may be room for greater variation than Dobson allowed. What in fact does medieval music require in the matter of regularity of the occurrence of word accent? Any answer to this question depends on our knowledge of the nature of rhythm in medieval music. This subject is, however, notoriously problematic. It is hardly surprising that the Music Editor of *Medieval English Songs* admits that 'rhythmic problems . . . occasioned long and often passionate discussion between the editors of the volume'.[16] With unmeasured music (that is, music of a plainsong kind) there are virtually no constraints with regard to regularity of verbal accent. Measured music, on the other hand, familiar in the 3/4 and 6/8 rhythms of modern performances of medieval songs, clearly has a regular beat. But even here, the implications of the musical rhythm for the stress-patterns of a verbal text are not self evident; one must be wary, as Harrison warns, of 'presuppositions about stress connected with the present-day use of bar-lines'.[17] Sometimes, it is uncertain from the medieval notation whether a tune is to be interpreted in a measured way or not. For instance, the tune of 'Man may longe lives weene' (*Medieval English Songs*, No. 6a) is written in unmeasured notation. Dobson nevertheless claims that it was 'presumably intended to be sung in a triple rhythm'. Having made this first assumption, he then adds a second, for it is only an assumption that music in triple rhythm 'demands a high degree of metrical regularity . . . in accentual rhythm'.[18] It is to be noted, however, that in this song, as in others, far from the music determining the word text, it is the word text, as edited by Dobson, that determines the interpretation

---

[13] *Medieval English Songs*, p. 34.

[14] See Gustave Reese, *Music in the Middle Ages* (New York, 1940), p. 243.

[15] I.e., by taking *ofte* as *oft* (with a silent final 'e') in line 2, and by removing *an* from the beginning of line 4.

[16] *Medieval English Songs*, p. 69.

[17] *Medieval English Songs*, p. 69.

[18] *Medieval English Songs*, p. 123.

of the music.[19] When, therefore, the interpretation of the tune derives not from the musical notation as such, but from the editor's views of the metre of the edited word text, the circularity of claims in terms of what 'the music . . . demands' is obvious. Accordingly, when Dobson emends to achieve strict coincidence of verbal and metrical accent,[20] this is not, as he claims, 'certainly what the music requires'.[21] Even in measured music, a singer has no difficulty in maintaining the rhythm of the tune against the natural stress-pattern of the odd word here and there.[22]

Nevertheless, it is clear that in a song, the words must fit the tune, and do so in all stanzas; this accordingly demands a considerable degree of regularity. This very match of words and music was the fundamental characteristic of continental songs from which the Middle English stanzaic lyric derives. In verse written by troubadours and trouvères, the 'most important single controlling factor is the number of syllables in any given line or stanza'.[23] This concern with number is central to the medieval concept of *musica* which Professor Stevens extensively explores in his recent book, *Words and Music in the Middle Ages*.[24] It may well be that in English stanzaic lyrics within this tradition (whether surviving with music or not) the major poetic constraint remained a syllabic match, line for line and stanza by stanza, but perhaps a match of syllables less strict and less tied to accentual regularity than Dobson envisaged.

Since, however, songs, in common with other Middle English lyrics, frequently survive 'lame and deformed'[25] after the hazards of scribal transmission, the syllabic count is often far from obvious at first sight. Sometimes it can be restored by taking into account alternative linguistic features such as variant forms of words in Middle English, final 'e', pronounced or silent, elision or hiatus, and full or syncopated forms.[26] When such possibilities have been exhausted, emendation may be the only way of restoring metrical form. Dobson's admirable and courageous commitment to the editor's duty to emend[27] contrasts markedly with Brook's conservatism.

In the light of the principles outlined above, some progress may be made towards a better appreciation of the sound and scansion of Middle English lyrics; and some indication of what may be achieved may be gathered from the following analysis of two penitential lyrics. It has not hitherto been noticed how,

---

[19] See *Medieval English Songs*, p. 298, where Harrison admits as much in his commentary on the music.

[20] E.g., the alteration in line 2 to allow for the accentuation of *liȝet* on the first syllable within strict trochaic metre.

[21] *Medieval English Songs*, p. 125.

[22] E.g., in *aȝee* (No. 6a, line 12) and *senful* (No. 6b, line 42, sung to the same tune as No. 6a).

[23] *Old Sound and the New*, p. 2.

[24] John Stevens, *Words and Music in the Middle Ages: Song, Narrative, Dance and Drama, 1050–1350* (Cambridge, 1986).

[25] Dobson, *Medieval English Songs*, p. 30.

[26] See G. V. Smithers, 'The Scansion of *Havelok* and the Use of ME *-en* and *-e* in *Havelok* and by Chaucer', in *Middle English Studies Presented to Norman Davis in Honour of his Seventieth Birthday*, ed. Douglas Gray and E. G. Stanley (Oxford, 1983), pp. 195–234, for a detailed account of the operation of such features in establishing metrical regularity.

[27] Thus, *Medieval English Songs*, p. 27: 'I would rather go wrong in the attempt than fail to make it'.

in the penitential lyric 'Mirie it is while sumer ilast',[28] one of the lyrics quoted by Professor Stevens in his Inaugural Lecture, the restoration of regularity in the syllable-count achieved by linguistic analysis is unusually and strikingly confirmed by a critical analysis of the surviving musical notation. The context in which this lyric with its accompanying music survived is significant. It seems probable that it occurred in a manuscript containing troubadour and trouvère songs. The sole surviving leaf contains, besides 'Mirie it is', two French songs, each of two stanzas, and each accompanied with music. Harrison considers it probable that further stanzas of the English poem would have followed in the complete manuscript. If, as seems likely, originally part of a French *chansonnier*,[29] 'Mirie it is' is thereby closely linked with the tradition of French song.

Professor Stevens prints the words and the music exactly as they appear in the manuscript.[30]

---

[28] In Carleton Brown (ed.), *English Lyrics of the Thirteenth Century* (Oxford, 1932), p. 14, No. 7.

[29] See Harrison, *Medieval English Songs*, p. 297.

[30] Except for the addition of *fast*, supplied, as by others, as the missing final word of the poem.

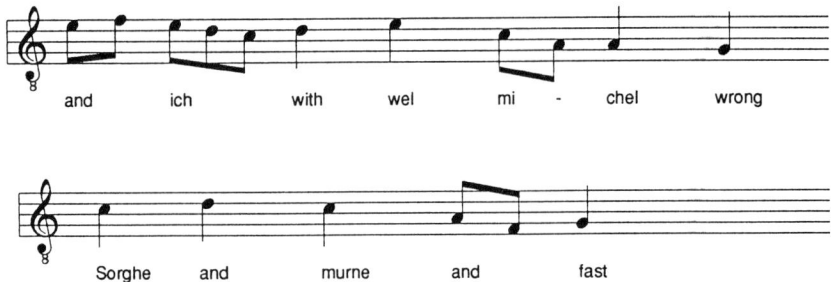

However, the metrical scheme reveals a striking irregularity. The first line, with 11 syllables, is distinctly odd viewed within the scheme of the stanza as a whole, which, as it stands, is: 11a, 5b, 7a, 4b, 7b, 7b, 7a. As part of an initial quatrain of lines riming a,b,a,b, the natural expectation would be that lines 1 and 3 would match in length as in rhyme. Nevertheless, it might be thought that the eleven syllables of the first line were guaranteed by the musical notes which accompany them in the manuscript. This, however, is not so. Musical notation was no freer from the taint of corruption than the verbal text. Where words survive with music, it appears that, in the majority of cases, the words were written first and the musical notes added thereafter. Furthermore, when adding the musical notes, scribes tended to place a note over every syllable of the text as written, repeating notes of the melody where necessary.[31]

On examination, it is evident that this first line may readily be reduced, without emendation, to seven syllables. *Miri*, without a final 'e', is an alternative Middle English form of the first word. By the kind of elision known as synizesis, a final /i/, coming before an initial vowel in the next word, becomes the corresponding semi-vowel /j/; this forms the first element of a diphthong with the following vowel, and, thereby, a single syllable.[32] The final 'e' of *while* may be omitted as silent. Finally, the last two words, *sumer ilast*, may be read as three syllables with the reduction of the second syllable of *sumer* by syncope. Most significantly, not only does the first line, by this means, match its rhyming partner in the quatrain in syllable-count, but the music of the first phrase, shorn of the repeated notes placed by the scribe to cover all the written syllables, now matches its repeat exactly.

Revisions of the manuscript readings in two other lines may be made in a similar fashion. By adopting the syncopated form *fughles* instead of the manuscript form *fugheles* in line two, this line, now of four syllables, becomes an exact match with line four, its rhyming partner. Likewise, by replacing the manuscript form *soregh* with the alternative *sorghe*, and with the elision of the final 'e's of *sorghe* and *murne* with the following *and* in each case, the final line of the poem may be read as

Sórghe ànd múrne ànd fást

[31] See Dobson, *Medieval English Songs*, p. 35.
[32] See Smithers, *Middle English Studies Presented to Norman Davis*, p. 202.

that is, with five syllables. Two significant points from the structure of the music testify to the validity of these changes. The first is the fact that no note thereby removed from the tune is other than a repeated note. The second is that when these notes are removed, it emerges that repeated notes are not otherwise characteristic of this melody; they occur only twice, once in the first phrase and once in the third phrase. The following is, therefore, arguably a more faithful presentation of the original music and text of this lyric.

Thus restored, the formal elegance of the matching of lines by syllable-count (now 7a, 4b, 7a, 4b, 7b, 7b, 5a) and of the matching of the musical phrases accords well with the characteristics of the French *chanson* and, therefore, with the context in which this penitential lyric survives.

But not all lyrics are songs. What of the others? As previously mentioned, Dobson distinguished what he called 'literary lyrics' from songs; whereas the latter were defined in terms of regularity of syllable-count, literary lyrics were characterised by the counting of stresses rather than syllables.[33] The assessment of line-length in terms of counting stresses has, of course, been a commonly adopted approach. G. L. Brook, as quoted above, dealt in terms of the number of stresses per line, as also, for example, did R. D. Stevick in his anthology entitled *One Hundred Middle English Lyrics*. This procedure has, however, two fundamental short-comings: first, it is often by no means clear what are to count as stressed syllables; and second, any consideration of the status of unstressed syllables, i.e. as metrical or merely scribal, is frequently left out of account.

In many cases, a more revealing approach, even with lyric verse which is not song-like in character, may be to focus on the assumption that a measure of regularity and symmetry in syllable-count was a more essential part of lyric verse-form than sometimes supposed. There is nothing inherently implausible about such an assumption; after all, a large corpus of non-alliterative verse in Middle English is written in couplets which are defined as octosyllabic or decasyllabic.

Chaucer's decasyllabic lines are most instructive. In characterising Middle English verse as 'very speech itself', Professor Stevens was at pains to emphasise that he included Chaucer's verse in this description. In support of his view, he appears to take issue with Robinson's practice of editing Chaucer's text according to decasyllabic lines by restoring final 'e's, and to favour C. S. Lewis's interpretation of Chaucer's verse in terms of four stresses. This line of support is, however, both dubious and unnecessary. M. L. Samuels has not only demonstrated the overwhelming linguistic case for the decasyllabic interpretation of Chaucer's lines, but his observation that 'it is a commonplace that decasyllabic verse abounds in the speech-rhythms of Sievers's half-line types' may be seen as telling support for Professor Stevens's basic contention.[34] Unlike poets from Spenser to Tennyson, it is, indeed, implausible to imagine Chaucer writing, any more than reading, his verse in terms of insistent iambic pentameters. The basic constraint determining the length of his line was its syllable-count; to 'mismetre' was rather, perhaps, a matter of number, of miscounting syllables, than of distorting metrical feet. As Professor Samuels further remarks, Chaucer's poetic medium differed from that of later poets: 'its higher proportion of genuinely unstressed syllables gave it a delicacy and lilt similar to that of the earlier Middle English lyrics'.[35] This description is not so very far from Professor Stevens's 'very speech itself'. However, to characterise Chaucer's verse in terms of 'delicacy and lilt' or speech-rhythm, and to read it

---

[33] Clearly Dobson is not referring specifically to lyrics in traditional alliterative verse form. The above discussion is not concerned with such lyrics.
[34] M. L. Samuels, 'Chaucerian Final "-e"', *Notes and Queries*, 217 (1972): 445–8 (p. 448).
[35] 'Chaucerian Final "-e"', p. 448.

with four stresses per line, are by no means the same thing. Nor, in order to register legitimate dissatisfaction with a reading of Chaucer in terms of iambic pentameters, is there any need to cast doubt on a count of ten syllables as the fundamental constraint of his line.

The problems which arise with a stress-counting approach to Middle English lyrics may be illustrated from 'Mirie it is' and 'Lord, thou clepedest me', the latter being the second lyric quoted by Professor Stevens. Both appear in R. D. Stevick's *One Hundred Middle English Lyrics*. Stevick's analysis of the stresses of the initial quatrain of 'Mirie it is' is as follows.

> Mírie it ís whil sómer y-lást
> Wyth fówel-es sóng;
> Bút now neígh-eth wín-des blást
> And wé-der stróng.[36]

Now, only by the most artificial and subjective notion of metrical stressing could the first word of line three be accented. This analysis runs counter to the demands of sense, whereby the stress would fall upon *now*, as well as the following *neigheth*: i.e.

> But nów neígheth wíndes blást.

Meanwhile, Stevick's analysis takes no account of the unstressed syllables further than to omit the final 'e' of *while*. Since this lyric was intended to be sung, the question as to how the poet might have expected it to be read is only of secondary importance. Nevertheless, it is to be noted that when, as above, the symmetry of the lines is restored in terms of syllable-count, the poem is still every bit as readable as 'very speech itself', and reading in such a manner has the merit of avoiding the influence of strained and artificial stressing.

With the second penitential lyric to be examined here, 'Lord, thou clepedest me', the inadequacy of attempting to assess metrical form solely on the basis of assumed stress patterns without due regard to syllable-count is again evident. Stevick comments at length on 'Lord, thou clepedest me' in his article, 'The Criticism of Middle English Lyrics'.[37] In his view, 'perhaps the most significant aspect of this poem is the relation of the linguistic structure to the metrical structure', a relation claimed to be 'at once appropriate and continually interesting'.[38] In the course of a linguistically exhaustive, not to say exhausting, analysis of this brief and seemingly simple poem, despite claims that this or that effect 'is achieved primarily through meter and the phrase structure', little, in fact, emerges as to precisely what the metre of this poem is. Indeed, little advance is made on the author's initial statement:

> The scansion is difficult, but it is obvious that there is no regularity in number of syllables or number of stresses per line; the nearest we can approach to regularity – by catching 'an ich' (1.2) under anacrucis – is to read three stresses in the first three lines, four stresses in the latter three.[39]

---

[36] *One Hundred Middle English Lyrics*, p. xxviii.
[37] R. D. Stevick, 'The Criticism of Middle English Lyrics', *Modern Philology*, 64 (1966): 103–17.
[38] 'The Criticism of Middle English Lyrics', p. 106.
[39] 'The Criticism of Middle English Lyrics', p. 106.

Once again, this kind of analysis turns out to be unsatisfactory, partly because the location of the stresses is so inherently subjective, and partly because the status of the unstressed syllables – metrical or merely scribal – is left out of account. Presumably Stevick's reading of the second line, 'catching "an ich" under anacrucis', would be:

An ìch nágt nè ánsuàrèdè thé.

This seems needlessly awkward. In view of the obvious chiasmic effect in the placing of the personal pronouns *thou / me* and *ich / thee* in the first two lines, it would be more appropriate to envisage the first stress as falling on *ich* in line two, even if, in line one, the stress must fall on *Lord* rather than on *thou*. Clearly this is a dramatic lyric rather than a song. Even so, there is no reason in principle why, in common with much Middle English non-alliterative verse, the length of the lines may not have been conceived at least partly in terms of syllabic constraints. An analysis, therefore, which works on the hypothesis that regularity or symmetry of syllable-count was recognised as a formal constraint for 'literary' lyrics and not only for songs, may prove illuminating. Put simply: does anything by way of plausible form emerge from an analysis of all the syllables and not just from the supposedly stressed syllables? In the case of this lyric, a pattern of four basically six-syllable lines (actually 6, 6, 7, 6) followed by two eight-syllable lines is clearly possible if the scribe's spellings *Louerd* (line 1), *ansuarede* (line 2) and *bute* (line 3) are replaced by the alternatives *Lord*, *answerd* and *but*, if in each occurrence of *thole* the final 'e' is elided with the following vowel, and if in line 6 *litel a* is reduced to two syllables by syncope. Thus:

> Lord, thou clepedest me,
> An ich noght n'answerd thee
> But wordes slow and slepy:
> 'Thole yet, thole a litel.'
> But 'yet' and 'yet' was endelis,
> And 'thole a litel' a long wey is.

In formal terms, this is attractive. The fourth line, with six syllables (or three stresses rather than four), is linked with the first three lines. This is in evident accord with the structure of the poem: the first four lines of implicit dialogue thereby form a unit contrasting with the final couplet of ominous comment in the form of two four-stress lines. By contrast, Stevick's division of the poem into two groups of three lines (with three of three stresses followed by three of four) runs counter to the rhetorical structure of the poem.

As a final example, brief mention may be made of Raymond Oliver's problem with the moral if not strictly penitential fifteenth-century lyric, 'What is this worlde but only vanyte?'.[40] Oliver believes that Middle English lyrics are 'at least roughly accentual, with varying numbers of slack syllables' and that 'the metrical stress is heavy'.[41] He quotes 'What is this worlde' as 'a good specimen

[40] In Carleton Brown (ed.), *Religious Lyrics of the Fifteenth Century* (Oxford, 1939), p. 260, No. 168.
[41] Raymond Oliver, *Poems Without Names: The English Lyric, 1200–1500* (Berkeley and Los Angeles, 1970), p. 90.

of Middle English meter, though perhaps more regular than usual' but 'can see no good reason why the sixth line should only have four main stresses'.[42] It is worth noting, however, that in his concern with stresses, the fact that this line has ten syllables, like the others,[43] escapes Oliver's attention. Furthermore, his approach to metrical analysis in terms of metrical feet is anachronistic; he fails to recognise the fundamental rhythmic freedom, the speech-like quality of Middle English verse.

In the end, it is perhaps not a surprising conclusion that all metrical syllables, and not just accented syllables, must be taken into account in the appraisal of Middle English lyric verse. Strange indeed are the results which can emerge from analysing lyrics line by line solely by counting stresses, not least when so much depends on the subjective response of the analyst, and when the notion of what counts as a stress – word stress, rhetorical stress, supposed metrical stress or rhyme stress – is so variable. And stranger effects still can arise from supposing that the verse should be read accordingly. But what are to count as genuine 'metrical' syllables? Obviously not simply all the syllables of the lyrics as they survive in copies which were often the product of the linguistic revisions and textual corruptions of successive scribes, not to mention the hazards of oral transmission. Literary criticism is attempted on the basis of such texts only at the risk of bizarre conclusions.[44] And even if Middle English lyrics had survived in autograph copies, judgements would still have to be made with regard to matters such as final 'e', elision, hiatus, syncope, and so on. Inescapably, then, the metrical analysis of Middle English lyrics remains a matter of interpretation, and can, therefore, only be approached on the basis of hypothesis. The hypothesis adopted here is that a major formal constraint in some Middle English lyric verse, as in French lyrics, was syllabic, and that this constraint was operative across a wider range of non-alliterative lyric verse than commonly supposed. This view harmonises well with the contention that the rhythm of Middle English verse was that of speech rather than any insistent pattern of metrical stress.

---

[42] *Poems Without Names*, p. 91.

[43] Granted the reduction of *ever* to one syllable in line 5.

[44] E.g., the metrical analysis of 'Mirie it is' in Edmund Reiss, *The Art of the Middle English Lyric* (Athens, Georgia, 1972), pp. 3–6, and critical comments by Reiss and by Stephen Mannyng discussed in Thomas G. Duncan, 'The Text and Verse-Form of "Adam lay i-bowndyn"', *RES*, 38 (1987): 215–221.

THE TRANSMISSION AND CIRCULATION OF
THE LAY FOLKS' CATECHISM

Sue Powell

In 1357 the Archbishop of York, John Thoresby, issued Injunctions to every archdeacon in the York province. To combat the ignorance of his priests, he had decided it was his duty to ensure that everyone in his diocese and province who was charged with the care of souls

> at least on Sundays should expound or cause to expound to the people in English, without any far-fetched subtlety of words, the articles of the faith, the commandments both of the New and the Old Testament, the deeds of mercy, the principal virtues, the sacraments of grace, and the deadly sins with their consequences; and that on our behalf they should enjoin their parishioners, men and women, that they themselves and each one of theirs should diligently hear and learn all these instructions; and that they should teach them clearly to their little ones, boys and girls, and compel them to learn them; and that at least at every Lent these curates I have spoken of should examine their parishioners as to whether they have learnt and got to know these things, and have instructed their children in this way, firmly imposing upon those who do not obey in this respect a healthy penance which they should be sure to increase to suit the circumstance, as their disobedience requires.[1]

And, so that nobody could plead ignorance, a very brief synopsis of the main points of these six tenets follows. The hierarchy is clear cut: Archbishop instructs archdeacon, archdeacon instructs those with care of souls, they in their turn instruct their parishioners, these layfolk in their turn instruct their children.

The above is a close paraphrase of the Latin. The Archbishop's Injunctions were of course issued in Latin and copied into his Register in Latin. But the Latin in the Register is preceded by what appears to be an English version of the same material, the only English in the whole of the Register. And both English and Latin form a separate quire of the manuscript, written in the hand of Thomas de Aldefeld, perhaps a relative of the earlier York notary, John de Aldefeld.[2]

---

[1] I am indebted to Mr Peter Howell of the Department of Classics, Royal Holloway and Bedford New College, University of London for assistance in this translation.

[2] The entry occurs on fols. 295ʳ-297ᵛ of York, Borthwick Institute of Historical Research, Register 11, described by D. M. Smith, *Guide to Bishops' Registers of England and Wales: a Survey from the Middle Ages to the Abolition of the Episcopacy in 1646* (London, 1981), p. 239, and by O. S. Pickering and S. Powell, *Index of Middle English Prose: Handlist VI* (Cambridge, 1989), pp. 33–34. The ascription of the hand was made by A. I. Doyle in 'The Manuscripts', in David A. Lawton (ed.), *Middle English Alliterative Poetry and its Literary Background* (Cambridge, 1982), pp. 88–100 and 142–47 (p. 142, note 6).

Thoresby's Injunctions exercised considerable influence on the character and matter of religious texts in the later Middle Ages, though the method of dissemination from priest to parishioner and the reduction of theological data to a number of basic but easily memorised tenets were not ideas original to him but taken from the 1281 Lambeth Constitutions of the then Archbishop of Canterbury, John Pecham (nor were they anyway original to Pecham).[3] Most present-day scholars of the religious literature of the fourteenth and fifteenth centuries need to refer to Thoresby from time to time, and they are served by a 1901 Early English Text Society edition which presents the Latin and English Injunctions, *en face* to Pecham's original Latin and a 'Wycliffite' version of the text.[4]

Dr Ian Doyle investigated the dissemination of the English version of the Injunctions in his doctoral thesis of 1952,[5] and Professor Anne Hudson has more recently exposed the fundamental inadequacies of the EETS edition and rejected the labelling of the Lambeth manuscript as Wycliffite.[6] The following discussion of the origins, transmission and circulation of the English version of Thoresby's Injunctions is indebted to the earlier researches of both Dr Doyle and Professor Hudson.

I.   *The Lay Folks' Catechism*

The English version of Thoresby's Injunctions appears in his Register without title or author, yet it is known to us as *The Lay Folks' Catechism* and its author as John Gaytryge. The title is editorial and presumably intended to match other

[3] For Pecham's canon 'Ignorancia sacerdotum', see F. M. Powicke and C. R. Cheney (eds.), *Councils and Synods with Other Documents Relating to the English Church, A. D. 1205-1313* (Oxford, 1964), ii.900-05. For details of Pecham's and Thoresby's material in the context of medieval pastoral instruction, see M. Gibbs and J. Lang, *Bishops and Reform 1215-1272* (Oxford, 1934), especially pp.94-179; L. E. Boyle, 'The Oculus Sacerdotis and some other works of William of Pagula', *Transactions of the Royal Historical Society*, 5th. series, 5 (1955): 81-110; R. M. Haines, 'Education in English Ecclesiastical Legislation of the Later Middle Ages', *Studies in Church History*, 7 (1971): 161-75; V. Gillespie, '*Doctrina* and *Praedicacio*: The Design and Function of Some Pastoral Manuals', *Leeds Studies in English*, n.s. 11 (1980): pp. 36-50; Jonathan Hughes, *Pastors and Visionaries: Religion and Secular Life in Late Medieval Yorkshire* (Southampton, 1988), Chapter 3, pp. 127-73. There are useful synopses of the two decrees in 'The Fourth Lateran Council and Manuals of Popular Theology' by Leonard Boyle and 'The Influence of Canonical and Episcopal Reform on Popular Books of Instruction' by Judith Shaw, in Thomas J. Heffernan (ed.), *The Popular Literature of Medieval England* (Knoxville, 1985), pp. 30-43 and 44-60 respectively.

[4] T. F. Simmons and H. E. Nolloth (eds.), *The Lay Folks' Catechism*, EETS OS 118 (London, 1901). *Verso* pages present the English text of the Register with the Latin at the foot of the page, and *recto* pages present London, Lambeth Palace Library, MS 408 with Pecham's Injunctions at the foot of the page.

[5] A. I. Doyle, 'A Survey of the Origins and Circulation of Theological Writings in English in the 14th., 15th., and early 16th. Centuries with Special Consideration of the Part of the Clergy therein', unpublished Ph.D. thesis (Cambridge, 1954).

[6] Anne Hudson, 'A New Look at the Lay-Folks' Catechism', *Viator*, 16 (1985): 243-58, and '*The Lay Folks' Catechism*: a Postscript', *Viator*, 19 (1988): 308-09. I would like to record my gratitude to Professor Hudson for her help and encouragement in the preparation of this paper.

publications of the EETS, *The Lay Folks* [*sic*] *Mass-Book and The Lay Folks' Prayer Book*.[7] Canon Nolloth, when he took over his friend's work on his death, had reservations about the title, though they are not quite the reservations we would have today. How far the work is and is not a catechism for layfolk is obvious from my translation of the beginning of Thoresby's Injunctions – neither the word 'layfolk' nor 'catechism' is wholly accurate and the two together smack today of fey antiquarianism.[8] As for the name of its author, despite variations in the manuscripts in which it occurs (four of them Catechism manuscripts), we can take it he was John of Gaytryge, a Benedictine monk at St Mary's Abbey in York.[9]

Though at first it may seem odd that the Register should not cite Gaytryge's name, on reflection it is quite natural. After all, it is the Archbishop's Register and they are his Injunctions, issued in his name, whether in Latin or English. But it is clear that the name of their author was known, and circulated for a while. The four *Catechism* manuscripts in which it is found are Northern, and amongst the earliest and the best. In one of them, the Thornton manuscript, Gaytryge's name is preserved even though the usual references to the Archbishop have been removed. In fact, it is from the Thornton manuscript that the name has achieved currency today, since it is there that the *Catechism* is called 'a sermon that Dan John Gaytryge made'.[10]

[7] Canon Nolloth's Prefatory Note to the edition of *The Lay Folks' Catechism* outlines the circumstances under which he undertook the completion of the work on Canon Simmons' death. In essence, Simmons would seem to have been responsible for the text and Nolloth for the Introduction. The title can be assumed to have been Simmons', since he had already published *The Lay Folks* [*sic*] *Mass-Book*, EETS OS 71 (London, 1879). The same formula had been used in the Society's publication of H. Littlehales (ed.), *The Prymer or Lay Folks' Prayer Book*, EETS OS 105, 109 (London, 1895, 1897). Where the titles are punctuated in these editions, it is in the idiosyncratic form (*Folks'*) reluctantly retained throughout this article.

[8] On 'layfolk', it is clear that instruction is to be of the clergy in the first instance, and then through them to the people; on 'catechism', the meaning, 'instruction by word of mouth' (OED *Catechesis*), is an acceptable description of the material here. However, in his lengthy discussion of catechism (pp. xxix–xxxix), Nolloth stresses the question-and-answer element prevalent in the meaning of the word as used in his own day (OED *Catechism* 2), though the structure of *The Lay Folks' Catechism* is not that of such a catechism (which did exist at the time, in, for example, John Mirk's *Instructions for Parish Priests*).

[9] The manuscripts of *The Lay Folks' Catechism* which cite the author's name are Oxford, Bodleian Library, MS Don.c.13 (fol. 165[va] 'Gaitrig'); London, British Library, MS Harley 1022 (fol. 73[v] 'Iohannem de Gaystek', not 'Taystek' as frequently cited); London, British Library, MS Arundel 507 (fol. 50[r] 'Iohannis de Caterig'), and the Thornton manuscript, Lincoln, Lincoln Cathedral Library, MS 91 (fol. 213[v] 'dan Iohn Gaytryge'). Hudson ('A New Look') has shown that the first of these manuscripts is the most authoritative of the extant texts. Doyle's suggestion ('A Survey', i.31, note 2) that Gaytryge's name derives from the place-name Catterick in North Yorkshire (cf. 'Caterig' cited above) has been disputed in a private letter to me from Dr Alex Rumble of the University of Manchester. Dr Rumble prefers the lost place-name 'Gaterigg' in Middlesborough (*The Place-Names of the North Riding of Yorkshire*, English Place-Names Society, v.161). For another recording of the name, see below and note 34. There would seem to be no confirmation of the name 'Graystok', a reading said to be derived from the Register by Canon J. S. Purvis and used by A. L. Kellogg and Ernest W. Talbert, 'The Wycliffite *Pater Noster* and *Ten Commandments*, with Special Reference to English MSS. 85 and 90 in the John Rylands Library', *Bulletin of the John Rylands Library*, 42 (1960): 345–77 (p. 356).

[10] The title 'Dan John Gattrynge's Sermon' (elsewhere 'Dan Jon Gaytryge's Sermon' and 'Dan Jon Gaytrigg') was given to the Thornton manuscript version of *The Lay Folks' Catechism* by G. G. Perry, *Religious Pieces in Prose and Verse*, EETS OS 26, rev. ed., (London, 1914). It has also been

Of course, Gaytryge's English has always been assumed to be a translation of Thoresby's Latin, although Canon Nolloth himself pointed out that 'the translation is really a very wide expansion of the original text'.[11] Professor Hudson in her paper on *The Lay Folks' Catechism* has questioned whether the two texts are as closely related as has been thought: 'Did Thoresby, or one of his officials, come across the vernacular text, perceive its usefulness, and then devise the injunction . . . to publicize an existing text? Or did the Archbishop seize on the English material as a neat vernacular rendering of what had already been promulgated in Latin?'[12]

There are certainly differences between the two. For example, the order of tenets in the Latin is not the same as in the English,[13] and the English deals with the spiritual deeds of mercy while the Latin of both Pecham and Thoresby does not.[14] Moreover, it has been suggested by both David Lawton and Anne Hudson that the Register version of the English is corrupt in comparison with other texts.[15]

If Gaytryge seems not to have been translating *verbatim* from Thoresby's Latin, and if the Register text is not the authorised *Ur*-text it has been assumed to be, it is at least possible that it was already circulating before it was used by the Archbishop.

II. The Genesis of the *Catechism*

Apart from their presence together on the same quire of the Register, the main reason why it has been assumed that Gaytryge was working to Thoresby's orders relates to a supposed visit by Gaytryge to the Archbishop's palace in the winter before the Injunctions were promulgated, during which collaboration on the *Catechism* took place. The letter providing this information is quoted by Canon Nolloth with this explanation: 'In the following letter it has been supposed that Thoresby refers to the monk of St Mary's Abbey [i.e. Gaytryge] . . . The supposition appears to lack foundation. But the letter is so graceful in itself, that it may fitly close our notice of the great Archbishop . . .' (p. xxi). Despite this disclaimer, later scholars have perpetuated what would appear to be a *canard*,

edited as 'John Gaytryge's Sermon' by N. F. Blake in *Middle English Religious Prose* (London, 1972), pp. 73–87.

[11] Simmons and Nolloth, p. xvii.

[12] Hudson, 'A New Look', p. 249.

[13] Pecham, Thoresby, and Gaytryge all differ in the order in which they deal with the tenets.

[14] Simmons and Nolloth, ll. 364–79.

[15] David Lawton, 'Gaytryge's Sermon, *Dictamen*, and Middle English Alliterative Verse', *Modern Philology*, 76 (1979): 329–43: 'By its very presence in the Register . . . *York* can be seen only as a copy of the text which was in fact transmitted throughout the archbishop's enormous diocese . . .' (p. 332). Hudson, 'A New Look', uses textual comparison to suggest that the Register may be corrupt: 'If it is allowed that the Thoresby register is defective, the explanation must lie in the existence of an original of the English copied inaccurately by Thomas de Aldefeld; the other manuscripts descend independently from this original and not from the Thoresby register' (p. 249). My own comparison of the manuscripts confirms Professor Hudson's suggestion that Oxford, Bodleian Library, MS Don.c.13 contains a text superior to that in the Register.

since their references lead us back only to Nolloth and Nolloth gives no reference for either the 'supposition' or the letter.[16]

The letter does, however, exist, and an explanation for Nolloth's rather infuriatingly qualified dismissal of it is available. It is in a York formulary of the fourteenth and fifteenth centuries.[17] Being a formulary, the letters are sample formulae to be emulated in similar circumstances, but this does not mean that they are not genuine letters. Where the Archbishop's letters were thought to be useful as models of style or composition in a certain situation, they would be copied into this ongoing manuscript, and this is where the letter referring to 'J de G' is found. It is undated, the Archbishop unspecified, and 'J de G' is not necessarily John of Gaytryge, but nevertheless the Archbishop is writing to the Abbot of York about one of his monks, and the inference that the monk is our John of Gaytryge is a reasonable one at least, though the facts are less certain than has been suggested.

In practice, whether we accept the evidence of the letter or not makes very little difference to our knowledge of how the *Catechism* came into being. If we accept it, then Gaytryge collaborated with the Archbishop over Christmas and Easter, and it is reasonable to assume that the visit was made in 1356/57. But Gaytryge might have been adapting an already existing work, rather than creating something new to the Archbishop's specifications. There is nothing in the texts to contradict such a theory. Though the supporting framework of both texts corresponds,[18] it has already been noted that there are differences in the body of the text.[19]

There is no reason, however, to assume that, where there are discrepancies between Gaytryge and Thoresby, they presuppose an already independently circulating English work (though it may to some extent have been independently composed). For one thing, the outline of the Injunctions might well still have been in Thoresby's head or only sketchily written down while Gaytryge was composing the English version, and in that sense the *Catechism* may indeed have 'pre-existed' the Injunctions. There would have been no reason for the Archbishop to follow Gaytryge's version closely – after all, the idea was his and Gaytryge merely following a commission. Pecham was the inspiration of course, but Pecham's canons were very sketchy anyway and might be independently developed in quite different ways.

---

[16] Cf. G. R. Owst, *Preaching in Medieval England: an Introduction to Sermon Manuscripts of the Period c.1350-1450* (Cambridge, 1926), p. 53, and Hughes, *Pastors and Visionaries*, pp. 149-50.

[17] York, Borthwick Institute of Historical Research, Register 13, fol. 18ʳ, described Smith, *Guide to Bishops' Registers*, p. 240. I am grateful to Dr Smith for the very helpful discussion which took place when this paper was still at an early stage of preparation.

[18] The English is very close to the Latin at the beginning and the end (ll. 33-76, 565-67) when it deals with Thoresby's intentions and his offer of 40 days' pardon, and within these sections there are three references to 'our father the Archbishop' (ll. 42, 74, 566).

[19] See above and notes 13 and 14. It would appear to be unwarranted to suggest that Gaytryge worked from Pecham rather than from Thoresby. He follows Pecham's order of the seven sins, citing gluttony fourth and sloth sixth (where Thoresby reverses this order), but he agrees with Thoresby in many more points. For example, Pecham specifies instruction four times a year, Thoresby and Gaytryge on Sundays; Pecham does not specify the chain of instruction from layfolk to their offspring; he does not demand an examination in Lent; he does not have the full discussion of the tenth commandment found in Thoresby and Gaytryge; he does not offer 40 days' pardon.

The fact that the Register text is not authoritative is easily explained and does suggest that it was already circulating, but not necessarily that it was circulating independently of the Injunctions. The Archbishop's business was copied up in batches every now and then. If we posit that the Injunctions were already in circulation when they were copied into the Register, then clearly one of the several copies made would have had to be procured and transcribed by Thomas de Aldefeld as a routine piece of business. (I have already pointed out that together the English and Latin form a separate quire in the Register.) Either the text was less accurate than it should have been or Aldefeld copied it inaccurately. Whatever the truth of the matter, it cannot be used as evidence of Gaytryge's text being in circulation before Thoresby's Injunctions.[20]

The routine circumstances under which Aldefeld was copying up the Archbishop's material might also explain why the Register version is written as prose, not verse (though Canon Nolloth somewhat confusingly reproduced it as verse in his EETS edition). There is some dispute as to whether Gaytryge wrote in unrhymed verse or rhythmical prose.[21] Without entering into the dispute, it can be said that it was variously interpreted as verse or prose in the manuscripts, though the earliest manuscripts (other than the Register) set it out as verse.[22] David Lawton has argued that the Register shows only a

---

[20] I have preserved the foregoing argument as it was delivered in my paper of July, 1991, although it has since been rendered redundant by a discovery by Dr R. N. Swanson of the University of Birmingham which confirms the tentative suggestions posited above and proves conclusively that Gaytryge was writing to Thoresby's commission and that his work was not circulating independently beforehand. In 'The Origins of *The Lay Folks' Catechism*', *Medium Aevum*, 60 (1991): 92–100, Dr Swanson discusses, edits, and translates Thoresby's original Latin mandate commissioning the translation. The commission occurs on fols. 73ᵛ–74ʳ of London, British Library, MS Cotton Galba E.x., the fragments of a letter-book relating to the archbishopric of York which may derive from the same volume as the letter from York, Borthwick Institute of Historical Research, Register 13 discussed above and at note 17. Thoresby's letter requests 'J. de Gaitrik' to translate 'decem precepta decalogi, et articulos fidei, et alia' (the ten commandments and the articles of faith, and other things) into English according to an enclosed schedule (presumably now lost) drawn up by the provincial council at York over which Thoresby had presided. Gaytryge is to translate 'grosso modo cum celeritate possibili', roughly with all possible speed.

[21] Skeat had 'not a doubt that the "Sermon" was originally in *verse*' and advised the editor of the Thornton version, G. G. Perry, that to print it as prose 'would be a mistake' (Perry, *Religious Pieces*, p. vi). Perry, however, confessed to doubts and disregarded Skeat's advice. Simmons and Nolloth merely assert (p. xvii) that the English version of the *Lay Folks' Catechism* is in 'rude verse' which would be easily committed to memory '(unpoetical though it be, and almost devoid of rhymes)'. There is no comment on the fact that they have transposed what is written as prose in the Register and in the Lambeth manuscript into lines of verse in their edition. David Lawton's argument in 'Middle English Alliterative Poetry: An Introduction', in Lawton (ed.), *Middle English Alliterative Poetry*, pp. 1–19 (p. 16) is that the work 'is constructed of *cursus* patterns and is derived from the *ars dictaminis*, the Latin art of epistolary rhetoric'. He expounds his theory most fully in Lawton, 'Gaytryge's Sermon', where he endorses Canon Simmons' verse format but points out, p. 336, that 'in an attempt to overregularize the text in accordance with uncertain principles there are occasional mistakes in lineation not derived from his copy'. Lawton's argument is disputed by Angus McIntosh in 'Early Middle English Alliterative Verse', in Lawton (ed.), *Middle English Alliterative Poetry*, pp. 20–33 (note 12).

[22] The Yorkshire manuscripts, which date from the late fourteenth to the mid fifteenth centuries, are all in verse. Complete texts in verse are: Oxford, Bodleian Library, MS Don.c.13; Oxford, Corpus Christi College, MS 155; Oxford, Queen's College, MS 389B (presumably once complete);Cambridge, Trinity College, MS B.10.12 (but the verse format begins only at Simmons and Nolloth, l.

'seeming prose framework',[23] since capitals and points normally mark off the verse lines. Certainly, it seems reasonable to assume that Gaytryge's original intention would have been to identify the rhythm (of his verse or prose) through the lay-out of the text. Certainly, the manuscript that Professor Hudson has identified correctly as the best, Oxford, Bodleian Library, MS Don.c.13, presents it in lines of verse. However, even if Gaytryge conceived of his work as such, it is probably not surprising that a notary like Aldefeld, used only to dealing with prose and routinely transcribing for the Archbishop's Register, did not bother to lay out the text as verse. Another factor, to be discussed in detail below, may be that there was a concern to fit both the English and the Latin onto the single quire at the scribe's disposal.

III. The Transmission and Circulation of the *Lay Folks' Catechism*

There are twelve manuscripts of *The Lay Folks' Catechism* which preserve Gaytryge's original text in full, eight which alter and adapt it fairly comprehensively (of which only two are interdependent), and another six which contain extracts.[24]

Of course the Register prepares us for ownership amongst priests, who were to use it to preach to their congregations. The evidence of the manuscripts shows that throughout its transmission the *Catechism* remained in

114, half-way through the articles of the faith); London, British Library, MS Harley 1022; Nottingham, Nottingham University Library, MS Middleton LM 9. London, British Library, MS Additional 25006 provides a prose prologue (up to and including Simmons and Nolloth, l. 76), but the main body of the text is written as verse (see note 35 below). The extracts and reworkings are in prose.

[23] Lawton, 'Gaytryge's Sermon', p. 336.

[24] To some extent I differ from Hudson ('A New Look', pp. 246–47) in my interpretation of reworked texts and extracts. In her list of seven 'Manuscripts in which an extract or extracts only were included', she includes Oxford, Bodleian Library, MS Bodley 789, fols. 51^v–68^v, which she notes has all but ll. 1–50, 59–71 of the Register text as edited by Simmons and Nolloth, that is, all but the preliminary explanation of the aims of the work and its method of distribution and use. Since the manuscript has all the main body of the text, and since Hudson lists amongst complete manuscripts London, British Library, MS Harley 1022, which also omits the preliminary material (ll. 1–82), I prefer to consider MS Bodley 789 a full manuscript rather than an extract. Because the text shows Lollard reworking ('later purged by orthodox ecclesiastical hands', Doyle, 'A Summary', i.34), I include it within Hudson's list of six 'Manuscripts which have a significantly reworked text'. To this list I also add the manuscripts which Hudson deals with on pp. 249–58 of 'A New Look', viz., London, Lambeth Palace Library, MS 408 and Oxford, Bodleian Library, MSS Eng.th.e.181/Douce 274/Douce 273 (on the relationship of these three manuscripts, which form a single text, see Hudson, '*The Lay Folks' Catechism*'). From the list I would, however, delete Lincoln, Lincoln Cathedral Library, MS 66, which admittedly has a significantly reworked text (after the first few lines 'unrecognizable', as Hudson says), but contains only the articles of the faith. I prefer to place this amongst the extracts. Thus, Professor Hudson's lists of seven manuscripts containing extracts, and six with a significantly reworked text are emended in my listing to seven of the first category (deleting MS Bodley 789 but adding MS Lincoln Cathedral 66), and eight of the second category (deleting MS Lincoln Cathedral 66 but adding MSS Bodley 789, Lambeth 408, and Eng.th.e.181/Douce274/Douce 273).

the hands of priests and was preached, but it also appears in the context of private devotional material, whether for religious or lay use. Robert Thornton, of course, made his copy for private reading but acknowledged its pastoral use by a prefatory statement emphasising its value in preparing for confession.[25]

Interestingly, the *Catechism* appears to have been popular amongst the regular, aswell as the secular clergy, who seem often to have taken an interest in *pastoralia* for conventual teaching. Gaytryge himself was, of course, a Benedictine monk. Of the clearly identifiable manuscripts, one belonged to the abbot of Rievaulx and one to a Durham monk, Richard de Segbrok.[26] The contents of the Rievaulx manuscript are pastoral, which might suggest that the work was intended for preaching within the abbey, whether to monks or lay employees, but Segbrok's miscellany would appear to be a personal selection for private devotion.[27] It can be dated to the last quarter of the fourteenth century and is therefore an interestingly early attempt at that rewriting and adaptation to which it is clear the *Catechism* was subject throughout its transmission.

Of the twelve manuscripts which represent the original and complete *Catechism*, seven were copied in the North, perhaps all of them in Yorkshire itself,[28] and, though Thornton copied from a Lincolnshire exemplar, he was of

[25] Lincoln, Lincoln Cathedral Library, MS 91, fol. 213ᵛ: 'Here begynnes a sermon þat Dan Iohn Gaytryge made, þe whilke teches how scrifte es to be made and whareof and in scrifte how many thynges solde be consederide'.

[26] Oxford, Corpus Christi College, MS 155 bears the original inscription 'Liber beate Marie de Rieualle ex procuracione domini Willelmi Spenser abbatis eiusdem' (fols. 2ᵛ and 274ᵛ). Doyle ('A Survey', ii.6, note 1) notes an abbot of this name in the periods 1436–39, 1471, 1487, and suggests the earlier date. London, British Library, MS Arundel 507 includes documents dating from 1374–96 concerning Richard de Segbrok, monk of Durham (Doyle, 'A Survey', ii.76, note 38).

[27] Doyle, 'A Survey', is the major source of information on ownership of *Catechism* manuscripts. Of the twelve complete texts, it may be estimated that, besides the Register, four were probably owned by secular clergy (Oxford, Bodleian Library, MS Don.c.13; Cambridge, Sidney Sussex College, MS 55; Cambridge, Trinity College, MS B.10.12; Oxford, Bodleian Library, MS Rawlinson C.288), two were for regular clergy (Oxford, Corpus Christi College, MS 155; London, British Library, MS Harley 1022), one (London, British Library, MS Additional 25006) 'probably for the use of a clerical tutor or school teacher in the Midlands' (Doyle, 'A Survey', i.35), and two for private use (the Thornton manuscript and Paris, Bibliothèque Ste. Geneviève, MS 3390). Amongst the reworked texts, one was certainly (London, British Library, MS Arundel 507) and another possibly (London, British Library, MS Harley 6615) owned by a monk, and two others (Yale, Yale University Library, MS Beinecke 317 and Cambridge, Trinity College, MS B.14.19) were used in preaching, though whether by priests or monks cannot be said. The fact that Oxford, Corpus Christi College, MS 155, a manuscript definitely commissioned for regular clergy, is pastoral in orientation clearly throws doubt on whether other manuscripts of *The Lay Folks' Catechism* with a pastoral orientation or showing evidence of preaching should necessarily be assumed to have belonged to priests.

[28] York, Borthwick Institute of Historical Research, Register 11, London, British Library, MSS Additional 25006 and Harley 1022, Cambridge, Trinity College, MS B.10.12, Oxford, Corpus Christi College, MS 155, Oxford, Bodleian Library, MS Don.c.13, and the fragments contained in Oxford, Queen's College, MS 389B. A. McIntosh and M. L. Samuels (ed.), *A Linguistic Atlas of Late Mediaeval English* (Aberdeen, 1986) place the first six in the North or West Ridings of Yorkshire. There is no analysis of the Queen's College fragments, but the dialect is clearly Northern. Details of dialect provenance throughout this article are dependent on McIntosh and Samuels.

course copying it in Yorkshire.[29] Two other manuscripts are from Lincoln-shire (which had close connections with York diocese), two from the Midlands and one from Norfolk.[30]

It has been noted that the *Catechism* circulated too in extracts (I would think more commonly than is suggested by the six extant manuscripts) and in various contexts and combinations, but, as we would expect, this is a late phenomenon and all but one of the manuscripts containing extracts is from outside the York province.[31] So too with the expanded and reworked *Catechisms*, only one is Northern, and that is the one copied by the Durham monk, which is an early and good copy with only minor interpolations. It is also one of the four manuscripts which give Gaytryge's name, associating him with nearby Catterick and calling him 'Caterig'.[32]

It has already been pointed out that the four *Catechism* manuscripts which bear Gaytryge's name were written (or, in the case of the Thornton manuscript, copied) in the Northern province. The evidence of the Register (which has no name) might suggest that Gaytryge's name did not travel with the copies of his *Catechism* and, where the name is known, we might assume some local knowledge. It was, however, perpetuated beyond the York province in an early fifteenth-century defence of Biblical translation, which was composed in Latin by Richard Ullerston at Oxford in 1401 and then abridged in English, probably before 1407.[33]

The tract defends scriptural translation by providing examples of official authorisation of teaching in the vernacular, and in its reference to *The Lay Folks' Catechism* it shows an awareness not only of Thoresby and Gaytryge but also of the circumstances of the dissemination of the *Catechism*:

> Also Sire Wiliam Thorisby, Erchebischop of ȝork, did do to drawe a tretys in Englisce be a worschipful clerk wos name was Gaytrik, in þe

[29] Some Yorkshire dialect features were perhaps misunderstood in the transmission of the text. For example, in two cruxes in the material on the ten commandments, Oxford, Bodleian Library, MS Don.c.13 reads 'for to tent ne trai withe þe werld' and 'þof al we do þat we may', where most other manuscripts, including the Register, read erroneously 'for to tent to/and/ne/or/nor tarry' and 'of/if all we do that we may'. Since the Register would appear to preserve the less authoritative readings, unless the variants are casual mistranscriptions rather than preferred variants, it would appear that some of Gaytryge's dialect features were unfamiliar to even a fellow Yorkshireman, Thomas de Aldefeld.

[30] Lincoln, Lincoln Cathedral Library, MS 91 and Nottingham, Nottingham University Library, MS Middleton LM 9 are from Lincolnshire, Paris, Bibliothèque Ste. Geneviève, MS 3390 and Cambridge, Sidney Sussex College, MS 55 are from the Midlands, and Oxford, Bodleian Library, MS Rawlinson C.288 is from Norfolk.

[31] The Northern manuscript is Oxford, Bodleian Library, MS Rawlinson C.285.

[32] London, British Library, MS Arundel 507. See note 9 above.

[33] The English version has been edited from Cambridge, Trinity College, MS B.14.50 by C. F. Buhler, 'A Lollard Tract: on translating the Bible into English', *Medium Ævum.* 7 (1938): 167–83. Buhler knew of seven manuscripts, but an eighth is cited in R. E. Lewis, N. F. Blake, A. S. G. Edwards (eds.), *Index of Printed Middle English Prose* (New York and London, 1985), p. 15, no. 37. The Latin tract survives in one manuscript, Vienna, Hofbibliothek, MS 4133. Its authorship, provenance, and date are established by Anne Hudson, 'The Debate on Biblical Translation, Oxford 1401', *English Historical Review*, 90 (1975): 1–18. Some alteration to my original paper has been occasioned by Professor Hudson's kindness in alerting me to her article and in furnishing me with a copy and a transcription of the Latin tract.

wiche weren conteyned þe articulis of þe feiþ, seuene dedli synnes, þe
werkes of mercy, and þe ten comandementes, and sente hem in smale
pagynes to þe comyn puple to lerne þis and to knowe þis, of wiche ben
ʒit manye a componye in Englond'.[34]

Even Canon Nolloth felt he could be a little snide ('an interesting and
ingenious conjecture') about Canon Raine's suggestion that these 'smale
pagynes' were pageants, though he spent some time airing the view, as have
others after him.[35]

It has already been pointed out that the *Catechism* and Injunctions fit neatly
onto a separate quire in the Register. There is a simple explanation available
for this. As has been made clear, it was the habit to copy up the Archbishop's
business every few weeks in batches from draft copies. As an extraordinary
piece of legislation, there was no obvious place in the Register for the
Injunctions. They did not fit amongst the territorial material at the beginning
nor in any other sections, such as those on ordinations or visitations, and so
they were inserted as a separate quire after the territorial passages and before
the bulk of the rest of the Register material.

There may, however, be an additional reason for the separate quire,
namely, that it represents one of these circulating *pagynes* which were
presumably sent out to Thoresby's archdeacons and which are referred to in
the tract quoted above as being sent to 'þe comyn puple'. Perhaps one of
these, one of a number routinely and not entirely accurately copied onto a
quire by Aldefeld, was sewn into the Archbishop's Register at what was felt to
be a suitable point. As we have seen, the Injunctions are preceded in the
Register by their English version, and the mere existence of English in
Archbishops' Registers is unusual. In practice, it must have been quite
common for Latin injunctions to be issued in a vernacular, since Latin, though
the official language of the Archbishop's records, might not be readily
understood by those for whom the injunctions were intended. For example,
visitation injunctions to nunneries might be issued in French or English,
though originally composed in Latin. Though this particular Register contains
no other English, other Registers have confessions or tithe details in English.
It seems, however, that it was not usual practice to copy the vernacular as well
as the Latin into Archbishops' Registers, and the sewing in of a conveniently-
available *pagyne* may be the explanation for the English on this occasion,

---

[34] Cambridge, Trinity College, MS B.14.50, fol. 28ᵛ. Thoresby's Christian name was, of course,
John, not William. The original Latin reads: 'Bone memorie dominus Willelmus Thoresbi
archiepiscopus Eboracensis quartus a presenti fecit fieri per quendam reuerendum uirum
cognomento Gaitrik quendam tractatum conscriptum in uulgari in quo continentur articuli fidei, in
quo eciam de septem peccatis mortalibus pertractatur, de septem operibus misericordie, quem
tractatum per paginas precepit laicis ad eorum instructionem' (Vienna, Hofbibliothek, MS 4133,
fol. 198ᵛ, col. b).
[35] Simmons and Nolloth, pp. xvii–xx. For more recent comments, see A. C. Cawley, 'Middle
English Metrical Versions of the Decalogue with Reference to the English Corpus Christi
Cycles', *Leeds Studies in English*, n.s. 8 (1975): 129–45 (pp. 131–32) and Lawton, 'Gaytryge's
Sermon', p. 331. MED *pagin(e* cites this passage to illustrate the definition 'a page or a leaf of a
book' (cf. OED *pagine*, a unit of paper), but the matter is anyway resolved by comparison with
the Latin original ('per paginas').

as it may explain both the cramped prose format of the *Catechism* and also the slightly odd fact that the English precedes the Latin.[36]

It has already been pointed out that Ullerston's tract originated in Oxford, and the English abridgement would appear to have been circulated by Lollards in the southern province throughout the fifteenth century.[37] In the sixteenth century it served Protestant purposes too and was printed twice, in 1530 and again in 1538, and was included by Foxe in his *Actes and Monuments* (1563). *The Lay Folks' Catechism* itself need not, of course, have been circulating in the south to have been used in this way as a valuable piece of Lollard/ Protestant evidence, but evidence suggests that in fact it was. The English version of the tract adds to the original Latin the comment that there are still many copies of the Catechism circulating in England[38] and the 1530 printed edition of the same tract has an interesting marginal gloss which shows that the *Catechism* was at that late date still in use in at least one London church: 'The same tretise is in þe church over agaynst London stone at this houre'.[39]

[36] The *Catechism* in Nottingham, University Library, MS Middleton LM 9 (fols. 248ʳ–56ʳ) is also on a separate quire (here of 10, not 8, in a different hand from the rest of the text, which is the *Speculum Vite*, fols. 1ʳ–247ʳ). The quire contains only the English text, which is copied out in lines of verse. It would seem that London, British Library, MS Additional 25006 originally contained the English version of the *Catechism* in a quire of 10, with 10 now missing (Hudson's quiring, 'A New Look', p. 246, note 11, appears to be incorrect). The prologue (fols. 1ʳ–1ᵛ) is prose but the text itself (fols. 2ʳ–9ᵛ) is in verse.

[37] The extant English manuscripts are southern/midland in dialect and amongst material added to the original Latin text is a reference to Thomas Arundel as Archbishop of Canterbury 'þat nowe is' (Bühler, 'A Lollard Tract', pp. 178–79, ll. 290–306). It is of some interest that *The Lay Folks' Catechism* appears fairly frequently in Lollard contexts. Though Hudson, 'A New Look', has shown that the description of London, Lambeth Palace Library, MS 408 as a Lollard version of *The Lay Folks' Catechism* should be abandoned, it nevertheless contains Lollard sentiments, while other texts associated with Lambeth are more heterodox. Oxford, Bodleian Library, MS Don. c. 13 is found in the context of the Wycliffite sermon cycle (Anne Hudson, *English Wycliffite Sermons* [Oxford, 1983–90], i.87–88). Lollard opinions are also found in Oxford, Bodleian Library, MS Bodley 789 and in the extracts from the *Catechism* in Cambridge, Cambridge University Library, MS Dd.xii.39 and London, British Library, MS Additional 24202, only the latter 'strongly Lollard' (Doyle, 'A Survey', i.34).

[38] See above and note 34. The word 'componye' ('of wiche ben ȝit manye a componye in Englond') would appear to be preserved in all the manuscripts, though the printed versions seem to use 'copye' instead. The matter is discussed by Cawley, 'Middle English Metrical Versions', p. 132. Either word would be appropriate in the context, and the mistranscription of either is easily explicable in scribal terms.

[39] A. W. Pollard and G. R. Redgrave, *A Short-Title Catalogue of Books Printed in England, Scotland and Ireland and of English Books Printed Abroad 1475–1640*, by W. A. Jackson, F. S. Ferguson, and Katharine F. Pantzer (London, 1976–86), i.130, item 3021, fol. Aiv verso. Perry, *Religious Pieces*, refers to this gloss in an addendum slip in his 1867 edition, whence it is cited in Doyle, 'A Survey', i.35 and note 7, but later editions omit the reference. For the church at London Stone (St Swithin's, Cannon Street), see T. Francis Bumpus, *Ancient London Churches* (London, undated), pp. 399–400.

IV. A Distinct Southern Version of the
Lay Folks' Catechism

It is commonly believed that the *Catechism* survives in 'distinctive Northern and Southern forms'[40] and that there is a 'distinct Northern and Southern manuscript tradition'.[41] Before subjecting these statements to scrutiny, it will be useful to investigate the further evidence for southern circulation.

There is some historical evidence that a work similar to the *Catechism* was officially distributed in the south in the same way and at the same time as the *Catechism* itself. Thoresby held the Northern province from 1353–73, during most of which time (1349–66) Simon Islip was Archbishop of Canterbury. The two Archbishops enjoyed a close and lasting friendship based on mutual concern for the pastoral welfare of the Church.[42] On 21 February 1361, just a few years after Thoresby issued the *Catechism* and his Injunctions, Islip ordered the commissary general of Canterbury to circulate local parish priests with a 'brevis libellus' of the seven deadly sins and ten commandments, ordering them to copy it, learn it, and teach it to their parishioners before his next visitation.[43] It is reasonable to assume that Islip was inspired by the example of the Archbishop of York, as Thoresby had been inspired by the example of an earlier Archbishop of Canterbury. Only the sins and commandments are specified, but the 'little book' (or *pagyne?*) might have contained more.[44] It is not known to survive and we do not know if it was in English or Latin, but it is probable that it was based on Thoresby's Injunctions and perhaps possible that it was the York *Catechism* itself which Islip circulated in the south.[45] The evidence is, however, too slight to suggest more than that material on the tenets, stimulated by Thoresby's Injunctions and the *Catechism*, was officially circulating in the southern province after 1357.[46]

An investigation of manuscripts of the *Catechism* which were copied in the southern rather than the northern province might be expected to reveal the existence of a distinct southern version of the text. Of the twelve full

---

[40] Albert E. Hartung (ed.), *A Manual of the Writings in Middle English 1050–1500*, vol. 7 (New Haven, 1986), p. 2271 [19].

[41] Lawton, 'Gaytryge's Sermon', pp. 331–32.

[42] See Hughes, *Pastors and Visionaries*, pp. 131–36.

[43] Hughes, *Pastors and Visionaries*, p. 154, who is dependent on W. A. Pantin, *The English Church in the Fourteenth Century* (Cambridge, 1955), p. 212. Islip's mandate survives in London, Lambeth Palace Library, Register of Simon Islip, fol. 182^{r-v}.

[44] Neither Ullerston's tract nor its English abridgement, for example, provides a full list of the tenets of the *Catechism*.

[45] It may be significant that when, from a base in the southern province, the mid fifteenth century reviser of John Mirk's *Festial* expanded Mirk's sermon for the Fourth Sunday in Lent with material on the ten commandments, he used a version of *The Lay Folks' Catechism* which, though in prose, retains one clearly southern rhyme ('also reuerence all men þat worshipfull be/do hem worship aftir her degree', London, British Library, MS Harley 2247, fol. 73^v). This rhyme is not found in any extant manuscript of the *Catechism*.

[46] V. Gillespie, 'Vernacular Books of Religion', in Jeremy Griffiths and Derek Pearsall (eds.), *Book Production and Publishing in Britain 1375–1475* (Cambridge, 1989), pp. 317–44 (p. 336, note 4), notes that in 1435 the Bishop of Bath and Wells issued a vernacular text of material of the Thoresby type.

manuscripts, five stem from within the jurisdiction of Canterbury,[47] whereas of the reworked texts all but one (London, British Library, MS Arundel 507) is of southern provenance. However, the textual evidence of these manuscripts shows no significant relationships amongst any of them which would mark them off as part of a scheme of organised distribution. What they do suggest is that individual copyists felt free to make emendations as they thought fit and that throughout its transmission the *Catechism* text remained flexible and adaptable to various uses.[48]

The treatment of the *Catechism*'s prefatory and concluding material may be used to exemplify this fact. As has been seen, the *Catechism* begins with an explanation of Thoresby's intention in circulating the *Catechism*, and it ends with the Archbishop's offer of forty days of pardon to those who learn the six tenets. In the course of this, the prefatory material contains two references and the concluding material one reference to 'our father the Archbishop'.[49] Neither province is specified, so that the text could well have circulated outside the York province without alteration. Cambridge, Sidney Sussex College, MS 55, was clearly in use by a priest in the southern province, since amongst its various prayers and materials for church use there is Archbishop Henry Chichele of Canterbury's English Sentence of Excommunication, prefaced by his decree of 1434. This *Catechism* text shows no alterations which would adapt it specifically for Canterbury circulation. Moreover, though we are certain of Northern circulation, one of the Northern manuscripts, Cambridge, Trinity College, MS B.10.12, alters and removes references to the Archbishop. This is clearly in fact because the text has been adapted for direct preaching to a congregation, and Thoresby's instructions to his priests were unsuitable in this context. It would seem likely that similar *ad hoc* decisions can explain other alterations in the text.[50]

Other manuscripts show a variety of different responses to this material. The Lambeth Palace Library manuscript which Simmons and Nolloth called a 'Wycliffite adaptation' of the *Catechism* retains the material intact, including (most strangely if it were indeed a Lollard adaptation) the archbishop's pardon.[51] One manuscript truncates the prefatory material but makes a specific reference

---

[47] Paris, Bibliothèque Ste. Geneviève, MS 3390 (West Midlands); Cambridge, Sidney Sussex College, MS 55 (Northants.); Oxford, Bodleian Library, MS Rawlinson C.288 (Norfolk); Nottingham, Nottingham University Library, MS Middleton LM 9 (Lincolnshire); Lincoln, Lincoln Cathedral Library, MS 91 (Lincolnshire). It is hard to know how to categorise the last of them, the Thornton manuscript, which was copied in Yorkshire but from a Lincolnshire prototype.

[48] This is true of all the manuscripts of the *Catechism*, as is clear from the existence of so many extracts, all, it seems, independent of each other. In general, the text is marked by the fluidity of its transmission, with much paraphrase and/or expansion of the basic text, sometimes clearly for preaching purposes (e.g. 'Loo, goode men and women' Yale, University Library, MS Beinecke 317, fol. 31ᵛ).

[49] Simmons and Nolloth, p. 4, l. 42; p. 22, l. 74; p. 98, l. 566.

[50] It would perhaps be in the nature of the network of dissemination posited for the *Catechism* by Dr Gillespie ('Vernacular Books', p. 317), whereby the archdeacons held the exemplars from which the priests copied the decrees, that such adaptation would take place.

[51] London, Lambeth Palace Library, MS 408, which is presented *en face* to the Register text of the *Catechism* in Simmons and Nolloth's edition. For Anne Hudson's argument against its being a Lollard reworking, and for its relationship with Oxford, Bodleian Library, MSS Eng.th.e.181/ Douce 274/Douce 273, see note 6.

to the 'archibischop of ʒork' and his pardon.[52] Two East Anglian manuscripts remove references to the archbishop and his pardon and refer instead to the 'consel of holy chirch'.[53] A manuscript now preserved at Hopton Hall retains the prefatory material but omits the final references to the Archbishop and his pardon. A Nottinghamshire monastic volume omits all the prefatory and concluding material, probably because the text was intended only for private reading.[54] The Thornton manuscript refers to 'bishop' rather than 'archbishop' throughout.[55]

David Lawton's comment on the evidence of the Thornton manuscript is of some interest: 'There is surely a possibility here that by Thornton's time the treatise was common knowledge, and in the Church common property, from time to time reissued in the name of one bishop for a particular diocese'.[56] Lawton presupposes a more official distribution of the *Catechism* than our information suggests, but two further manuscripts, Midland in origin, one currently in Paris and the other at Yale, are of particular interest in that they alter the neutral references to 'our father the archbishop' to specify the Archbishop of Canterbury.[57] The Paris manuscript dates from the early fifteenth century and the Yale manuscript from up to a century later, and they show no textual interdependence, but they are comparable in one other way too. Both of them refer to seven, rather than six, tenets. 'Refer' is the crucial word, since the Paris manuscript refers to seven tenets at the beginning and end of the text[58] but deals with, and refers to, only six in the body of the text, but the Yale manuscript refers to and also treats seven tenets in all, albeit that the extra tenet, the gifts of the Holy Ghost, is dealt with rather perfunctorily.[59]

---

[52] Oxford, Bodleian Library, MS Bodley 789, fol. 68ʳ.

[53] Oxford, Bodleian Library, MS Rawlinson C.288, fols. 85ʳ, 85ᵛ; London, British Library, Harley 6615, fol. 127ᵛ.

[54] Cambridge, University Library, MS Additional 6686. This manuscript is listed amongst Hudson's 'Manuscripts in which an extract or extracts only were included' ('A New Look', p. 246), since it also omits the commandments and the deadly sins. Doyle ('A Summary', i.33 and ii.122, note 54) suggests that the hand is too small to allow reading aloud.

[55] Lincoln, Lincoln Cathedral Library, MS 91, fol. 214ʳ ('oure ffadire þe byschope'), fol. 214ʳ⁻ᵛ ('oure haly ffadir þe beschope'), fol.218ʳ ('oure ffadir þe beschope').

[56] 'Gaytryge's Sermon', p. 333.

[57] Paris, Bibliothèque Ste. Geneviéve, MS 3390, fol. 38ᵛ ('oure fader þe erchebisschop of Caunterbyri'), fol. 39ᵛ ('oure fader þe holi erchebischop'), fol. 52ʳ ('oure fader þe erchbisschop'); Yale, University Library, MS Beinecke 317, fol. 21ᵛ ('oure holy fadir þe archebysshop of Cawntirberye'), fol. 22ʳ ('oure holy fadire þe archebysshop'), fol. 34ʳ ('oure fadire þe Archebysshop of Cawnterberye').

[58] Fols. 38ᵛ, 52ʳ.

[59] The extra tenet is introduced in the fourth position, in place of the deeds of mercy, which come last (the positions of the deadly sins and the corresponding virtues are transposed). It is so brief as to be easily reproduced: 'And nowe þe fourth þynge to knowe by God almygthy be þe vij gyftes of þe Holy Gost, þe which been þise: þe gyfte of wysdom and of kunnynge, þe gyfte of cownceyle and of strength, þe gyfte of kunnynge [sic] and of pyte, and the gyfte of þe drede of our lorde. Thise gyftes may not perfyʒtly be geete withoute specyall prayer, þe whych comprehendyth þe vij petycionys of the Pater Noster be þe which we put out of oure sowle þorough þe vertu of þe gyftes of þe Holy Gost þe vij dedly synnes. And so as towchynge to þe vij petycyones of þe Pater Noster and also þe vij gyftes of þe Holy Goste, I passe ovyre to speke of as at þis tyme tylle at more leysere, and purpose me to speke of þe vij dedly synnes, þe whych is þe fyfte þynge þat we shulde knowe God almygthy by . . .' (fol. 32ʳ).

These two manuscripts will form part of the final discussion as to whether a distinct southern version of the *Lay Folks' Catechism* exists, but it may be concluded at this stage that amongst the extant manuscripts there is no evidence of a southern manuscript tradition. If then, there is no manuscript evidence to support it, why is it commonly believed that the *Catechism* survives in 'distinctive Northern and Southern forms' and that there is a 'distinct Northern and Southern manuscript tradition'?[60]

In his 1954 thesis Dr Doyle referred to the printed text known as the *Quattuor Sermones* as 'a distinct southern provincial version' of the *Catechism* and suggested that some of the Midland texts of the *Lay Folk's Catechism* 'approximate more or less closely' to it.[61] This would appear to be the origin of the belief that distinct northern and southern forms survive.

V. The *Quattuor Sermones*

In the printed form in which it circulated as the *Quattuor Sermones*, it would be true to say that we are dealing with a southern form of the *Catechism*.

The *Quattuor Sermones* was printed by Caxton three times, twice in (probably) 1483 and again in 1491. It is normally found in the company of the *Festial*, the late fourteenth-century collection of sermons by the Austin canon, John Mirk, also printed by Caxton in 1483 and 1491.[62] No exact counterpart of the work exists in manuscript, but the printed form was based on a reworked version of the *Catechism* such as that extant in Cambridge, Trinity College, MS B.14.19, which is the most southerly in dialect of all the *Catechism* manuscripts and was copied in Suffolk.

The Trinity College manuscript, though fuller than the *Quattuor Sermones* and with numerous variant readings, is certainly the basis of about two-thirds of the *Quattuor Sermones*.[63] The manuscript presents a version of the *Catechism*, known only in this one manuscript, which includes the Pater Noster and the Ave Maria as an extra tenet and which ends with the five bodily and ghostly senses and the nine pains of hell. Two other manuscripts of the *Catechism* include material on the Pater Noster, Ave Maria, and five senses, but they bear no relation to the Trinity College manuscript.[64] The manuscript does, however,

---

[60] See above and notes 40 and 41.

[61] Doyle, 'A Summary', i.35 and note 8.

[62] The *Quattuor Sermones* has been discussed by Norman F. Blake and L. Reffkin in 'Caxton's First Edition of "Quattuor Sermones" ', *Gutenberg-Jahrbuch* (1974): 77–82, and has been edited by Professor Blake in *Quattuor Sermones*, Middle English Texts 2 (Heidelberg, 1975). Some of the statements in the earlier article would seem to have been altered or modified in the edition.

[63] This is acknowledged by Blake, *Quattuor Sermones*, p. 16: 'This contains the introduction and seven tenets of Christian belief as given in QS, but as a general rule this text is much wordier than QS.'

[64] They are London, Lambeth Palace Library, MS 408 and Oxford, Bodleian Library, MSS Eng.th.e.181/Douce 274/Douce 273 (see note 48). The material (the Pater Noster, Ave Maria, Creed, five bodily and ghostly senses) is a true interpolation, inserted after the preface and before the six tenets, and the text continues throughout to refer to only six tenets.

bear some relation to the Paris and Yale manuscripts mentioned above, in that all three stem from the province of Canterbury (and Paris and Yale specifically refer to the Archbishop of Canterbury), and all three cite (and Yale and Trinity College specifically deal with) seven tenets.

It must be clearly stated that there is no textual interdependence amongst these manuscripts. The Trinity College manuscript is mid-fifteenth century in date, stems from Suffolk, and is an extensively reworked text, which divides the seven-fold material into sermons for two successive Sundays. However, it may be suggested that the three manuscripts, different as they are, illustrate a fifteenth-century tendency in the southern province to expand the *Catechism* to include the Pater Noster as a separate tenet. The very differences amongst the manuscripts would seem to illustrate that this was in each case an *ad hoc* production, rather than part of a manuscript tradition. I would suggest, in fact, that no southern manuscript tradition of the *Catechism* ever existed, and that, though it would be true to say that a distinctive southern version of the *Catechism does* exist, it exists, as Dr Doyle has suggested, in the form of the *Quattuor Sermones*, and in that printed form alone.

The final question that may be addressed is whether the *Quattuor Sermones* existed in manuscript form before Caxton's printing. Apart from the version of the *Catechism* already described, the Quattuor *Sermones* consists of a treatise on contrition, confession and satisfaction, *The Clensyng of Mannes Sowle*.[65] It concludes with the Sentence of Excommunication in English and Latin and the Bidding Prayers for Sundays in English. Both the Sentence and the Bidding Prayers are specifically adapted for Canterbury use.[66]

Latin versions of the Sentence date from the early thirteenth century. Even though priests were enjoined to expound it to their parishioners four times a year and English translations were stipulated from time to time, there was no official English version until Archbishop Chichele issued his for Canterbury in 1434. But even before Chichele the quarterly obligation meant that it was a common component in manuscripts of pastoral material. It has already been noted that the Sidney Sussex College manuscript contains the Chichele's Sentence and the Bidding Prayers, as well as the *Catechism*. Moreover, Dr Oliver Pickering in his seminal article on the Sentence of Excommunication has pointed out that the form of the Sentence in that manuscript has a brief addition at the end which is 'especially close' to the Sentence in the *Quattuor Sermones* and which is not found normally in Chichele's Sentence.[67]

Though there is therefore manuscript evidence for the combination of *Catechism*, Sentence and Bidding Prayers, the evidence does not presently exist to argue that the whole make-up of the *Quattuor Sermones* existed before Caxton printed it. There is, however, precedent for the whole combination of material it contains. What is known as the *Sacerdos Parochialis*, which circulated in the south in the fifteenth century, has in its fullest form almost exactly the same

---

65 See Hartung, *A Manual*, p. 2299 [84].

66 References to the province of Canterbury occur at Blake, *Quattuor Sermones*, p. 84, l. 24 and p. 86, l. 17.

67 O. S. Pickering, 'Notes on the Sentence of Cursing in Middle English; or, A Case for the Index of Middle English Prose', *Leeds Studies in English*, n.s. 12 (1981): 229–44 (p. 243, note 43).

make-up – Pater Noster, Ave, Creed, Commandments, Sins, Virtues, Precepts of the New Testament, Sacraments, five senses, Sentence and Bidding Prayers.[68]

The *Sacerdos Parochialis* does not contain a discussion of contrition, confession and satisfaction, as, it has already been noted, the *Quattuor Sermones* does. However, the pastoral aims of the *Catechism*, and indeed the specific comment in the Thornton manuscript that the *Catechism* 'teches how scrifte es to be made and whareof and in scrifte how many thynges solde be consederide'[69] make it apparent that the context is entirely appropriate. Whether Caxton found all these *pastoralia* together or not, they were certainly all circulating in the same contexts and might easily have been copied or bound together in various combinations.[70]

VI. The *Festial*

It has been noted that the other component of nearly all the copies of the *Quattuor Sermones* is the *Festial* and that both were printed by Caxton in 1483 and in 1491. Caxton normally issued them together and always with separate signatures, but after 1495 the *Festial/Quattuor Sermones* was usually set up as one text with one set of signatures. The version of the Sentence closest to that in the *Quattuor Sermones* is one which appears in a manuscript of the *Festial*.[71] Moreover, the version of the Bidding Prayers closest to the *Quattuor Sermones* is one which appears in a manuscript of the *Festial*.[72]

The *Festial* and the *Quattuor Sermones* are of directly comparable origin, both written for priests to deliver to layfolk in an attempt to correct mutual ignorance. Both stem from the initiative of Thoresby's *Catechism*. The possibility presents itself that the Sentence and Bidding Prayers which occur at the end of the *Quattuor Sermones* were present, together with the *Lay Folks' Catechism* (in its Trinity College form, with the treatise on penance), in the manuscript of the *Festial* used by Caxton.[73] The separate signatures of the *Festial* and the *Quattuor Sermones* argue against this, together with the fact that none of the thirty-plus *Festial* manuscripts extant contains the *Catechism*. However, I would not want to dismiss completely the possibility of some prior link between the *Festial* and

---

[68] Hartung, *A Manual*, pp. 2272–73 [23].

[69] See note 25.

[70] Blake, *Quattuor Sermones*, p. 11, notes that Caxton is unlikely to have been responsible for bringing together the separate components of the *Quattuor Sermones*, 'since when he linked texts together he either made some reference to the fact or else used different sets of signatures for each part'.

[71] Pickering, 'Notes', p. 236. The Sentence occurs on fols. 1ᵛ, col. a–2ᵛ, col. b of Oxford, Bodleian Library, MS Rawlinson A.381, a manuscript which contains several items of *pastoralia* and was clearly compiled for or by a priest.

[72] Oxford, Bodleian Library, MS Hatton 96, fols. 135ʳ–136ʳ.

[73] No extant manuscript of the *Festial* is comparable to either Caxton's first or his second editions, which were set up from different sources, though it is clear that he used a Group B version of the text. On the division of the *Festial* manuscripts into an earlier, westerly Group A and a later Group B, see Martyn F. Wakelin, 'The Manuscripts of John Mirk's *Festial*', *Leeds Studies in English*, n.s. 1 (1967): 93–118.

the *Quattuor Sermones* and would query whether it really is the case that the main reason why the two works were printed together must have been 'simply that both were available in print'.[74]

At any rate, it can be said that, whether they were previously connected or not, the decision to issue together the *Festial* and the *Quattuor Sermones* was a sound one, clearly assessed as such by Wolfgang Hopyl and the later printers who set them up together.[75] As Dr Doyle has said, 'the number of impressions was nearer that of Church service-books and scholastic text-books than that of other English didactic compositions'.[76]

It would seem appropriate to conclude by rejecting the received opinion that the *Lay Folks' Catechism* survives in 'distinctive Northern and Southern forms' and that there is a 'distinct Northern and Southern manuscript tradition'. What can be said is that the *Quattuor Sermones* represents a distinct Canterbury version of the York *Catechism*. It presented a complete pastoral guide for the priest, though private religious and lay devotion were not excluded either.[77] In combination with the *Festial* and, from 1491, together with the *Hamus Caritatis*, a text on the ten commandments and the two precepts of the Gospel, which is addressed specifically to the householder,[78] it sold very well indeed up to Wynkyn de Worde's final printing in 1532.

In these late editions can be seen the final stage of the transmission of the *Lay Folks' Catechism* prepared by John of Gaytryge in York in 1356/57 at the command of his Archbishop, John Thoresby. It has been augmented and expanded to seven tenets, and *The Clensyng of Mannes Sowle* and the Sentence and Bedes have been added to form the *Quattuor Sermones*. Its marketability has been increased by the addition of the sermons of the ever-popular *Festial*. Finally, there has been added an extra exhortation specifically directed at the responsible layman, aware of his duty to his family and household. The whole transmission shows in fact the evolution of the *Catechism* from a mid fourteenth century circulating *pagyne* for the parish priest to a weighty *vade mecum* which reflects the needs of a lay as well as clerical readership in the late fifteenth century. Of this great volume, of course, the *Quattuor Sermones* is just a small part, but even at this stage it is clearly recognisable, in Dr Doyle's original statement of 1952, as 'a distinct southern provincial version' of the *Lay Folks' Catechism*.

[74] Blake, *Quattuor Sermones*, p. 13. For further discussion of the *Festial* in relation to the *Quattuor Sermones*, see S. Powell, 'John Mirk's *Festial* and the Pastoral Programme', *Leeds Studies in English*, n.s. 22 (1991): 85–102, especially pp. 90–92.
[75] Blake and Reffkin, 'Caxton's First Edition', p. 81, credit James Ravynell with first issuing the texts as one volume, but Blake, *Quattuor Sermones*, p. 13, notes correctly that they were first printed in one volume with one set of signatures by Wolfgang Hopyl in 1495.
[76] Doyle, 'A Summary', i.36.
[77] Doyle, 'A Summary', i.36 comments on the paucity of surviving copies as evidence of the 'degree of hard practical employment of these works'. He is able to cite one copy belonging to a priest, one to a monk, and two to laymen (note 11).
[78] For further details, see Powell, 'John Mirk's *Festial*', pp. 91–92.

'MEDDLING WITH MAKINGS' AND WILL'S WORK

Ralph Hanna III

I will read a small excerpt from what people today would call a more extensive project. This seeks to situate within fourteenth-century discourses Langland's expansive revisions to the 'Visio' in the C Text of *Piers Plowman*. Most particularly, I am interested in the 'autobiographical passage' of C passus V, which has been largely ignored since E. Talbot Donaldson's seminal discussion forty-odd years ago.[1] As will become evident, I am engaged in revising Donaldson's views, arguing that Langland represents Will through the discourse associated with a recognizable medieval profession, that of hermits. And, of course, my arguments have particular relevance to this occasion, since our honoree Ian Doyle, while perhaps not the twentieth-century Godric, shares with him an almost eremitic attachment to Durham; and like many medieval hermits – Wulfric of Haselbury Plucknett or Christina of Markyate among them – he has a universal reputation as the seer (in this case codicological) who could resolve all our problems, were he willing to speak (or just write us a letter back).

My study begins by taking very seriously the one set of lines from *Piers Plowman* which everyone knows:

> In a somer seson, whan softe was þe sonne,
> I shoop me in shroudes, as I a sheep weere,
> In habite as an heremite, vnholy of werkes;
> Wente wide in þis world wondres to here.   (B Prol.1–4)[2]

As a guide to what seems to me extraordinary about this passage, and about authorial self-representation in this poem,[3] I take a comment Jean Leclercq once made about hermits:

> It's necessary to distinguish two quite general categories of hermits in the Middle Ages: those of whom one speaks and those of whom one doesn't. These last constitute the normal and most frequent cases: men of whom we

---

[1] *Piers Plowman: The C-Text and Its Poet* (New Haven, 1949), pp. 201–19.

[2] All citations are from George Kane and E. Talbot Donaldson (eds.), *Piers Plowman: The B Version* (London, 1975). Here I retain the archetypal B reading of line 2 (confirmed in C.Prol.2; as frequently, Kane and Donaldson have intruded the reading of A.

[3] By this locution I place myself uneasily between New Critical readings which rigidly distinguish a godlike Langland the Poet from an ironized Will and such a demolition as George Kane's 'The Autobiographical Fallacy in Chaucer and Langland Studies', reprinted in *Chaucer and Langland: Historical and Textual Approaches* (Berkeley, 1989), pp. 1–14. Will is not obviously so different from his maker as Geoffrey is from Chaucer; and, as I implicitly argue near the end of the paper (more explicitly in my longer project), the poem as Will/Langland's significant biography is precisely what is served through this representation.

know nothing, or almost nothing, because they have 'done' nothing; they are contented 'to be' in the presence of God.[4]

Thus, the very entry to the poem, its first identification as the speech of one who presents himself as at least like a hermit, is quite ambivalent. The normal eremitic case, as Leclercq describes it, is to be beyond discourse – isolated in contemplation within the savage cell, traditionally, as Langland knows (B.XV.269–306), situated in a forest or a cave. Thus hermits should be removed from the world, from the ken of observers who would describe them, entrap them in discourse: significantly most efforts of this kind represent posthumous *Vitae*. And hermits themselves should be nondiscursive, silent, without any need for writing: their 'being' should be imbricated in the non- or pre-linguistic, in pure presence, proximity to the divine. Insofar as such being is discursive at all, it claims a language explicitly nonreferential, a meditative sequence of approximations like Rolle's 'dulcor'/ 'calor'/ 'canor'; such discourse only gestures toward an ultimate reality, which some might take to be the ground of Langland's poem.

But the opening lines of *Piers* suggest that one should examine Will within actual human discourse, that contemporary limited discussion which describes hermits. In the later Middle Ages, such a profession is essentially a lay one: it is a profession of desire, specifically a desire for closer contact with and understanding of God; this desire, as much as any form of ecclesiastical sanction, creates a hermit. Moreover, the visible manifestation of such a desire is presented as the assumption of a special, but not necessarily standardized, dress, a habit. Hermits are frequently self-created ('*I shoop me* in shroudes'), and they create their own habits, both their clothes and their own ways of life.[5] The opening lines of the poem describe the moment of Will's vocation – the moment in which, like many contemporary hermits, he makes himself, out of devotion, into a new person, reclothes and thereby commits himself, without the sanction of orders, to a form of the religious life.[6] And such moments, insofar as

[4] *L'eremitismo in occidente nei secoli XI e XII*, Miscellanea del centro di studi medioevali 4 (Milan, 1965), p. 28 (my translation).

[5] The only direct precursors to my work are Malcolm Godden's two studies, 'Plowmen and hermits in Langland's *Piers Plowman*', *RES*, 35 (1984):129–63; and *The Making of Piers Plowman* (London, 1990), both of which note such self-creation and appropriately cite the office of Richard Rolle, e.g. the article at pp. 161–62. As my subsequent argument indicates, Godden overemphasizes the contemplative features of fourteenth-century eremiticism and, consequently, fails to see that this life is not separated from the Plowman's world of work: indeed, as I argue below, eremitical discourse quite frequently problematizes one goal of the profession, contemplation.

[6] Cf. Hawkin, 'Yhabited as an heremyte, an ordre by hymselue, / Religion saunz rule and resonable obedience' (B.XIII.284–85). For the importance of the new life, see Virginia Davis, 'The Rule of St Paul, the First Hermit, in Late Medieval England', *Studies in Church History*, 22 (1985): 203–14, at 209, note 24. This citation, in fact from an *ordo* which seeks to regularize the profession, is paralleled in virtually all the other surviving examples (only seven, listed Davis, p. 207, note 15); see the text printed by Rotha Mary Clay, in her still-standard *Hermits and Anchorites of Medieval England* (London, 1914), p. 199; the Bainbridge Pontifical, Surtees Society, 61.141; Ralph Barnes (ed.), *Liber Pontificalis of Edmund Lacy, Bishop of Exeter* (Exeter, 1847), p. 130; Oxford, Bodleian Library, MS Tanner 5, p. 97; Oxford, Bodleian Library, MS Rawlinson C.549, fol. 6ᵛ. What Davis claims to be a 'rule' of St Paul in fact is simply part of the *ordo*; cf. Rawlinson C.549, fol. 8ᵛ, where her 'rule' materials follow upon this direction to the bishop: 'Et antequam recedat heremita, quia sub

they are succeeded by wilderness withdrawal, by something like a pilgrimage out of the *saeculum* ('Wente wide in þis world'), form a standard representation of the origins of the medieval hermit's life.[7]

Yet, as I have indicated, such a commitment is ambivalent. As Leclercq's language would indicate, the eremitic ideal, the life of the true hermit, is to be, to exist in divine presence. And Leclercq implicitly identifies language, the language both of documentary sources and of autobiography, as what distinguishes such hermits from those like Will, 'unholy of works'. In Langland's telling, Will becomes a hermit, not to evade notice, but precisely to demand it – to enter into language as speaker and subject of his poem. The ambivalence of his unregulated status, that simultaneous presence of desire and absence of warrant (which he shares with, for example, Richard Rolle)[8], conditions both his religious vocation and his determination to perform an action, to write his own words (rather than simply to copy authoritative texts, the manual labour of Carthusian monk/hermits). The effort by a hermit to appropriate a human discursive space is problematic – as Rolle's constant edgyness and Will Langland's difficulties with his poetic vocation indicate.

It's within such a construction that I consider a well-known passage from passus XII of the B text, Ymaginatif's rebuke of the dreamer.[9] This moment in Langland's earlier version I consider to have enabled the C text's much more detailed and problematic discussion of Will's poetic vocation, a function of his eremitic profession:

> 'And þow medlest þee wiþ makynges and my3test go seye þi
>   sauter,
> And bidde for hem þat 3yueþ þee breed, for þer are bokes
>   ynowe
> To telle men what dowel is, dobet and dobest boþe,
> And prechours to preuen what it is of many a peire freres'.
> I sei3 wel he seide me sooþ, and somwhat me to excuse
> Seide, 'Caton conforted his sone þat clerk þou3 he were,
> To solacen hym somtyme; so I do whan I make:

---

aliqua certa regula minime debet coartari, ideo ne ignorans ignoretur, exponatur ei aliquis modus uiuendi cum certis obseruanciis'. However (in spite of Davis's claims, p. 208 note 18), this text may only be borrowed from a 'regula Pauli'; its hermit makes a vow of chaste life 'iuxta regulam beati .N.' (fol. 5ʳ), which I take to indicate that the individual chose a sanctified sponsor ad lib. (The Middle English rules claim to be for 'orders' of Pope Celestine V – as London, British Library MS. Addit. 34193, fol. 131ʳ, notes 'the wylke pope Celestine whas an heremyte or he whas pope' – and of St Linus.)

[7] See Henrietta L. Leyser, *Hermits and the New Monasticism: A Study of Religious Communities in Western Europe 1000–1150* (New York, 1984), pp. 23–24. Perhaps significantly, William of Malmesbury alleges that Little Malvern priory (O.S.B.) owed its foundation to two such eremitic wanderers; see Hubert Dauphin, in *L'eremitismo*, p. 277. I ignore, in the context of this presentation, a further pressing issue about Prol. 4, Will's wending and his association with the gyrovague – that he enters the wilderness, not to exist, to be – but to act, and to act errantly.

[8] Cf. Richard Rolle, ed. E. J. F. Arnould, *The Melos Amoris* (Oxford, 1957), p. 4/3.

[9] In the discussion which follows, I am especially indebted to Anne Middleton, 'Narration and the Invention of Experience', in Larry D. Benson and Siegfried Wenzel (eds.), *The Wisdom of Poetry: Essays in Early English Literature in Honor of Morton W. Bloomfield* (Kalamazoo, 1982), pp. 91–122.

Interpone tuis interdum gaudia curis.
And of holy men I here', quod I, 'how þei ouþerwhile
In many places pleyden þe parfiter to ben.
Ac if þer were any wight þat wolde me telle
What were dowel and dobet and dobest at þe laste,
Wolde I neuere do werk, but wende to holi chirche
And þere bidde my bedes but whan ich ete or slepe'.

(B.XII.16–28)

At this point in the poem, Ymaginatif, his own image-making power, ignored for forty-five years, has caught Will in his first moment of shame. This emotion has at last seized the dreamer after a lengthy series of rebukes for his refusal to 'suffer': in his intellectual arrogance – a disguise, a habit, put on to mask a deep despair – Will has refused to keep his mouth shut and to exist in silence, to be a proper eremitic subject who would be invisible to us.[10] At the opening of this passage (B.XII.16–17), Ymaginatif tells Will he should be ashamed that he adds to the world's already extensive discourse, simply because he desires to do so: 'þow medlest þee wiþ makynges and myȝtest go seye þi sauter / And bidde for hem þat ȝueþ þee breed, for þer are bokes ynowe'. Praying, repeating the holy words of one's Psalter, is fine; constructing an individuated, pseudo-learned discourse for oneself is not.

Will acknowledges this charge, this assertion that his action has no warrant ('I seiȝ wel he seide me sooþ' 20). But he also, as he will again in passus V of the C text, undertakes an evasive defence of what seems indefensible, his status, not as an orant but as a speaking hermit-poet. This defence responds to Ymaginatif's 'medlest þee': Ymaginatif means 'You meddle, intrude yourself into what's not your business', 'intermit,' as Chaucer's Summoner claims the Friar does.[11] But Will, quite typically, counts on some fast footwork to deflect Ymaginatif's charge and turns that figure's moral absolutism polyvocal. Ymaginatif claims that there are people in society who are truly learned and who thus have warrant to enter discourse ('many a peire freres', for example). But in contrast to that charge that he is a meddler, Will misconstrues, responds as if Ymaginatif has used a second sense of the verb *medlen*, 'to intermix'. He first cites (23ª) Cato, *Disticha*, iii.6: 'Stick in/interpose some joys amidst your cares'; the citation continues, 'so that you may *sufferre animo*, endure with spirit, any labor'.[12] And he then goes on to make a more expansive claim, which insists on the power of 'interposition', of interchanging work and play: 'of holy men I here . . . how þei ouþerwhile ('sometimes, at times'; cf. *somtyme* in line 22) / In manye places pleyden þe parfiter to ben'.

It's in this second claim, that Cato's alternating or 'interponential' life (sometimes one thing, sometimes another) – what Hilton, for example, calls 'medled' or mixed and what Will depicts as holyness alternating with joy, prayer

---

[10] B.XI.413 defines suffering as silence; cf. B.XI.416ª (from Boethius): 'You'd have been a philosopher, if you'd kept your mouth shut'.

[11] *Canterbury Tales* D.834.

[12] Cato reads: 'Interpone tuis interdum gaudia curis / Ut possis animo quemvis sufferre laborem'. The citation is a foretaste of Will's claims to be a learned hermit at C.V.35–39: he's been through grammar school (cf. B.XII.21 'clerk þouȝ he were'). Cf. the translation of 'Interpone' as

with making – that Will evokes the practice of hermits, of 'holy men', in order to claim that his poeticizing might be licit activity.[13] For medieval discussions of the eremitical life insist upon an 'interponential' quality which that life should share with those imperatives Will derives from Cato. At the center of eremitic devotion is supposed to be, as Ymaginatif points out, recitation of the Psalter.[14] But saying the psalms, although it forms a central religious act, is always perceived within this discourse as potentially dangerous – as contributing to possible sloth (a state in penitential lore intimately connected with the despair which has dogged Will for two passus). The danger of sloth the wise hermit avoids precisely by 'meddling', by an alternation among appropriate tasks (reading, manual labour, meditation or contemplation, perhaps simply taking a walk).[15]

In England, the seminal example of this discourse appears in ch. 9 of the instructions Aelred of Rievaulx prepared for his sister. Aelred's words were appropriated by the author of the oldest and longest English rule for hermits, 'The Cambridge Rule':

> Idleness is that enemy of the soul which a hermit should avoid above all other things. It is the parent of all evils, the artificer of lust, the solace of sloth and the nurse of vices. It begets the worst thoughts and instills a dread of being in one's cell. Therefore, the hermit should flee it through a variety of spiritual exercises.[16]

Aelred's – and his adaptor's – first clause alludes to the ultimate ground for this suspicion of any protracted and unalloyed devotional effort, ch. 48 of Benedict's

---

'entirmedle' in the Middle English translation of Christine de Pisan at Alexandra Barratt, *Women's Writing in Middle English* (London, 1992), p. 157/350. See further Glending Olson, *Literature as Recreation in the Later Middle Ages* (Ithaca, 1982), pp. 109–15, which sees monastic recreation as extra-regiminal effort (and thus different from the eremitic prescriptions, all built into the regimen, which I will describe).

[13] I think Will's claim here is distinguishable from that grammar-school tradition exemplified by Henryson's *Moral Fables*, ll. 19–21 (pointed out to me by Priscilla Bawcutt). Henryson's playful use of Cato is primarily directed to the activity of readers, not that of poets (although it surely licenses them as well); and Henryson imagines (*Fables*, l. 25) the hardship which requires amelioration as inherent in a different textual situation – the study appropriate to a grammar school, not Will's psaltering, central to the hermit discourse I will describe below.

[14] A point I examine in greater detail in my longer study; for my purposes here, see Leclerq, *L'eremitismo*, p. 39; 'The Oxford Rule' for hermits (Oxford, Bodleian Library, MS Rawlinson C.72), ed. Livarius Oliger, *Antonianum*, 3 (1928):318–19, 320; Clay's *ordo*, *Hermits*, pp. 201–02 (cf. Davis, 'Rule', p. 211 and note 29); Rolle's routine reliance upon and impressive interest in both Latin and English psalters.

[15] Cf. the standard list of activities which appears in most of the hermit *ordos*: 'monemus te vivere . . . in vigiliis, in jejuniis, in laboribus, in precibus, in misericordie operibus' (Clay, *Hermits*, p. 199; similarly Bainbridge Pontifical, p. 287; Lacy Pontifical, p. 130; Tanner 5, p. 97; Rawlinson C.549, fol. 7ʳ, with variants). The stroll in one's garden is recommended by Stephen of Tournai, Epistola 159 (*PL* 211.448).

[16] 'Ociositas inimica est anime, quam pre ceteris debet cavere heremita. Est enim omnium malorum parens, libidinis artifex, fomentum accidie et nutrix viciorum. Ipsa pessimas cogitationes seminat et horrorem incutit celle. Ideo exerciciorum fuganda est varietate'. I cite 'The Cambridge Rule' (Cambridge, University Library, MS Mm.vi.17) from Oliger, *Antonianum*, 3 (1928): 306–07. The author here quotes Aelred of Rievaulx's *De Institutione inclusarum*, cap. 9, which I cite from Charles Dumont, *La Vie de recluse* (Paris, 1961), pp. 62–66.

Rule.[17] But where Benedict clearly speaks of filling spaces in the day, a schedule, Aelred shows a deliberated interest in variety, alternation, change of duties. Aelred's description of a recluse's ideal regimen from All Saints' until Lent is taken over into 'The Cambridge Rule' as if a universal prescription; this passage insists upon the possibly debilitating effect of excess prayer, most particularly excessive engagement with the Psalter:

> And the hermit should beware, lest too extensive prayer give birth to distaste; it is more useful to pray more often and briefly, rather than all at once and for too extended a period, unless an inspired spirit of devotion prolongs prayer. Also he should beware imposing on himself any rule about saying a certain number of psalms, but so long as they please him, he should say them. If, however, they begin to be burdensome, let him pass on to reading, just as (if he's exhausted by those duties) he can proceed to manual labour, so that by such a healthy alternation he may recreate his spirit and drive away sloth.[18]

Rather than lose the salutary effects of prayer, one should alternate one's practice – break up oration with reading or manual labor.

And further touches of the 'salubris alternacio' typify other aspects of the hermit's daily schedule. Before Terce, for example, the hermit should engage in an 'alternation between reading, prayer, and manual labour' ('alternaci[o] lectionum, orationum, et operis manuum'). After lunch (here I cite Aelred's somewhat more explicit language), 'he should return to that switching off I have already prescribed, casting spiritual exercises among bouts of manual labour until Vespers' ('ad praescriptam vicissitudinem redeat, spiritualibus exercitiis opus corporale interserens usque ad vesperam'). Not only do both Aelred and the redactor of 'The Cambridge Rule' vary *alternacio* with *vicissitudo*, but Aelred's participle *interserens* recalls Cato's similar prefixed form *interponere* and, in context, further reminds one that 'meddling' is a state of mutuality: prayer offers as great a break from manual labor as does the reverse 'vicissitude'. Finally, *interserere*, in the company of another parallel form, *intermittere* (recall Chaucer's Friar and Summoner), recurs in the description of labours appropriate to a brother 'qui literas non intelligit'. ('The Cambridge Rule' has only the second of these verbs.)[19]

Moreover, this material has a surprisingly wide English distribution. I have identified Aelred's *Institutio inclusarum*, written for his sister, as merely one

---

[17] 'Idleness is the enemy of the soul, and therefore the monks ought to be occupied at set times in manual labor, and contrariwise, at other set times in holy reading' ('Otiositas inimica est animae, et ideo *certis temporibus* occupari debent fratres in labore manuum, *certis iterum horis* in lectione divina').

[18] 'Et caveat ne prolixior oratio fastidium pariat; utilius est enim sepius orare breviter quam semel nimis prolixe, nisi orationem prolongaverit devocio inspirata. Caveat etiam ne de numero Psalmorum aliquam sibi legem imponat, sed quamdiu delectant, utatur illis. Si ceperint esse oneri, transeat ad lectionem, sicut ad opus manuum, hiis fatigatus pergens, ut salubri alternacione spiritum recreet et pellat accidiam'.

[19] And Aelred's further discussion (ch. 11, p. 74) of the afternoon manual labor all should practice during Lent offers a further example: they should work 'casting brief prayers into their space of labor from time to time' ('breves per intervalla orationes interserens').

example of a general twelfth-century interest in eremitic discipline. This text has, of course, a distinguished life in English as a source of instruction for enclosed women, in *Ancrene Riwle*, for example. One of the two Middle English translations of Aelred, that in Oxford, Bodleian Library, MS Bodley 423, includes this portion of the text and dutifully translates the passage about interspersing the Psalter with other duties.[20] And traces of Aelred's formulation recur in writings for women such as the *Chastising of God's Children* and *The Orchard of Syon*.

But, like *Ancrene Riwle*, Aelred's instructions for women were also appropriated for male use, in this case for the unregulated state of hermits,[21] as in 'The Cambridge Rule'. This rule was subjected to further rewriting in the Latin 'Oxford Rule': the passage I have been discussing does not appear there, nor in three separate English adoptions of the latter rule composed *c.* 1500 (London, British Library, MSS Sloane 1584 and Additional 34193; Bristol, Public Library, MS 6), although they all insist upon the importance both of the psalter and of a variegated eremitic regimen. But later traces appear, in the *Speculum inclusorum*, in Richard Methley's epistle 'To Hew Heremyte', and in several copies of the half-dozen surviving *ordo*s for sanctifying a hermit.[22] If one considers Leclercq's point with which I began, that the lives of hermits should not be the subject of discursive formulations, that in fact no such language, descriptive or proscriptive, should exist, these references represent a veritable plethora of riches.

But why should such an insistence on 'meddling', alternation, exist? Why should psalming be dangerous, so dangerous as to require limitation? What is there about recitation of the biblical text which leads Aelred to describe it as *onerus* and Will to see that it requires the interspersed play of poetry? In this essentially rote reading, the mind can wander, can stray from devotional thoughts to other things. Such mental wandering already constitutes what Aelred calls *fastidium* (distaste), a turning from *delectatio devotionis*. But, as the discourse associated with the twelfth-century revival of the eremitic life suggests, the real danger resides in the quality of such thoughts – what another seminal passage (this time from St Jerome) calls *perniciose cogitationes*, and what Ivo of Chartres will explicitly call *phantasia* and *vana imaginatio*.[23] In these descriptions, when his less than fully occupied consciousness wanders, the

---

[20] EETS 287.6/215–24; for references to other English uses, see p. 70, 219–20n, 223n.

[21] Another topic I consider at length elsewhere: what Felicity Riddy tells me she considers the 'feminization' of hermits, through their appropriation to a male state of instructions originally applicable to female recluses.

[22] See James Hogg's edition of Methley's epistle, ch. 12, *Analecta Cartusiana*, 31 (1977): 119; and Clay's *ordo*, *Hermits*, p. 202: 'suis laboret manibus *temporibus intermediis* circa victualia acquirenda' (similarly Rawlinson C.549, fol. 9ᵛ; and the English of bishop Waynflete's register cited Davis, 'Rule', p. 212: put commas after 'laboure' and 'reherced' in her citation).

[23] Jerome, 'Ad Rusticum monachum', Epistola 125.11 (*PL* 22.1079), part of the passage cited in 'The Cambridge Rule', ed. Oliger, p. 312; and Ivo, Epistola 256 (*PL* 162.261). Examples to much the same point but less explicit in their language occur fairly widely, given that such discourse should not exist; cf. Peter the Venerable, Epistola 20, in Giles Constable (ed.), *The Letters* (Cambridge, 1967), at pp. 37–38; Peter Damian, opusculum 15.22 (*PL* 145.354); Stephen of Tournai (note 14 above); Adam of Dryburgh, 'De Quadripertito exercitio cellae' 15–16, 36 (*PL* 153.826–27, 880–82); and Aelred.

insufficiently devout hermit grows to despise his calling and his cell, becomes slothful in the traditional monastic sense. By allowing his mind to wander, by exercising an immoderate and ungoverned imagination, such a figure, for the theorists of the eremitical life, easily becomes the unrestrained Will the poet, the man who can fall asleep praying in order to give his own undisciplined thoughts free reign (and then wake up to give them permanence, to write them down).[24] These clearly are not what one might construe as legitimate hermit visions, like the prognostications Christina or Wulfric received and which are appropriate to another portion of the 'interponential' life, contemplation.

Hence Will's emphasis on that mixture appropriate to the eremitical life. But informatively, that alternation most frequently poises against prayer, not Will's play, but manual labor. Unlike recluses, according to theorists of this state, hermits are expected to work for their sustinance (B.XV.290–93).[25] But the discourse of medieval hermit life presents this oscillation between devotion and labour positively, as something more than the mere economic necessity that one must labour for one's food:[26] within this discourse, labour is a form of grace which contributes equally as much to spiritual excellence as do purely devotional occupations. The presence of labour within hermit biography is not simply itself beneficial but confers value on that activity with which it alternates and which initially appears greater, oration associated with saying the psalms: the potential alternation between prayer and manual labour removes from such prayer its gravest danger (the lapse into fantasy which Will calls poetic play). Thus, manual labour potentially creates the actual value of such devotion.

Ultimately, one should see Will's appeal as witty yet evasive. Hermit discourse is, of course, peculiar: following Leclercq, it is what should not exist. Indeed, it would not, were it not for souls like Will – those who claim the calling for themselves with no supervision and, consequently, no assurance they are getting it right. It follows, then, that the discourse of eremiticism is entirely regulatory, disciplinary: it addresses those who would only err, were it not for instruction.

Eremitical discourse defines this peculiar form of life through the distinction 'hard devotion in psaltering'/'interposed physical labour'. In doing so, it seeks to extirpate *vana cogitatio* through the exercise of thought control: to regulate a human consciousness depraved by its own vague imaginings; to suppress human subjectivity, too embroiled in the purely experiential, and in the eremitical situation (unlike the monastic) unsupervised by any superior;[27] and it relies upon a system of physical discipline, manual labor, to assert such control.

---

[24] Cf. B.V.5–8 (and the more pointed C.V.105–08), B.XIX.1–5.

[25] Recluses, primarily female, were not expected to work and thus subjected to extensive regulation and licensing in order to assure that they had trust funds adequate for their maintenance. See Ann K. Warren, *Anchorites and their Patrons in Medieval England* (Berkeley, 1985).

[26] For which, cf. 'The Cambridge Rule', ed. Oliger, pp. 311–12, with citations of Acts 18.10 and II Thes. 3.10; 'The Oxford Rule', ed. Oliger, p. 318, with citations of Ps. 127.2 and II Thes. 3.10 again.

[27] Rolle, as he was well aware, was thus a great – and dangerous – model in his absolute suppression of any requirement either for supervision or for labour; compare Jonathan Hughes' discussion of various efforts at denaturing (or domesticating) his message, *Pastors and Visionaries: Religion and Society in Late Medieval Yorkshire* (Woodbridge, 1988), passim.

But Will, as he will again in C.V (cf. C.V.45: 'The lomes þat y labore with and lyflode deserue'), re-engages himself in precisely the misprision which 'interposition' of tasks has been designed to avoid. His distinction, 'work at the psalter'/'play at poetry', conflates the discursive context to which he appeals – alternate the multiple forms of your work/set off psalming against physical labour – into one member of a newly-created distinction. For Will, prayer becomes a total work, as harsh as anything manual. And what such a conflation – which evades material manual labour altogether[28] – opens out as the second member of its distinction is precisely the forbidden – the space of vain imagining, of *Piers Plowman* itself.

Moreover, as the concluding response to Ymaginatif (XII.25–28 'Ac if þer were any wight . . .') indicates, Will cannot conceive any actual improvement of his state. Were someone to explain even Dobest for him, the then compulsive psalming he promises here would, following this eremitical discourse I outline, find him thoroughly entrapped within that same posture he claims here wittily to avoid: excessive psalming, broken only by what the poem at other moments sees as the ultimate self-indulgence, eating and sleeping,[29] predictably would produce yet more *vanae cogitationes*, more *slepe*, more *phantasmata* and dreams, more poem still – stretching on toward infinity. And indeed, the locution 'neuere do werke' (B.XII.27) gives the game away, exposes Will's smokescreen of self-justification for what it is, since it implies that Will views the poem, not as the 'play' he has claimed in his initial defensiveness, but in fact as his unique form of labor.

Thus, I take Will's response to be a qualified triumph. He will win, be a poet as he wants, violate the eremitic rule of being outside discourse, whatever happens. And his evocation of the interpositional power of 'play' for him justifies, establishes as licit, the poem as activity. But it situates *Piers Plowman* as a conditioned second-best action, and does so quite deliberately. Will's investing himself in the cope of the hermit presents his poem as a repeated episodicness, because vicissitudinal; it will always occur in interstices, as a nonacknowledgement of those responsibilities he alternately (especially when pressed) claims for himself. For there can be no poem if Will behaves, practises the actual alternation of prayer and work enjoined by eremitic discipline. Instead, his episodic work-play, which always turns back to other bits of his existence, represents only half a life – and in terms of the discourse from which it appropriates, the worse half, the errant, the turning from the sober and socially meaningful religious duty of divine praise to some murkier effort. One might think of the other great poet who cites Will's bit of Cato in a passage which also

---

[28] Bella Millett points out to me that twelfth-century monastic rules seem caught between contentiously opposed two- and three-member patternings of the religious life: asceticism/variousness v. asceticism/variousness/amusement (Langland's play). My argument sees Langland as seizing upon the problematic three-part distinction and then collapsing it into what appears the less contentious and more ancient two-part system, although with a shuffling of terms which keeps amusement, generally maligned in monastic writings, according to Millett, central to the entire discussion. As my evocation of C.V at the head of the paragraph indicates, another area of interest in my longer study is the interface between eremitical discourse and fourteenth-century discourses on labour, omnipresent in the self-defence of the C version.

[29] Cf. C.V.9, or the temptation of Need in B.XX.

concerns troubled poetic vocation: 'For so to interpose a little ease, / Let our frail thoughts dally with false surmise' ('Lycidas', 152–53). Langland is our great poet of 'false surmise': his Will writes the otiose intervals which surround a centre of useful action, one which, so far as the poem goes, cannot, and so far as the eremitic discourse on which it draws claims, should not exist.[30]

[30] This paper is indebted to a variety of persons who have offered suggestions and demanded clarifications. I received particularly helpful readings in draft from my colleagues David Lawton and John Ganim. And unusually searching feedback came from a variety of York conference participants, whose suggestions I have tried to take into account as I have revised for publication: among them I would single out Felicity Riddy, as well as Priscilla Bawcutt and Bella Millett.

THY WILL BE DONE: *PIERS PLOWMAN* AND THE *PATERNOSTER*

Vincent Gillespie

I

At the end of passus XI of most A text manuscripts of *Piers Plowman*, Will resoundingly affirms the power of simple faith and the sanctity of the working poor, contrasting their devotion and dedication with the inflated learning and *scientia* of the educated and 'clerkes':

> *Ecce ipsi ydiote rapiunt celum vbi nos sapientes in infernum*
> *mergemur.*
> And is to mene in oure mouþ, more ne lesse,
> Arn none raþere yrauisshid fro þe riȝte beleue
> þanne arn thise [k]ete clerkis þat conne many bokis,
> Ne none sonnere ysauid, ne saddere of conscience,
> þanne pore peple, as plouȝmen, and pastours of bestis,
> Souteris & seweris; suche lewide iottis
> Percen wiþ a *paternoster* þe paleis of heuene,
> Wiþoute penaunce at here partyng, into [þe] heiȝe blisse.
>
> (A.XI.305–13)[1]

The potency of the *Pater Noster* clearly fascinated Langland. Like the power of love described by Holy Church, the prayer is 'portatif and persaunt as the point of a nedle' (B.I.157): *brevis oracio penetrat celum*.[2] Will asserts in the A and B texts that many clerks have lived to curse the time that they ever knew more than their Creed 'and principally hir paternoster' (B.X.465).[3] The Lord's Prayer looms large in the prayer life of the poem. Spiritual inadequacy is revealed by Sloth's ignorance of its contents:

---

[1] All references are to the following editions of *Piers Plowman*: A text: G. Kane (ed.), *Piers Plowman: The A Version* (London, 1960); B text: A. V. C. Schmidt (ed.), *The Vision of Piers Plowman: A Complete Edition of the B-Text* (London, 1978); C text: D. Pearsall (ed.), *Piers Plowman by William Langland: an Edition of the C-Text*, York Medieval Texts, second series (London, 1978).

[2] The tag, also found in *The Cloud of Unknowing* and *Dives and Pauper*, is appended to this passage in C-text versions and in some A-text copies, though not printed by Kane; see J. A. Alford, 'Some Unidentified Quotations in *Piers Plowman*', *Modern Philology*, 72 (1974–5): 390–9, p. 390. A citation of the tag in *Fasciculus Morum* perhaps predates all these occurrences; see S. Wenzel (ed. and trans.), *Fasciculus Morum: A Fourteenth-Century Preacher's Handbook* (London, 1989), p. 511.

[3] On the revisions of this passage in B and C, see D. F. Johnson, ' "Persen with a Pater-Noster Paradys Oþer Hevene': *Piers Plowman* C.11 296–98a', *The Yearbook of Langland Studies*, 5 (1991): 77–89.

> I kan noght parfitly my Paternoster as the preest it syngeth.
>
>   (B.V.395)

Haukyn's preoccupation with the things of the world reveals itself in his careless attention to the prayer's recitation:

> Ne nevere penaunce parfournede ne Paternoster seide
> That my mynde ne was moore on my good in a doute
> Than in the grace of God and hise grete helpes.
> *Ubi thesaurus tuus, ibi et cor tuum.*   (B.XIII.396–98a)

But for Will himself the *Pater Noster* is one of the means by which he earns his daily bread, as he reveals in the 'autobiographical' passage added in the C text:

> The lomes þat y labore with and lyflode deserue
> Is *pater-noster* and my prymer, *placebo* and *dirige*.   (C.V.45–46)

Moreover his literal bread is supplemented by a supersubstantial bread: the spiritual profit and food that the prayer and its teachings make available to ordinary people.[4] As he argues in self-defence to Reason and Conscience in the same C text episode:

> 'Preyeres of a parfit man and penaunce discret
> Is the leuest labour þat oure lord pleseth.
> *Non de solo,*' y sayde, 'for sothe *vivit homo,*
> *Nec in pane et in pabulo,* the *pater-noster* wittenesseth;
> *Fiat voluntas dei* – þat fynt vs alle thynges.   (C.V.84–88)

Indeed Will's dedication to the search for 'a gobet of his grace' (C.V.100) begins in the C text with a waking-state episode where he acts out the commitment to the prayer he has already described:

> And to þe kyrke y gan go, god to honoure,
> Byfore þe cros on my knees knokked y my brest,
> Syȝing for my synnes, seggyng my *pater-noster*,
> Wepyng and waylyng til y was aslepe.   (C.V.105–8)

Clearly the prayer has a particular power and significance for Will, especially in the C version of the poem. Why is this?

The *Pater Noster* enjoyed a special place in the devotional life of the English church.[5] It is increasingly common to find in pastoral manuals of the fourteenth- and fifteenth-centuries vernacular and Latin treatises which are specifically

---

[4] St Matthew's version of the fourth petition reads 'Give us this day our supersubstantial bread' (6.11: Douay-Rheims). St. Luke has the more familiar daily bread (11.3), but many patristic and medieval commentators follow Matthew.

[5] For a superficial survey, see M. Hussey, 'The Petitions of the Paternoster in Medieval English Literature', *Medium Ævum,* 27 (1958): 8–16. A fuller account is found in F. G. A. M. Aarts, *Þe Pater Noster of Richard Ermyte* (The Hague, 1967), pp. cii–cxiv; see also R. Raymo, 'Works of Religious and Philosophical Instruction', in *A Manual of the Writings in Middle English 1050–1500,* ed. A. Hartung, 7 (1986), pp. 2279–82 and bibliography. Latin commentaries on the *Pater Noster* are listed in M. W. Bloomfield *et al., Incipits of Latin Works on the Virtues and Vices 1100–1500 AD,* Medieval Academy of America Publication No. 88 (Cambridge, Mass., 1979), hereafter *Incipits.*

devoted to the explication of the significance of the prayer and its seven constituent petitions. Ad hoc pastoral manuals covering the catechetic syllabus routinely came to include discussion of it, and older Latin expositions are quarried and reformulated for the needs and abilities of the new and expanding audience for vernacular didacticism.[6]

From early in the church's history, the division of the prayer into seven petitions had encouraged their association with the seven capital or deadly sins, the virtues, the gifts of the Holy Spirit and (skilfully reduced) the Beatitudes.[7] These linked sequences of septenaries were the basis of frequent verbal and visual catechetic schematisations.[8] One of the most popular, Hugh of St Victor's *De Quinque Septenis*, is preserved in a tabular version in Oxford, University College, MS 45, accompanied by a metrical exposition of the *Pater Noster* and by an A text of *Piers Plowman*. A further schematic representation of the prayer in a 'table ypeynted' is found in the Vernon Manuscript along with another A-text of *Piers Plowman*.[9] These linked septenaries of catechetic material formed

[6] Recent surveys of vernacular manuals include Raymo; G. H. Russell, 'Vernacular Instruction of the Laity in the later Middle Ages in England: Some Texts and Notes', *Journal of Religious History*, 2 (1962–63): 98–119; V. Gillespie, '*Doctrina* and *Predicacio*: The Design and Function of Some Pastoral Manuals', *Leeds Studies in English*, New Series, 11 (1980 for 1979): 36–50; F. Kemmler, 'Synodalia and Vernacular Literature: A Note on Methods of Religious Instruction in Early Fourteenth-Century England', in G. K. Jember (ed.), *Tuebingen Studies in Literature and Language: Language and Its Manipulation* (Denver, 1980), pp. 79–89; Kemmler, *Exempla in Context: A Historical and Critical Study of Robert Mannyng of Brunne's 'Handlyng Synne'*, Studies and Texts in English, 6 (Tübingen, 1984), pp. 24–59; J. Shaw, 'The Influence of Canonical and Episcopal Reform on Popular Books of Instruction', in T. J. Heffernan (ed.), *The Popular Literature of Medieval England*, Tennessee Studies in Literature, 28 (Knoxville, 1985), pp. 44–60; L. E. Boyle, 'The Fourth Lateran Council and Manuals of Popular Theology', in Hefferman, pp. 30–43; C. A. Martin, 'Middle English Manuals of Religious Instruction', in M. Benskin and M.L. Samuels (eds.), *So Meny People Longages and Tonges: Philological Essays . . . presented to Angus McIntosh* (Edinburgh, 1981), pp. 283–98; Gillespie, 'Vernacular Books of Religion' in J. Griffiths and D. Pearsall (eds.), *Book Production and Publishing in Britain 1375–1475*, Cambridge Studies in Publishing and Printing History (Cambridge, 1989), pp. 317–44; A. Barratt, 'Works of Religious Instruction', in A. S. G. Edwards (ed.), *Middle English Prose: A Critical Guide to Major Authors and Genres* (New Brunswick, 1984), pp. 419–20, discusses the *Pater Noster* and the influence of Hugh of St Victor (see note 9 below).

[7] A. Katzenellenbogen, *Allegories of the Virtues and Vices in Medieval Art*, Medieval Academy of America Reprints for Teaching, 24 (Toronto, 1989; original edition London, 1939); M. W. Bloomfield, *The Seven Deadly Sins* (Michigan, 1952), pp. 83–91.

[8] One of the finest and most elaborate of these schematisations is the *Speculum Theologie*, discussed and illustrated in L. F. Sandler, *The Psalter of Robert de Lisle in the British Library* (London and Oxford, 1983), pp. 23–27 and Appendix III; F. Saxl, 'A Spiritual Encyclopedia of the Middle Ages', *JWCI* 6 (1943): 82–134, pp. 107–15.

[9] fol. 47r; for the Latin text (*Incipits* 8999), see *PL* 175.405–14; J. Krochalis and E. Peters, *The World of Piers Plowman* (Philadelphia, 1975), pp. 170–6. Hugh's *Expositio in Abdiam* (*PL* 175.400–1) contains substantially the same exposition of the prayer. A further Victorine commentary on the prayer (*Incipits* 9122) is preserved in *Allegoriae in Novum Testamentum*, Liber 2, *In Matthaeum* (*PL* 175.774–89, esp. 769–70, 781–2). In Vernon the table accompanies the *Speculum Vitae* which is structured round an extensive linking of the septenaries; see Hussey, 'Petitions', 12–13 and plate; A. I. Doyle, *The Vernon Manuscript : A Facsimile of Bodleian Library, Oxford, MS. Eng. Poet. a.1* (Cambridge, 1987), p. 9; A. Henry, ' "The Pater Noster in a table ypeynted" and Some Other Presentations of Doctrine in the Vernon Manuscript', in D. Pearsall (ed.), *Studies in The Vernon Manuscript* (Cambridge, 1990), pp. 89–113. Ian Doyle must take some of the blame for this paper as it was a request from him to check the Univ. manuscript for his Vernon introduction that started me thinking about this topic.

part of an influential repertoire of visual aids to which Langland occasionally alludes.[10]

Popular lay devotion to the prayer is suggested by the *Pater Noster* guild of York, which was committed to the erection and maintenance of 'a certain drawing which hangs above a column in the cathedral church . . . and depicts the layout and usefulness of the Lord's prayer'. The York guild also supported the now lost *Pater Noster* play, and there was a similar play in Beverley.[11]

There can be little doubt that the inclusion of the prayer in the catechetical regimes specified in the pastoral legislation of thirteenth-century English bishops gave substantial impetus, and was in part a response, to theological study of its pastoral potential.[12] English decrees – even some predating the Fourth Lateran Council of 1215, such as Langton's for Canterbury, now dated 1213/14 – specified a syllabus of instruction that was often repeated and gradually refined. The Creeds (including *Quicumque vult*, fundamental to the catechetic structure of the *Visio*), the *Pater Noster*, the Commandments and the Deadly Sins, sometimes supplemented by the Sacraments and later joined by the *Ave Maria*, were to be expounded regularly to the laity, whose knowledge of them was to be tested in confession.[13]

Robert Grosseteste's highly influential decrees for Lincoln (?1239) codified this syllabus, while his own pastoral writings, particularly the valuably schematic *Templum Dei*, addressed the needs of priest and people alike in

---

[10] e.g the apparent reference to a Tree of Vices at C.VIII.70, and to a Wheel of Virtues at C.XV.160-62; see R. E. Kaske, ' "Ex vi transicionis" and its passage in *Piers Plowman*', *JEGP*, 62 (1963): 32–60, pp. 55–57; E. Salter, '*Piers Plowman* and the Visual Arts', in D. Pearsall and N. Zeeman (eds.), *English and International: Studies in the Literature, Art and Patronage of Medieval England* (Cambridge, 1988), pp. 256–66, p. 262.

[11] At some point before the sixteenth-century, a *Pater Noster* window was erected in Malvern Priory and could perhaps have been known by Langland. A. F.Johnston and M. Rogerson (eds.), *Records of Early English Drama: York* (Manchester, 1979), ii.646–7 (Latin) and 864 (translation); Johnston, 'The Plays of the Religious Guilds of York: The Creed Play and the Pater Noster Play', *Speculum*, 50 (1975): 55–90, prints the same texts with discussion. On Beverley, see A. F. Leach, 'Some English Plays and Players, 1200–1548', in *An English Miscellany presented to F.J. Furnival* (Oxford, 1901), pp. 220–1. On the plays and related art, see M. D. Anderson, *Drama and Imagery in English Medieval Churches* (Cambridge, 1963), pp. 60–71, who notes (p. 64) Thomas Habington's sixteenth-century reference to the now destroyed *Pater Noster* window in Malvern Priory. It is unclear whether this window would have been present in Langland's lifetime.

[12] The most recent account is J. Goering, *William de Montibus (c.1140–1213): The Schools and the Literature of the Pastoral Care*, Pontifical Institute of Mediæval Studies, Studies and Texts, 108 (1992).

[13] M. Gibbs and J. Lang, *Bishops and Reform, 1215–1272, with Special Reference to the Lateran Council of 1215* (Oxford, 1934); C. R. Cheney, *English Synodalia of the Thirteenth Century* (Oxford, 1941, reprinted with a new introduction 1968); Cheney, 'The Earliest English Diocesan Statutes', *English Historical Review*, 75 (1960): 1–29; Cheney, 'Some Aspects of Ecclesiastical Legislation in England in the Thirteenth Century', in *Medieval Texts and Studies* (Oxford, 1973), pp. 185–202; R. M. Haines, 'Education in English Ecclesiastical Legislation of the Later Middle Ages', in G. J. Cuming and D. Baker (eds.), *Councils and Assemblies* Studies in Church History, 7 (Cambridge, 1971), pp. 161–75. The legislation is available in F. M. Powicke and C. R. Cheney (eds.), *Councils and Synods, II (1205–1313)* (Oxford, 1964), hereafter *CandS*. For Langton's syllabus, see *CandS*, p. 31. On the influence of the legislation, see Kemmler, *Exempla*, pp. 28–59; Shaw, 'Influence'; Gillespie, 'Design and Function' and 'Vernacular Books'.

developing the interactive relationship between the septenaries.[14] Walter de Cantilupe's ambitious legislation for Worcester (1240), which still had canonical force when Langland was moving about the diocese, reflect this new catechetical impulse which was finally given Provincial force by the synthetic decrees of Archbishop Pecham in 1281.[15]

The centrality of the *Pater Noster* in the catechetic framework is obvious. As an evangelically sanctioned prayer, proceeding from the mouth of God, it had unchallenged authority. The *Glossa Ordinaria* cites Augustine's comment that if we pray properly it is not possible to say more than is contained in the prayer.[16] Innocent III, in a formulation soon to become formulaic, emphasises that it excells in the authority of its teaching, the brevity of its words, the sufficiency of its petitions and the fecundity of its mysteries.[17] Hugh of St Cher claims that it excells in dignity, because it proceeds from God himself; in brevity, so that it can be more easily remembered, more frequently repeated and so that none can excuse themselves from ignorance of it; and in fecundity, because it contains all

---

[14] *CandS*, pp. 268-9; on their influence, see Cheney, *Synodalia*, pp. 124-41; the instruction to examine the laity on confession is amusingly illustrated by the lyric *How the Ploughman Learned His Paternoster* (*IMEV* 3182), printed in C. and K. Sisam (eds.), *The Oxford Book of Medieval English Verse* (Oxford, 1970), pp. 514-21. J. Goering and F.A.C. Mantello (eds.), *Robert Grosseteste: Templum Dei*, Toronto Medieval Latin Texts (Toronto, 1984), esp. the table of septenaries on p. 38. A similar table is used later by Simon Hinton, see A. Dondaine, 'La Somme de Simon de Hinton', *Recherches de Théologie Ancienne et Médiévale*, 9 (1937): 5-27, 205-18, p. 11. Similar schematic tables are used to order the information the priest should elicit and impart in a fourteenth-century confession manual in Cambridge, University Library MS Gg. 4. 32, fols. 25ʳ-47ʳ, perhaps alluding to the *Templum Dei*.

[15] Cantilupe's statutes show the probable influence of Lincoln in their catechetic provisions (*CandS*, p. 304), including the prescription of knowledge of *Quicunque vult* (though there is no specific mention of the *Pater Noster*). The influence of these decrees on several other sets of diocesan legislation is discussed by Cheney, *Synodalia*, pp. 96-109, though *CandS*, p. 266 recants and inverts the earlier claim that Worcester influenced Lincoln; R. M. Haines, *The Administration of the Diocese of Worcester in the First Half of the Fourteenth Century* (London, 1965), p. 45. Pecham's decrees are printed in *CandS*, pp. 892-918; the famous *De informatione simplicium sacerdotum*, better known by its opening words *Ignorancia sacerdotum* (pp. 900-5), spells out the catechetic syllabus in detail but is largely summarising the work of earlier legislators. The relative paucity of catechetical prescriptions in the legislation of the fourteenth century suggests that earlier legislation was still significant. The most significant exception is the catechetic instructions issued in Latin and the vernacular by Archbishop Thoresby for the northern province (1357), closely modelled on Pecham's canons for the southern province, and later expanded to include a commentary on the *Pater Noster*; see Gillespie, 'Design and Function', pp. 43-6; A. Hudson, 'A New Look at the Lay Folk' Catechism', *Viator*, 16 (1985): 243-48 and 'The Lay Folks' Catechism: A Postscript', *Viator*, 19 (1988): 308-9; R. N. Swanson, 'The Origins of *The Lay Folks' Catechism*', *Medium Ævum*, 60 (1991): 92-97. Perhaps significantly, Thoresby had been translated from Worcester in 1353.

[16] *Biblia Sacra cum Glossa Ordinaria* (Antwerp, 1617), v.128: 'Si recte et congruenter oramus nihil aliud dicere possumus quam quod in ista oratione dominica positum est', glossing Matthew 6.

[17] *Incipits* 8386; *De Sacro Altaris Mysterio Libri Sex*, 5, caps xvi-xxviii (*PL* 217. 897-906, 897). Cf. the similar account of the prayer in the hugely popular thirteenth-century *Speculum Ecclesie* of Edmund of Abingdon (*Incipits* 6441/8177), which was widely circulated throughout the period in Latin, Anglo-Norman and Middle English versions. For the Latin text, see *Edmund of Abingdon: Speculum Religiosorum and Speculum Ecclesie*, Auctores Britannici Medii Aevi, 3 (London, 1973), pp. 73-81. For two Middle English versions from later fourteenth-century manuscripts, see C. Horstman, *Yorkshire Writers: Richard Rolle of Hampole and His Followers* (London, 1895), i.219-61.

things that need to be asked for.[18] According to Richard Wetheringsett's thirteenth-century English pastoral manual *Qui bene praesunt*, which may have been known to Langland, the excellent sufficiency of the *Pater Noster* arises because it contains everything necessary for life.[19]

Such views are widely repeated and refracted in English manuscripts and texts. A fourteenth-century *Tabula de Utilitate Oracionis Dominice* argues that the prayer also has 'sentencia longa . . . ut maijoris devocio habeatur', is 'facilis dicenda' to encourage frequent repetition and is 'subtilia intelligenda' so that we will more diligently apply ourselves to understand it.[20] As the Wycliffite exposition puts it 'in so schort a preier is conteyned so myche witt, þat no tunge of man can telle it al here on erþe'.[21] These pithy formulations achieved widespread penetration into the vernacular didactic and homiletic literature of fourteenth-century England, and apparently into the devotional lives of its people. Alexander Stavensby's thirteenth-century Statutes for Coventry and Lichfield prescribed that every layman and woman should recite seven *Pater Nosters*, seven *Ave Marias* and two Creeds every day. Illiterate religious were allowed to substitute *Pater Nosters* for the Office psalms. Rolle uses it paraliturgically in his *Meditations on the Passion*. Hilton recommends it in his advice to women religious in *The Scale of Perfection*.[22] Moreover it featured in the early stages of literacy training, and *The Book of Vices and Virtues* exploits this pedagogic tradition in suggesting that childlike humility, not masterful knowledge, is necessary to gain access to the proper *clergie* of the prayer:

> Whan men setteþ first a child to lerne lettrure, men techeþ hym his pater
> noster. Who so wole lerne þis clergie, hym behoveþ become meke and

---

[18] *Domini Hugonis Cardinalis, Postilla*, v, (Paris, 1545), fol. 21 rb, glossing Matthew 6. J. B. Allen, 'Langland's Reading and Writing: *Detractor* and the Pardon Passus', *Speculum*, 59 (1984): 342–62, suggests the influence of Hugh's Psalter commentary on Langland, and Hugh's exegetical works are aslo deployed by B. H. Smith, *Traditional Imagery of Charity in Piers Plowman*, Studies in English Literature, 21 (The Hague, 1966). I have found Hugh's commentary on Matthew to be usefully comparable to *Piers Plowman*, without wishing to suggest direct influence, especially as the commentary tradition on *fiat voluntas tua* contains many commonplaces. Bonaventure has a similar formulation: 'Oratio haec privilegiata est in tribus: in dignitate, quia a Christo composita; in brevitate, ut citius sciatur, melius retineatur et frequentius dicatur; in fecunditate, quia omnes petitiones continet et utriusque vitae necessaria complectitur', *Expositio Orationis Dominicae*, in *S. Bonaventurae Opera Omnia*, 7 (Quarracchi, 1895), pp. 652–5, p. 652 (*Incipits* 8927).

[19] *Incipits* 4583; Oxford, New College MS 94, fol. 33ᵛ. The work survives in at least 56 copies, attesting to its widespread popularity. For Langland's possible knowledge of this work, see S. Wenzel, 'Medieval Sermons' in J. A. Alford (ed.), *A Companion to Piers Plowman* (Berkeley, 1988), pp. 155–72, p. 161.

[20] *Incipits* 8834; London, British Library MS Additonal 15237, fol. 79ʳ.

[21] Oxford, Bodleian Library, MS Bodley 938, fol. 25ʳ; for a printed text of this largely orthodox commentary, see T. Arnold (ed.), *Select English Works of John Wyclif*, 3 (Oxford, 1871), pp. 98–110. See the similar comments in W. N. Francis (ed.), *The Book of Vices and Virtues*, EETS, OS 217 (London, 1942), p. 97; W. O. Ross (ed.), *Middle English Sermons*, EETS, OS 209 (London, 1940 for 1938), pp. 9–12, p.10; *Pore Caitif* (Jolliffe F.8), as in Oxford, Bodleian Library, MS Bodley 3, fol. 79ʳ.

[22] For Stavensby (Coventry I, 1224x1237), see *CandS*, p. 213. Stavensby was one of a number of English bishops who composed short manuals on the deadly sins and confession to be circulated with their decrees. S. J. Ogilvie-Thomson (ed.), *Richard Rolle: Prose and Verse*, EETS, OS 293 (Oxford, 1988), pp. 64–83. J. P. H. Clark and R. Dorward (eds., trans.), *Walter Hilton: The Scale of Perfection*, The Classics of Western Spirituality (New York, 1991), 1.27, pp. 98–9.

umble as a child, for to suche scolers techeþ oure goode maister Ihesu Crist þis clergie, þat is þe faireste and þe profitableste þat is, who-so wel vnder-stondeþ it and holt it.[23]

The prayer's role in the spiritual leechcraft of the increasingly forensic pastoral care of the thirteenth- and fourteenth-centuries is explicit in Innocent III's medical analogy: Man is the patient; God is the doctor; the Deadly Sins are the ailments; the petitions of the *Pater Noster* are the complaints and groans of the patient; the gifts of the Spirit are the antidotes; the virtues are the signs of a return to health; and the Beatitudes are the resultant joyful celebrations. Spiritual health is the governing metaphor for the diagnostic charts and septenaries that linked together the *Pater Noster* and other catechetic categories. Indeed Grosseteste says of his own table in the *Templum Dei* 'in hoc tabula est tota cura officii pastoralis'.[24] It is within the matrix of such pastoral interactions and catechetic schema that Langland's exploration, understanding and affirmation of the power of the *Pater Noster* can best be grounded.

II

The *Pater Noster* was no simple talisman or magic charm for Langland. The enthusiasm displayed for the prayer by Will does not go unchallenged by other figures in the poem. His A text eulogy of the prayer's potency is, perhaps significantly, reassigned in the C text to Rechelessnesse. In the B text, Will's advocacy of patient poverty, simple faith and reliance on the *Pater Noster* is immediately questioned by Scripture:

> Thanne Scripture scorned me and a skile tolde,
> And lakked me in Latyn and light by me sette,
> And seide, *'Multi multa sciunt et seipsos nesciunt'*.   (B.XI.1–3)

This application to Will of a commonplace which might be thought to support the very 'anti-intellectual' point he was making highlights Langland's unease with glib formulations and over-schematic resolutions. For Will at this point in his

---

[23] Francis, p. 97; the same phrase is found in the *Pore Caitif* commentary (MS Bodley 3, fol.79ʳ). On the *Pater Noster* in primers and elementary schooling, see N. Orme, *English Schools in the Middle Ages* (London, 1973), pp. 62–63. The penetration of the catechetic syllabus into schools is illustrated by Bishop Grandisson of Exeter's decree of 1357 forbidding pupils to advance to higher studies until they have mastered the Lord's Prayer, *Ave Maria*, Creeds, Matins and Hours of the Virgin; see C. Brown, 'Chaucer's "Litel Clergeon" ', *Modern Philology*, 3 (1906): 467–91, p. 485. Primer texts often precede simple catechetic and pastoral manuals: see, for example, *The Winchester Anthology: A Facsimile of British Library Additional Manuscript 60577*, intro. by E. Wilson (Cambridge, 1981), items 180–203, including (item 196) a Middle English version of the *Speculum Ecclesie* commentary on the *Pater Noster*; G. A. Plimpton, *The Education of Chaucer* (London, 1935), plates IX.1–IX.15; Manchester, John Rylands Library MS English 85, fol.2ʳ, described by G. A. Lester, *The Index of Middle English Prose: Handlist II: Rylands and Chetham's Libraries* (Cambridge, 1985), p.15.
[24] *PL* 217.899. Goering and Mantello, p. 38; Grosseteste's table uses the headings Infirmitas, Planctus, Preparacio, Medicina, Sanitas and Gaudium to organise his septenaries.

and the poem's development, to attempt to retreat behind a facade of 'povere commune laborers' is naive and unduly utopian. Scripture is forcing him to realise that his own situation is more complicated than that of the 'lewed juttes', a realisation that provokes a response that itself displays the limitations of Will's understanding and his self-control:

> Tho wepte I for wo and wrathe of hir speche.   (B.XI.4)

Indeed Will's advocacy of the *Pater Noster* is somewhat vitiated by his own anger, which strikes at the heart of the meekness and patience invoked by the prayer, 'for þe holygost seiþ þat in to yuel willid soule schal no wisdom entre'.[25] As with so many other aspects of the poem, Will's journey from an abstract and idealistic advocacy of the merits of the *Pater Noster* to a *kynde knowynge* of its efficacy will be painful and troubled, and will address and redress intimate details of Will's own psychological makeup.

Similarly, in the C text autobiographical passage, Will's certainty of his own rectitude:

> Forthy rebuke me ryhte nauhte, Resoun, y ȝow praye,
> For in my conscience y knowe what Crist wolde y wrouhte,
>   (C.V.83–84)

is brusquely questioned by Conscience's challenge to what looks like an irregular way of life, and his assertion that the theory and the reality do not in any case marry up:

> Quod Conscience, 'By Crist, y can nat se this lyeth;
> Ac it semeth no sad parfitnesse in citees to begge,
> But he be obediencer to prior or to mynistre'.   (C.V.89–91)

Will's romantic self-projection is once again open to scrutiny and assessment.[26] Like Haukyn in the B text, Will has effectively been accused of being:

> Yhabited as an heremyte, an ordre by hymselve –
> Religion saunz rule and resonable obedience.   (B.XIII.284–85)

But, in a striking paradox, the solution offered by Patience for Haukyn's failings and misdemeanours is that same clause of the *Pater Noster* cited by Will as a defence of his own way of life:

> *Fiat voluntas dei* – þat fynt us alle thynges.

Fiat voluntas tua, the *viaticum* offered by the pilgrim Patience to Haukyn at the beginning of his own pilgrimage of faith, offers a *vitaille* of surpassing power and resourcefulness in resolving Haukyn's (and Will's) problems with the

---

[25] *Pore Caitif*, MS Bodley 3, fol.79ʳ.

[26] K. Kerby-Fulton, ' "Who Has Written this Book?": Visionary Autobiography in Langland's C Text', in M. Glasscoe (ed.), *The Medieval Mystical Tradition in England*, V (Cambridge, 1992), pp. 101–16, offers a persuasive reading of this passage as fulfilling the criteria of a process of spritual *probatio*, strengthening the sense one has of Will trying on different spirtual *personae* and striking different spirtual attitudes. The passage is clearly linked to the justification of 'God's minstrels' in C.IX, discussed below.

world. But what pertinence does this clause of the *Pater Noster* have to their predicament, and why is it entrusted to Patience?[27]

The whole of Will's encounter with Patience and their meeting with Haukyn (B.XIII–XIV) explores the practical contemporary application of the pastoral teachings of the Gospels, especially those of St Matthew and St Luke.[28] Matthew chapter 6, for example, contains the injunction to lay up treasure in heaven; the verse 'where thy treasure is there is thy heart also', already quoted from Haukyn's speech of self-condemnation; and, in particular, the teaching of the *Pater Noster* to the Apostles. These resonances are essential to our understanding of the scene when Patience offers Haukyn *fiat voluntas tua* as food for the spiritual journey.

The opening of B.XIII marks Will's meeting with Patience who arrives at Conscience's court seeking sustenance. Will, the 'heremite unholy of werkes' (B.Pr.3) who is described as wandering 'in manere of a mendynaunt' (B.XIII.3), is seated at a side table with Patience, who is strikingly similar in dress, manner and appearance:

> Ac Pacience in the paleis stood in pilgrymes clothes,
> And preyde mete *par charite* for a povere heremyte.   (29–30)

Will and Patience are treated alike in this episode, probably because they are dressed in a similar way and possibly because the validation of Will's mode of life and poetic mission depends upon an imaginative identification with Patience, whose shadow he becomes for the episode with Haukyn. Their appearance makes them comparable to the apostles and disciples as sent out by Christ on their pastoral mission to the world:

> And he said to them: Take nothing for your journey; neither staff, nor scrip, nor bread, nor money; neither have two coats.   (Luke 9.3)[29]

St Matthew echoes the terms of the injunction:

[27] My approach to this episode – in particular my use of commentaries on *fiat voluntas tua* – somewhat parallels an earlier paper by L. K. Stock, 'Will, Actyf, Pacience and *Liberum Arbitrium*: Two Recurring Quotations in Langland's Revision of *Piers Plowman* C Text, Passus V, XV, XVI', *Texas Studies in Literature and Language*, 30 (1985): 461–77, which was unknown to me when this paper was delivered. Other important recent discussions of this theme in the meeting between Patience and Haukyn, which also summarise and refer to earlier scholarship, include: A. C. Spearing, 'The Development of a Theme in *Piers Plowman*', *RES*, n.s., 11 (1960): 24–53; J. A. Alford, 'Haukyn's Coat: Some Observations on *Piers Plowman* B.XIV. 22–7', *Medium Ævum*, 43 (1974): 133–8; J. Mann, 'Eating and Drinking in *Piers Plowman*', *Essays and Studies*, n.s., 32 (1979): 26–43; A. V. C. Schmidt, 'Langland's Structural Imagery', *Essays in Criticism*, 30 (1980): 311–25; M. Godden, 'Plowmen and Hermits in Langland's *Piers Plowman*', *Review of English Studies*, n.s., 35 (1984): 129–63; M. Godden, *The Making of Piers Plowman* (London, 1990), pp. 101–16, 194–200; J. Simpson, *Piers Plowman: An Introduction to the B-Text* (London, 1990), pp. 133, 140–66, 229.
[28] H. Barr, 'The Use of Latin Quotations in *Piers Plowman* with special reference to Passus XVIII of the "B" Text', *Notes and Queries*, n.s., 33 (1986): 440–48, observes that in Passus XIII 'More quotations are worked into the line because of a change in the role of the quotations themselves. At points in this part of the poem, the quotations become allegorical food. They are physically consumed rather than expounded' (p.444).
[29] W. Scase, *'Piers Plowman' and the New Anti-Clericalism*, Cambridge Studies in Medieval Literature, 4 (Cambridge, 1989), p. 20, points out the importance of this text for the friars' defences of mendicant poverty.

> Do not possess gold nor silver, nor money in your purses: Nor scrip for your journey, nor two coats, nor shoes, nor a staff; for the workman is worthy of his meat.　(Matthew 10.9–10)

The apostles are commissioned to continue the mission of John the Baptist. His cry 'Do penance for the kingdom of heaven is at hand' (Matthew 3.2) is echoed in the injunction to the apostles 'Preach, saying 'the kingdom of heaven is at hand' (Matthew 10.10), or as St Mark records it 'And going forth they preached that men should do Penance' (6.12).

Agite penitenciam, the cry of John the Baptist, is that very same 'soor loof' placed before Patience and Will at the beginning of the banquet. Its teaching is both directly addressed to them – particularly to Will – and, in a typically Langlandian finessing of a difficult problem, represents Patience (whose enthusiasm for it is marked and in contrast to Will's mourning) being given the phrase by Scripture (who serves the meal), as a reward for his labours (the labourer is worthy of his meat/hire). But most significantly this bread of penance is also a message being committed to Patience for him to pass on to others.

This scene at the court of Conscience is a foreshadowing of a discussion unique to the C text, where the the prophetic force and apostolic mission of wandering hermits are explored more explicitly.[30] While rejecting false beggars and confidence tricksters, Langland carefully delineates another liminal group:

> The whiche aren lunatyk lollares and lepares aboute,
> And madden as þe mone sit, more other lasse.
> Careth they for no colde ne counteth of non hete
> And aren meuynge aftur þe mone; moneyles þey walke,
> With a good will, witteles, mony wyde contreyes,
> Riht as Peter dede and Poul, saue þat þey preche nat
> Ne none muracles maken – ac many tymes hem happeth
> To profecye of þe peple, pleyinge, as hit were . . .
> Hit aren as his postles, suche peple, or as his priue disciples.
> For a sent hem forth seluerles in a somur garnement
> Withoute bagge and bred, as þe book telleth:
> > *Quando misi vos sine pane et pera.*
> Barfoot and bredles, beggeth they of no man . . .
> Suche manere men, Matheu vs techeth,
> We sholde haue hem to house and helpe hem when they come.
> > *Et egenos vagosque induc in domum tuam*
> For hit aren merye-mouthed men, munstrals of heuene,
> And godes boys, bourdyors, as the book telleth . . .
> Ryht so, ȝe ryche, ȝut rather ȝe sholde
> Welcomen and worschipen and with ȝoure goed helpen

---

[30] Recent studies of this crucial episode are D. Pearsall, ' "Lunatyk Lollares" in *Piers Plowman*', in P. Boitani and A. Torti (eds.), *Religion in the Poetry and Drama of the Late Middle Ages in England* (Cambridge, 1990), pp. 163–78; K. Kerby-Fulton, *Reformist Apocalypticism and 'Piers Plowman'*, Cambridge Studies in Medieval Literature, 7 (Cambridge, 1990), pp. 126–32, who links it with the autobiographical episode in C.V, as does Scase, pp. 125–60. Still important is the seminal study by E. T. Donaldson, *Piers Plowman: The C-Text and its Poet* (New Haven, 1949), pp. 140–55.

Godes munstrals and his mesagers and his mery bordiours,
The whiche arn lunatyk loreles and lepares aboute,
For vnder godes secret seal here synnes ben keuered.
For they bereth none bagges ne boteles vnder clokes
The whiche is lollarne lyf and lewede ermytes.

(C.IX.107–21;124–27;134–40)

What is striking about this passage is the way that Langland assimilates 'God's minstrels' to an apostolic role model. Like Will in C.V, they mimic the apostles and disciples in their dress. They do not usurp the canonical authority of priests in presuming to preach (112–4), but they acquire a prophetic status, becoming the mouthpieces – 'pleyinge, as hit were' – for God's message to reach mankind. Such figures, he argues, are more suitable for the support of rich men than secular minstrels.

Seen in the perspective of this C-text discussion, Patience's treatment at the house of Conscience in the B-text thus depends for its full effect on a recognition of the gospel echoes it invokes. The serving of the Evangelists, St Augustine and St Ambrose to the guests at the feast is supported by a quote from the same verse (10.7) of St Luke's gospel describing the commissioning of the apostles and later used by Langland in his discussion in C.IX:

Edentes et bibentes que apud eos sunt

Like God's minstrels, Patience does not preach or work miracles. But the message of his bread has a prophetic resonance throughout the rest of this episode. Just as the apostles were commissioned to preach penance and the coming of the kingdom, Patience's sour loaf fuels his pilgrimage and mission to the world as a minstrel of God.[31]

When, with the wanderlust characteristic of his functions in Langland's poem, Conscience decides to accompany Patience and Will, he assimilates himself to their eremitical (and apostolic) appearance:

Conscience tho with Pacience passed, pilgrymes as it were.

(B.XIII.215)

Conscience's departure involves him in a gentle brush with Clergye that reminds us of the apparent anti-intellectualism of the end of the A text, and certainly recalls Will's spiritual idealism about the poor at the end of B.X:

'Me were levere, by Oure Lord, and I lyve sholde,
Have pacience parfitliche than half thi pak of bokes!'

(B.XIII.200–1)

But whereas Will's idealism is clearly too neat to be satisfactory to Langland, here Conscience's recognition that the combination of Patience and Clergye would indeed be spiritually formidable suggests that a more sophisticated model of spiritual development is in the process of construction. Clergye will, we are told await Conscience 'Til Pacience have preved thee and parfit thee maked' (214). Learning is deferred rather than despised, and the rest of this episode

---

[31] Cf. Simpson, *Introduction*, pp. 152–6.

explores the social, spiritual and personal implications of Patience's apostolic modes of proving and perfecting.[32]

In keeping with their obedience to the evangelical commands, Conscience and Patience carry only metaphorical bread with them on their journey:

> Thanne hadde Pacience, as pilgrymes han, in his poke vitailles:
> Sobretee and symple speche and soothfast bileve,
> To conforte hym and Conscience if thei come in place
> There unkyndenesse and coveitise is, hungry contrees bothe.
>
> (B.XIII.216-9)

They act as messengers for the *vox clamantis*. The *vitailles* in their pouch embody the instructions that Christ gave to the apostles as he launched them on their public ministry:

> Behold I send you as sheep in the midst of wolves. Be ye therefore wise as serpents and simple as doves . . . But when they shall deliver you up take no thought how or what to speak for it shall be given you in that hour what to speak. For it is not you that speak but the Spirit of your Father that speaketh in you.   (Matthew 10.16,19)

Christ's mission to the apostles is that they become bearers of the word, God's minstrels, messengers on his behalf. The *vitailles* carried by Patience and Conscience represent the sustaining effects of the message which the Father will speak through them and make manifest in them. The pilgrim-hermit figure, represented in this episode in different degrees of development and perfection by Patience, Conscience and Will, is thus both a signifier of the truth and a seeker for that same truth ('With Pacience wol y passe, parfitnesse to fynde', C.XV.185).

In tentatively blending the roles of apostolic teacher and pilgrim for truth in B. XIII and XIV, Langland explores how ordinary men of good will can become vehicles for the word and work of God. *Fiat voluntas tua*, and the matrix of moral and catechetic teachings traditionally associated with it, have a decisive role to play in this process. They provide a familiar mnemonic framework for Langland's cautious and painful construction of a psychological model of willed selflessness. This model becomes a paradigm for the kenotic openness which both liberates the individual from worldly self-concern and becomes a vehicle for this grace to pass into the wider community. As such it lies close to the poem's fundamental concern with individual salvation and the perfection of the social order. *Fiat voluntas tua*, the prayer of selfless charity, thus becomes a bridge between the ideal obedience of the apostles in relinquishing worldy security to follow Christ and the more difficult mediation of Christ's injunction *Ne soliciti sitis* in the social condition's of Langland's own time.[33] *Fiat voluntas tua* comes to represent both the message to be transmitted and the effects of that message on bearer and recipient alike. The immediate recipient of the message

---

[32] Cf. J. Simpson, 'The Role of *Scientia* in *Piers Plowman*', in G. Kratzmann and J. Simpson (eds.), *Medieval English Religious and Ethical Literature* (Cambridge, 1986), pp. 49–65; Simpson, *Introduction*, pp. 142–52.

[33] Scase, pp. 54–83; Pearsall, 'Lunatyk Lollares'.

is, of course, Haukyn whose transition from errant sinner in the B text to the misguided but well-meaning apprentice of Piers in C owes much to the process explored in this meeting with Patience.

Haukyn, as has often been pointed out, is one of those secular minstrels that secular lords are wont to support.[34] If Patience is partly a prototype of the 'God's minstrel' figure who will emerge fully in the C text, he is, therefore, implicitly to be contrasted with Haukyn. Indeed there are striking ways in which they are mirror images of each other. Christ commanded the apostles to take only one coat: Haukyn complains that he has only one coat and finds the effort of keeping it clean overwhelming on top of his worldly responsibilities. Haukyn is a waferer whose goods are greatly in demand. Patience also has a bag full of *vitailles* that he makes available to people that he meets. They stand at opposing poles of the social and spiritual world yet they have much in common with each other and with Will, who shares many characteristics of both of them. Dressed like Patience, his basic attitudes and behaviour are echoed in Haukyn's solicitous worldliness: Will has the habit of one and the *habitus* of the other. He shares Haukyn's eagerness for spiritual advancement and enlightenment along with his easily disheartened and readily distracted motivation.

Haukyn is an embodiment of another gospel type: the seed that falls among the thorns:

> And he that received the seed among thorns is he that heareth the word;
> and the care of this world and the deceitfulness of riches choketh up the
> word and he becometh fruitless.   (Matthew 13.22)

Haukyn is Active – indeed he is almost hyper-active. He is the poem's archetype of over-solicitousness about the things of the world, and his mind is seldom on the things of the spirit:

> Ne nevere penaunce parfournede ne Paternoster seide
> That my mynde ne was moore on my good in a doute
> Than in the grace of God and his grete helpes.
> *Ubi thesaurus tuus, ibi et cor tuum*   (B.XIII.396–8a)

Patience's remedy for Haukyn's deficiencies is to promise him flour and dough from which Haukyn can make food *for himself* if he is rightly disposed. Recalling Will's recurrent concern about *lyflode*, Patience firmly and unequivocally returns to one of the poem's main themes:

> We sholde noght be to bisy abouten oure liflode,

supporting it with further quotations from Matthew and elsewhere:

> *Ne soliciti sitis &c; Volucres celi Deus pascit &c;*
> *Pacientes vincunt &c.*   (B.XIV.34–34a)

Haukyn, with world-weary incredulity, laughs at Patience's naivety, at which Patience, in an action which embodies and enacts the virtue of the gift he is about to make, *paciently* pulls out of his poke:

---

[34] See most recently Godden, *Making*, pp. 109–15; Simpson, *Introduction*, pp. 157–9.

> Vitailles of grete vertues for alle manere beestes,
> And seide, 'Lo! here liflode ynogh, if oure bileve be trewe.
> (B.XIV.38–9)

These *vitailles of gret vertues* must be the same ones given to him by Scripture at Conscience's court: 'sobretee and symple speche and soothfast bileve.' Patience buttresses them with further quotations from the gospels of John ('Whatever you ask in my name shall be given to you'.) and Matthew again ('Man shall not live by bread alone but by every word that proceeds from the mouth of God'.). On closer inspection Will sees that the food is not real bread. The metaphorical *vitailles* in Patience's sack have coalesced into 'a pece of the Paternoster – *Fiat voluntas tua*' (49). The raw materials of the bread of life are revealed as being words which do indeed proceed from the mouth of God.

The *Pater Noster* had such authority precisely because it had come *ex ore dei*, as the context in Matthew's gospel makes clear. The prayer could be said to be asking specifically 'in God's name' because Christ put the words of the prayer into the mouths of his disciples. Such a potent prayer could easily deliver the spiritual results promised by Patience. But why does Patience particularly offer the third petition *fiat voluntas tua*? Commentaries on the *Pater Noster* generally see this clause as recommending that sinful men should cooperate in allowing God's will to be done on earth 'þoruz amending of her lif'.[35] The 'soor loof' *Agite penitenciam* given by Scripture to Patience has been passed on to Haukyn as the raw material for his own penitential reformation in preparation for the kingdom of heaven. Hence Conscience is fulfilling the apostolic imperative of the gospels in his subsequent exposition of the meaning of contrition, confession and satisfaction (B.XIV.16–35). But such a generalised movement to sorrow and repentance is hardly a satisfactory explanation for so precise a citation, even if it grounds the passage firmly in the penitential eremiticism of the apostolic mission of God's minstrels. It is necessary to explore the catechetical hinterland of *fiat voluntas tua* to get a sharper sense of the local force of its invocation.

III

The bulk of the commentary and pastoral tradition, including the *Glossa Ordinaria*, links *fiat voluntas tua* with the sin of Wrath, because it 'lettiþ a man knowe goddus wil'.[36] Both Hugh of St Victor's influential commentaries on the *Pater Noster* set *fiat voluntas tua* against the sin of wrath.[37] The standard view of

---

[35] MS Bodley 938, fol. 30ʳ; Arnold, *Wyclif*, iii.104. *Þe Pater Noster of Richard Ermyte*, ed. Aarts, pp. 35–40, esp. pp. 37–8, places significant emphasis on *Ne soliciti sitis* and the theme of food in its exposition of *fiat voluntas tua*.

[36] J.H.L. Kengen (ed.), *Memoriale Credencium* (Nijmegen, 1979), p. 198, apparently following Thomas of Chobham's thirteenth-century *Summa Confessorum*, ed. F. M. Broomfield, Analecta Medievalia Namurcensia, 25 (Louvain/Paris, 1968), p. 38: 'Et sic excluditur ira que impedit cognoscere que sit voluntas dei'.

[37] *Expositio in Abdiam*, PL 175.400–1; *De Quinque Septenis seu Septenariis*, PL 175.405–14. The pseudonomous *Speculum Ecclesie* (*Incipits* 9103), PL 177.371–73 makes the same association, as do, e.g., Hugh of Strasbourg's *Compendium Theologicae Veritatis* (*Incipits* 6399); the *Summa Virtutum de Remediis Anime (Postquam)* (*Incipits* 3988); Wyclif's main Latin commentary (*Incipits*

the petition was that it did not call for God to do as he wished, but rather for it to be possible for us to do as God wishes. As Hugh of St Cher puts it, just as man cannot do good unless he has the help of God, so likewise good cannot be done in man unless man wills it. Recalling the parable of the sower (and, incidentally paralleling our sense of Haukyn as a seed in stony ground), Hugh emphasises the reciprocity of the relationship between the wills: just as a seed cannot flourish without soil, so soil will not bear fruit without a seed.[38]

A subsidiary view was that *fiat voluntas tua* related to the sin of Envy. Robert Grosseteste's popular *Templum Dei* links it with *odium* or ill-will, a subsection of Envy that clearly indicates the common ground existing between the sins. Richard Wetheringsett's *Qui bene praesunt* similarly claims that the petition removes all species of envy, as do the schematic tables of the *Speculum Theologie*. Furthermore *odium* in Chobham's *Summa* (a copy of which was in Great Malvern Priory and might, on one biographical model, have been available to Langland[39]) is seen as a branch of Wrath and is prohibited by St Matthew's report of Christ's words:

> If therefore thou offer thy gift at the altar and there thou remember that thy brother hath anything against thee; leave there thy offering and go first to be reconciled to the brother; and then coming thou shalt offer thy gift. (V.23–24)

Odium, nestling in the shadow of envy and wrath, cuts a man off from the sacramental grace of the eucharistic meal. Archbishop Pecham's famous and influential 1281 canon *De informacione simplicium sacerdotum* sees *odium* as the outstanding common factor between the two sins.[40]

But why should these two sins be any more applicable to Haukyn than the other deadly sins with which he is shown to be afflicted and against which he is later given explicit instruction? The B text gives us a clear picture of Haukyn's ill will and tendency to wrath in his long initial portrayal and in the discussion of the branches of that prime spiritual sin Sloth. It has often been pointed out that

---

8137) and the vernacular commentaries; Simon of Hinton (*Incipits* 8136); the Middle English sermons printed by Ross; the *Pore Caitif*; the Vernon table.

[38] *Postilla*, v, fol. 22rb. Some commentators (e.g. Innocent III, Bonaventure and the commentator in London, British Library, MS Additional 15237) relate the petition to the sin of avarice, but see it as a function of a desire to possess and control.

[39] The manuscript is now Oxford, Queen's College MS 326. On Langland's probable connection with Great Malvern, see most recently M. L. Samuels, 'Langland's Dialect', *Medium Ævum*, 54 (1985): 232–47; Samuels, 'Dialect and Grammar' in Alford (ed.), *Companion*, pp. 201–21. On whether Langland's education extended beyond the cathedral or monastic school level, see N. Orme, 'Langland and Education', *History of Education*, 11 (1982): 251–66; J. M. Bowers, *The Crisis of Will in Piers Plowman* (Washington, 1986), pp. 19–24. Langland uses several canon law maxims that occur in Chobham's *Summa* (among other sources), see N. Gray, 'Langland's Quotations from the Penitential Tradition', *Modern Philology*, 84 (1986): 53–60, to which should be added Chobham's use of *Redde quod debes* (Broomfield, p. 563). Gray notes (p. 59) that Chobham's version of the three elements of Penance is echoed by Conscience in B.XIV.17a–21a.

[40] *CandS*, p. 904: 'Invidia vero est odium felicitatis aliene; de qua oriuntur detractio, murmuratio, dissencio, perversa iudicia et similia. Ira est appetitus vindicte et nocumenti alieni que, cum perseverat in corde, fit odium, de qua oriuntur persecutiones verborum et factorum, plage, homicidia, et similia'.

Haukyn shares and displays many of the failings and weaknesses that afflict Will earlier in the poem. They are presented schematically in his coat of many metaphors:

> He hadde a cote of Cristendom as Holy Kirke bileveth;
> Ac it was moled in many places with manye sondry plottes –
> Of pride here a plot, and there a plot of unbuxom speche,
> Of scornyng and of scoffyng and of unskilful berynge.
>
> (B.XIII.273–6)

He deceives by appearance, he boasts and brags, he is disobedient, a detractor of learned and lewd alike, he is a 'liere in soule', a hypocrite who wishes people to think him intellectually and spiritually superior. Patience's offered *vitailles* of soberness, simple speech and steadfast belief are thus clearly applicable to the circumstances of his moral predicament.

In his unbuxom speech and lack of reasonable obedience, Haukyn's portrait refers back to the description of Wrath in the earlier confession of the Deadly Sins. Especially in the B text version, Wrath is concerned with the effects of wicked words in religious environments. Wrath's restlessness ('I Wrathe reste nevere') is comparable to Haukyn's hyperactive lifestyle, and both exclude the possibility of reflection and introspection. But with Langland's characteristic dislike for categoric distinction, it is not Wrath who is most like Haukyn, but Envy, whose ill will towards his fellow men causes his body 'to-bollen for wrathe, that he boot hise lippes' (B.V.83). Like Haukyn, Envy has a cloak ('clothed in a kaurymaury . . . In kirtel and courtepy' (B.V.78–79)), and his character expresses itself in an anger for revenge:

> And wryngynge he yede with the fust – to wreke hymself he
>   thoughte
> With werkes or with wordes whan he seyghe his tyme.
> Ech a word that he warp was of a neddres tonge;
> Of chidynge and of chalangynge was his chief liflode,
> With bakbitynge and bismere and berynge of fals witnesse.
>
> (B.V.84–8)

This is closely reflected in Haukyn's behaviour:

> Al that he wiste wikked by any wight, tellen it,
> And blame men bihynde hir bak and bidden hem meschaunce
>   . . .
> And made of frendes foes thorugh a fals tonge.
>
> (B.XIII.323–24,327)

Significantly, in the C text this passage is reappropriated to form part of the characterisation of Envy. Envy and Wrath are, indeed, blended together explicitly in Will's account of his closer examination of Haukyn's coat:

> It was fouler bi fele fold than it first semed.
> It was bidropped with wrathe and wikkede wille,
> With envye and yvel speche entisynge to fighte,
> Lying and lakkynge and leve tonge to chide.   (B.XIII.319–22)

Wrath and Envy, are in effect Haukyn's 'head sins' which govern and characterise his behaviour. They are linked by a common disorder of the will, and Langland, like other commentators, was sensitive to the fluidity of the boundaries separating them. In the A text version of the Deadly Sins passage Wrath does not appear, perhaps because many of his main attributes were initially subsumed under the presentation of Envy. But Wrath assumes increasing importance in B and C.[41] Although Envy is reduced in C, Wrath is further increased, partly by taking over some of the ill-will attributes of Envy's portrait. By C, Wrath and Envy follow directly after Pride in the sequence of the sins, just as they do in the descriptions of Haukyn's coat in B.[42] All three are linked together by Langland at the end of Piers' directions to the castle of Truth:

> Ac be war thanne of Wrathe, that wikked sherewe:
> He hath envye to hym that in thyn herte sitteth,
> And poketh forth pride to preise thiselven.   (B.V.609–11)

In the C text, this warning is immediately preceded by a citation of John 16.23: 'Whatever you ask in my name shall be given to you.' In the B text account of Haukyn, this same citation immediately precedes Patience's offer of *fiat voluntas tua*.

Wrath and Envy buttressed by Pride are said to attack man's earthly riches in the *Glossa Ordinaria* commentaries on the Sermon on the Mount, and this identification is repeated by Hugh of St Cher.[43] Patience's guarantee to Haukyn, derived from the Sermon on the Mount:

> Shal nevere myte bymolen it ne mothe after biten it,   (B.XIII.23)

emerges directly, then, from the confidence with which he is able to offer *fiat voluntas tua* as an antidote to this nexus of sins. Indeed in offering it, he is effectively offering himself. Commentaries on *fiat voluntas tua* consistently see Patience as the virtue which counteracts the wrathfulness addressed by the petition. Hugh of St Victor firmly teaches that one must not become angry against the Creator 'sed per omnia patientiam exhibere'.[44] Neighbouring Norman fonts in the Malvern Hills have figures of Patience beating Wrath and Mercy opposed to Envy. Grosseteste's *Templum Dei* says that wrath is counteracted by Patience and envy by Charity – an intriguing combination in the light of Langland's subsequent development of the Haukyn episode to include discussion of Charity.[45] Hugh of St Cher comes close to the teaching of *Piers Plowman* in his claim that patience is capable of transforming the stones of vituperation into the sweet bread of fulfilling food, a function

---

[41] On these revisions, see G. H. Russell, 'The Poet as Reviser: The Metamorphosis of the Confession of the Seven Deadly Sins in *Piers Plowman*', in M. J. Carruthers and E. D. Kirk (eds.), *Acts of Interpretation: The Text in its Context 700–1600* (Norman, Oklahoma, 1982), pp. 53–65.
[42] The fourteenth-century York Augustinian John Waldeby's commentary on the *Pater Noster* (*Incipits* 9123) links Pride with *fiat voluntas tua*, saying that *superbia* has two sons: *invidia* and *ira*; Oxford, Bodleian Library MS Laud Misc. 296, fol. 18[va].
[43] Cf. Alford, 'Haukyn's Coat', 135; *Glossa*, v.135–6; *Postilla*, v., fol. 23[rb].
[44] *PL* 175. 403 and 408.
[45] On the fonts, see R. Kaske, '*Piers Plowman* and Local Iconography', *JWCI*, 31 (1968): 159–69, p. 162. *Templum Dei*, p. 48.

performed by Langland's Patience for the stony-hearted Haukyn.[46] Patience's offer of the *Pater Noster* implicitly relates his teaching to observance of the commandments.[47] Obedience is commonly seen by the commentaries on *fiat voluntas tua* as a prerequisite for and a function of the Holy Spirit's gift of Counsel which (along with the closely related gift of Knowledge) is usually associated with the third petition: 'spiritus consilii ad obediencie condimentum'.[48] Rolle's commentary on the *Pater Noster* follows the *Glossa Ordinaria* in praising counsel, by which our will is filled so that we can fulfill the will of God, which is 'preceptorum eius custodia'.[49] Counsel teaches us to comform our will to the will of God, while Knowledge enlightens us and teaches us how to convert our lives.[50]

If we receive the gift of counsel, according to the commentary tradition, we will be made humble and merciful in our dealings with our fellow men, obeying the evangelical commandment clearly breached by Haukyn: to love our neighbours as ourselves. Mercy manifests itself in a variety of ways. Innocent III's influential *Pater Noster* commentary points out that while avarice consistes of *acquirendo et retinendo*, mercy manifests itself by *dando et dimittendo*. In letting go of the things of the world we can conform our will to the will of God and set our spritual sights on the homeland of heaven, though Innocent stresses that this process can only imperfectly be achieved in this world and will reach its

---

[46] *Postilla*, v, fol. 14[vb]: 'Beati ergo mites quia mitites lapides vituperationis convertit in panis suavissime refectionis'. The voluminous medieval literature on the subject of Patience, and in particular the *Glossa Ordinaria* commentary on the book of Job, frequently makes an explicit contrast between the patient enduring of tribulation by the virtuous and the more common tendency for suffering to produce *tristitia*, *ira* and *odium*. See E. D. Kirk, ' "Who suffreth more than God?": Narrative Redefinition of Patience in *Patience* and *Piers Plowman*', in G. J. Schiffhorst (ed.), *The Triumph of Patience: Medieval and Renaissance Studies* (Orlando, 1978), pp. 88–104, esp. p. 91; A. P. Baldwin, 'The Triumph of Patience in Julian of Norwich and Langland', in H. Phillips (ed.), *Langland, the Mystics and the Medieval English Religious Tradition* (Cambridge, 1990), pp. 71–83.

[47] Commentaries on the Commandments often describe wrath and envy, either severally or together, as offences against the command Thou Shalt Not Kill: e.g. R. C. Dales and E. B. King (eds.) *Robert Grosseteste: De Decem Mandatis*, Auctores Britannici Medii Aevi, 10 (Oxford, 1987), pp. 62–64, which includes a pertinent discussion of *odium*; Francis (ed.), *The Book of Virtues and Vices*: 'þe þridde maner of monslauhtre is in herte: whon eny wiȝt bereþ envye or hattrede in herte to heore euencristne' (p. 326). St Matthew's gospel also links murder and anger against fellow men (Mt. 5.21–22).

[48] *Speculum Theologie*, ed. Sandler, p. 129. For the division over the Gift received, see e.g. Counsel: Innocent III; Bonaventure; *Glossa Ordinaria*; Rolle; some copies of Chobham; *Speculum Theologie*; Hugh of St Cher; *Somme le Roi* tradition (e.g. *Book of Vices and Virtues*; *Speculum Vitae*, *Mirror to Lewd Men and Women*). Knowledge: Augustine; *Speculum Ecclesie*; Hugh of St Victor; most copies of Chobham; Aquinas; the Vernon table.

[49] *Incipits* 8395; Oxford, Bodleian Library MS Bodley 861, fol.143[rb]; *Glossa*, 5.130: Hic petitur spritus consilii, per quem voluntas dei inquiritur, vt a nobis impleatur.

[50] e.g. Aquinas, *In Orationem Dominicam Expositio*, in *S. Thomae Aquinas, Opuscula Theologica*, 2 (Turin/Rome, 1954), 227–9, clause 1061: 'Docet ergo hoc Spiritus sanctus per donum scientiae, ut scilicet non faciamus voluntatem nostram, sed voluntatem Dei' (*Incipits* 8515). Aquinas also stresses obedience to the commandments (clause 1065), linkage which goes back at least as far as Augustine's *De Sermone Domini in Monte* (*Incipits* 8140). Knowledge is particularly effective against envy because, as *Qui bene praesunt* asserts, *Invidus enim dicitur quasi non videns* (MS New College 94, fol. 40[r]); but it also works against wrath, as Chobham argues: 'Et sic excluditur ira que impedit cognoscere que sit voluntas dei, et introducitur donum scientie que docet equanimiter conversari' (Broomfield, p. 38).

consummation in the next.[51] Counsel and mercy together produce compassion for our fellow men – another moral facet singularly lacking in Haukyn's makeup – and compunction for our own sins. Compassion is an effective antidote for envy and compunction for wrath, as Hugh of St Victor argues.[52] This process of moral reformation will earn the accolade of the beatitudes, and indeed it is usually 'Blessed are the merciful, for they shall receive mercy' that is associated with *fiat voluntas tua*.[53]

Haukyn is not unwilling to enter into a process of reformation. But, unlike the apostolic Patience, whose habit and *habitus* obey Christ's instructions, Haukyn's limited wardrobe is a hindrance to his active life in the world. His sacramental confessions are never sustained because he is held back from the spiritual banquet by his worldliness: *Uxorem duxi, et ideo non possum venire* (B.XIV.3a). Like Will, Haukyn asks questions and repents for past sorrows. He receives the gift of counsel and the gift of knowledge from Patience's *pacient* exposition of the virtues of the proferred *vitaille* which, as one commentary puts it, 'techith to fulfil pacentlich godis wil'.[54] When man is aware of the grace and mercy of God and appreciates that all of his goods proceed from God, then he becomes better able to ride out the vicissitudes of life, less buffeted by the variations of good and bad events. In this state he will not become angry against God, but will exhibit patience. As the thirteenth-century Latin treatise *Postquam* puts it: 'Patience is the chest in which the treasure of virtues is kept'.[55] St Matthew and Langland put it more aphoristically: 'Ubi thesaurus tuus, ibi et cor tuum' (B.XIII.398a). The working of God's will in us manifests itself in three ways: conversion from sin; confirmation of that conversion; and the glory or reward that follows from the conversion.[56] In the light of all this it is worth remembering Patience's claims for *fiat voluntas tua* when he offers it to Haukyn:

'Have, Haukyn,' quod Pacience, 'and et this whan the hungreth,
Or whan thow clomsest for cold or clyngest for drye;
And shul nevere gyves thee greve ne gret lordes wrathe,
Prison ne peyne – for *pacientes vincunt*.
By so that thow be sobre of sighte and of tonge,

[51] *PL* 217. 903: Da nobis spiritum consilii, ut faciamus voluntatem tuam, maxime misericordiam consequamur, secundum illud: Beati misericordes . . . Sicut enim avaritia consistit in acquirendo et retinendo, ita misericordia consistit in dando et dimittendo. Bonaventure follows Innocent here. Hugh of St Cher makes a similar point (*Postilla*, fol. 22[ra]): Da nobis spiritum consilii quo misericordes effecti, tuam voluntatem in tua impleamus pro modulo viae, sicut impletur in celo pro modo patriae. Postquam vero homo iam misericordiam consecutus est et se totum subiicit voluntati domini statim ad altiora suspirat, ut scilicet illum videat, cuius voluntati obtemperat remotis omnibus nebulis phantasmatum, quod non implebitur nisi in futuro.

[52] Hugh's analysis offers an interesting parallel to the moral turpitude of Haukyn in B: 'Optime ergo per compunctionem cordis (quae spiritu scientiae operante, interius ex humilitate nascitur) ira et indignatio animi mitigatur quia e converso stultum ira interfecit, quando in adversis per impatientiae vitium agitatus, atque caecatus, vel malum quod patitur se meruisse, vel bonum quod habet per gratiam accepisse non agnoscit' (*De Quinque Septenis*, *PL* 175.408).

[53] E.g. by Innocent III; Chobham; Grosseteste; Bonaventure; Hugh of St Cher; the *Somme le Roi* tradition.

[54] Kengen (ed.), *Memoriale Credencium* p. 198, probably paraphrasing Chobham.

[55] *Incipits* 3988; S. Wenzel (ed.), *Summa Virtutum de Remediis Anime*, The Chaucer Library (Athens, Georgia, 1984), p. 164: 'ipsa est archa in qua seruatur thesaurus virtutum.'

[56] Waldeby on the *Pater Noster*, MS Laud Misc. 296, fol. 16[vb].

> In ondynge and in handlynge and in alle thi fyve wittes,
> Darstow nevere care for corn ne lynnen cloth ne wollen,
> Ne for drynke, ne deeth drede, but deye as God liketh . . .
> *Si quis amat Christum mundum non diligit istum.*
>
> (B.XIV.50–57, 59a)

What Patience offers to Haukyn, in his message and through the example of his own life, is a poverty of disengagement, an enactment of *ne soliciti sitis*. *Qui bene praesunt*, Wetheringsett's pastoral manual, concludes its discussion of *fiat voluntas tua* with a Pauline quotation of clear relevance: 'Nolite conformari huic seculo sed reformamini in novitate sensus vestri'.[57] Forsaking possession, wedding oneself to patience and poverty liberates the spiritual riches otherwise denied:

> So poverte propreliche penaunce is to the body
> And joye also to the soule, pure spiritual helthe,
> And contricion confort, and *cura animarum*.   (B.XIV.283–85)

As *Postquam* argues, humility is the mother of obedience, but patience is the nurse of obedience.[58] Langland's Patience nurtures Haukyn's incipient reformation by unfolding for him (and for Will and the reader) a deeper understanding or *kynde knowynge* of the interaction between the vices, virtues, remedies and beatitudes commonly associated with this petition for disengagement from the world. Langland's citations of *fiat voluntas tua* invoke not only the immediate context of the Lord's Prayer but also the submerged matrix of interacting moral and psychological imperatives encoded within it by the catechetic tradition. Patience offers both an allegorical embodiment of that matrix and a means of access to it, as Langland suggests in the C text revision where Patience describes himself in terms that allude to the portable mnemonic septenaries of the Wheel of Virtues:

> For, by hym þat me made, myhte neuere pouerte,
> Meseyse ne meschief, ne man with his tonge
> Tene þe eny tyme and þou take pacience
> And bere hit in thy bosom aboute wher þou wendest
> In þe corner of a cart-whel, with a crow croune.[59]
>
> (C.XV.158–62)

But, as so often in the poem, Langland explores the anxious tension between the codified idealisms of moral reformation and the difficult struggle to bring

---

[57] MS New College 94, fol. 36ᵛ, quoting Romans 12.2: 'And be not conformed to this world; but be reformed in the newness of your mind, that you may prove what is the good, and the acceptable, and the perfect will of God' (Douay-Rheims). See the discussion of patient poverty in Donaldson, *C-Text*, pp. 175–80. For a pertinent discussion of the spiritual benefits of voluntary poverty, see S.Wenzel (ed.), *Fasciculus Morum: A Fourteenth-Century Preacher's Handbook* (London, 1989), pp. 386–94.

[58] Wenzel (ed.), *Summa Virtutum*, p.218, which also cites a Bernardine definition of obedience as 'the virtuous carrying out of a just command by a mind that takes counsel'. Hugh of St Victor comments: 'si quid autem boni habuerit ex misericordia Dei procedere, ac per hoc discat, sive in malis, quae sustinet, sive in bonis, quae non habet, contra Creatorem non irasci, sed per omnia patientiam exhibere' (*De Quinque Septenis*, PL 175.408).

[59] See the references in note 10.

them to fruition, a struggle which the commentaries on *fiat voluntas tua* recognise will not be completed in this life. Thus Haukyn's repentance is posited on the recognition that the life of the world carries with it the inevitability of sin:

> 'Allas,' quod Haukyn the Actif Man tho, 'that after my
>   cristendom
> I ne hadde be deed and dolven for Dowelis sake!'
>
> (B.XIV.320–21)

This is a sophistication of the simplistic and idealistic faith in the power of the *Pater Noster* expressed by Will at earlier stages of the poem. Even though 'povere commune laborers' may pierce heaven with a *Pater Noster* and pass through Purgatory 'penauncelees . . . for hir pure bileve' (B.X.457–62), the reality for most men in the active life is rather different:

> 'So hard it is,' quod Haukyn, 'to lyve and to do synne.
> Synne seweth us evere,' quod he, and sory gan wexe,
> And wepte water with his eighen and weyled the tyme
> That evere he dide dede that deere God displesed. (B.XIV.322–5)

Haukyn's mournful repentance is the result of the effects of knowledge, counsel and good will combining to make him aware of his need for mercy and for his life to be conformed to the will of God.[60] The seeds of this reformation are contained in *fiat voluntas tua*, the 'pece of the Paternoster' offered by Pacience. The power of the *Pater Noster* traditionally lies in its focussed and concentrated articulation of the catechetic bedrock of the Church's teachings. Like the dough and flour offered by Patience, it contains the basic ingredients for salvation. But something more is needed to catalyse the development into *kynde knowynge*.

This may help to explain why Haukyn's first words to Patience after his receipt of *fiat voluntas tua* puzzlingly ask about the location of Charity. *Fiat voluntas tua* is often linked to charity, for example by Grosseteste, by the Wycliffite commentary and by Rolle who defines charity as full conformity to the will of God. In B, Patience's answer goes some way to explaining the local significance of charity in Haukyn's reformation:

> Ther parfit truthe and poor herte is, and pacience of tonge –
> There is Charite, the chief chaumbrere for God hymselve.
>
> (B.XIV.99–100)

But the C text reformulation of this exchange identifies more clearly the relevance of Haukyn's question and the wider spiritual significance of *fiat voluntas tua* both for Will and for the poem:

> 'What is parfit pacience?' quod *Activa Vita*.
> 'Meeknesse and mylde speche and men of o will,

---

[60] Some commentaries on *fiat voluntas tua* link it with the beatitude 'Beati qui lugent' (e.g. *Speculum Ecclesie*, Aquinas and some copies of Chobham). Aquinas explains this as a function of longing for Heaven, a mourning for the constraints of the body, and a result of the battle between body and spirit: 'Et qui sic plorant, perveniunt ad patriam, ad quam nos perducat Deus' (*Expositio*, clause 1069). Chobham comments: 'Inde sequitur tertia virtus, id est luctus pro peccatis propriis et alienis, et impetrat consolationem eternam' (Broomfield [ed.], *Summa*, p. 38).

> The whiche wil loue lat to oure lordes place,
> And þat is charite, chaumpion, chief of all vertues;
> And þat is pore pacient, alle perelles to soffre'.   (C.XV.274–78)

The linking of Charity and Patience here explains why Patience's exposition of his powers earlier in this passus ends with the Joannine authority 'Caritas expellit omnem timorem' (C.XV.165a: 1 John 4.18). The pertinence of charity/love casting out fear to the moral and spiritual predicament of Haukyn/*Activa Vita* is clear from the full context in John's epistle, which explores the relationship between faith and works:

> Perfect charity casteth out fear, because fear hath pain. And he that feareth is not perfected in charity. Let us therefore love God, because God first hath loved us. If any man say I love God, and hateth his brother; he is a liar. For he that loveth not his brother, whom he seeth, how can he love God whom he seeth not? And this commandment we have from God that he, who loveth God, love also his brother.   (I John 4.18–21)

Haukyn/*Activa*'s wrathful and envious behaviour is contrasted with the evangelical commandments which have formed the moral backbone of the poem since Holy Church's speech.[61] Patience and charity offer potent antidotes by teaching renunciation and willed loss of control: *fiat voluntas tua*, the prayer that invokes the fulfillment of God's will through our will, links these virtues implicitly at first, but increasingly explicitly as the C text progresses.

In C.XVI, *Liberum Arbitrium* responds to Will's questions about the nature of Charity with an account of his works and teachings that emphasises his reliance on the basic prayers of the church and his embodiment of the faithful patience articulated by several petitions of the *Pater Noster*. Just as many commentaries on the prayer emphasise that 'unless you become like little children you will never enter the kingdom of heaven' (Matthew 18.3), so Charity is described as 'a childische thyng', a description supported by the same gospel citation (C.XVI.296–96a). Charity responds to the changing moods and humours of mankind with self-effacing and self-emptying empathy and generosity. Characteristically, Will is concerned about Charity's *lyflode*:

> 'Who fynt hym his fode?' quod y, 'or what frendes hath he,
> Rentes other richesse to releue him at his nede?'
> Of rentes ne of oþere rychesse ne recceth he neuere.
> A frende he hath þat fynd him þat faylede hym neuere:
> Oen *Aperis-tu-manum* alle thynges hym fyndeth;
> *Fiat-voluntas-tua* festeth hym vch a daye.
> Also a can clergie, *credo-in-deum-patrem*,
> And purtraye wel þe *pater-noster* and peynten hit with *auees*.
>   (C.XVI.313–20)

Liberum Arbitrium's reply encodes the specific and general attributes of the *Pater Noster* in his account of Charity's childish trust in God and his teachings:

---

[61] Hilton notes that envy and wrath 'hinder the love and charity you ought to have toward your fellow christians' (Clark and Dorward [ed.], *Scale of Perfection*, 1.64, p. 135). The symptoms of wrath and envy are well described in *Scale* i.69, and the antidote in love in *Scale* ii.38.

he is emphatically not solicitous for his own well being; indeed he embodies and makes manifest ('a can . . . purtraye wel þe *pater-noster*') the kenotic prayer at the heart of the *Pater Noster*, yielding the initiative to the Almighty.

Charity's roots lie not only in the basic prayers of the church, though the catechetic syllabus is never far from the mind of the poem in its search for *kynde knowynge*, but also in the optimism and utopianism of Will's faith in the power of the *Pater Noster* at the end of the A text. But unlike the clerks in that episode who regretted their learning and longed to return to the basic syllabus outlined by *Liberum Arbitrium*, Charity combines his faith and reliance on the basic teachings of the church with *clergie* that enables him to understand and articulate them at a profounder level. Thus Charity represents something akin to the blending of Patience and Clergye foreshadowed when Conscience leaves his court to go on pilgrimage with Patience and Will. The exploration of the deeper moral and spiritual implications of *fiat voluntas tua* in the Haukyn/*Activa* episode leads inevitably (if not inexorably) to their realisation in the portrait of Charity.

Grosseteste asserts that the Creed is linked to Faith, the *Ave Maria* to Hope and that the *Pater Noster* should be known by the laity *ad caritatem*. Indeed, he argues, charity helps us specifically both to invoke and to implement the petition *fiat voluntas tua*:

> Caritas dat nobis Spiritus Sancti uoluntatem, vnde petimus eius uoluntatem fieri in nobis, et non nostram.[62]

It is not surprising that the willing submission of the human will to the will of God is a matter of considerable interest to a character called *Liberum Arbitrium*.[63] Indeed the transformation from *Anima* in the B text to *Liberum Arbitrium*, described as the *ledare* of *Activa Vita* (the transfigured Haukyn), may owe something to Langland's awareness of the emphasis on free will in commentaries on *fiat voluntas tua*. Hugh of St Cher, for example, glosses the petition as an invocation of divine help in making the *liberum arbitrium* consent to the working of grace in the soul by the power of the gift of counsel.[64]

The passus ends with *Liberum Arbitrium* returning to the recurrent theme of covetousness, emphasising the need to let go of our grasping tight-fisted ways on earth if we are to enjoy the open-handedness of God's mercy and the freedom that comes with serving his will. The false *conseil* of Covetousness will prevent Charity from entering in:

---

[62] Goering and Mantello (ed.), *Templum Dei*, pp. 50, 67. Grosseteste notes that by the first three petitions of the *Pater Noster* 'inuocamus in humilitate, paciencia, obediencia ad fidem, spem, caritatem optinendam et conseruandam' (p. 67). The diagnostic chart included by Grosseteste illustrates the skeletonic psychology of the commentary tradition: '*Infirmitas*: Odium; *Planctus*: Fiat voluntas; *Preparacio*: Misericors; *Medicina*: Obediencia; *Sanitas*: Caritas; *Gaudium Intra*: Vnitas; *Gaudium Extra*: Misericordiam consequentur' (p. 38). The relevance of this kind of schema to Langland's procedures in this section of the poem is, I hope, by now apparent.

[63] Cf. Donaldson, *C-Text*, pp.87–96; A. V. C. Schmidt, 'Langland and Scholastic Philosophy', *Medium Ævum*, 38 (1969): 134–156; B. Harbert, 'A Will with a Reason: Theological Developments in the C-Revision of *Piers Plowman*', in Boitani and Torti (eds.), *Religion in the Poetry and Drama*, pp. 149–61, esp. pp. 156–61.

[64] *Postilla*, fol. 22ra.

> And ho-so coueyteth to knowe him, such a kynde hym foleweth
> As y tolde þe with tonge, a litel tyme ypassed;
> For noþer he ne beggeth ne biddeth, ne borweth to ȝelde.
> He halt it for a vyce and a foule shame
> To begge or to borwe, but of god one.
> *Panem nostrum cotidianum, etc.*   (C.XVI.367–71a)

The echo of the apostolic perfection of Patience and the God's minstrels is clear.
God will 'fynt us alle thynges':

> By clothyng ne by carpynge knowe shaltow hym neuere,
> Ac thorw werkes thow myhte wyte wher-forth he walketh.
> *Operibus credite.*   (C.XVI.338–39a)

Once again the invocation of a specific clause of the *Pater Noster* is
significant. The commentaries usually associate *panem nostrum* with the gift of
fortitude, sometimes attributing to it patience as an antidote to wrath, the virtue
of temperance and a thirst for justice. All these manifest themselves in good
works. In effect the invocation of this petition at the very end of C.XVI pulls
together much of the passus's teaching about the nature of Charity and its
mediation through the active life. Charity's works display the judicious fortitude
traditionally ascribed to *panem nostrum*, relating these virtues to the dominant
petition *fiat voluntas tua* by the emphasis on renunciation and trust that
characterises them both. Hugh of St Cher makes the link between the petitions
explicit when he describes *panem nostrum* as the *viaticum* for the pilgrim who is
in search of the kingdom of heaven.[65] Like Haukyn before him, Charity is
feasted by *fiat voluntas tua*, which becomes, in a sense, that supersubstantial
bread that provides all that is necessary for the pilgrimage of the human will.
Whereas the first two petitions invoke Faith and Hope, the third asks for 'parfit
charite to god and to oure evencristen'. As Rolle comments in his exposition,
charity consists 'in plena conformitate domine voluntatem'.[66]

IV

Langland's invocations of the *Pater Noster* allude to and finesse the prayer's
commentary tradition by exploring the difficulties of enacting its teachings in the
world of the poem and by examining how the schematic and two-dimensional
matrix of the catechetic tradition might be catalysed and realised in the notably
more complex and rounded moral psychology of his characters. Fundamental to
that exploration is Will's (and perhaps Langland's) growing understanding of the
transfiguration of the human will implicit in *fiat voluntas tua*, the essence of
which is captured in Cyprian's commentary:

> The will of God is just as Christ did and taught: humility in conversation;
> stability in faith; truthfulness in words; justice in actions; mercy in works;

---

[65] *Postilla*, fol. 22ra.
[66] Wycliffite commentary, MS Bodley 938, fol. 29r; Rolle commentary, MS Bodley 861, fol. 143rb.

discipline in morals; not knowingly doing harm; being tolerant where possible; holding peace with your brethren. This is to aim for oneing with Christ; this is to carry out God's commandments; this is to fulfill the will of God.[67]

Langland is more succinct, but no less comprehensive:

> *Fiat voluntas dei* – þat fynt vs alle thynges. (C.V.88)

---

[67] *Incipits* 8302; *Liber de Oratione Dominice*, *PL* 4.535-62, 546. The point is made mnemonically in the *Expositio Magistralis* (*Incipits* 8799), a brief clausal commentary on the *Pater Noster*, mainly preserved in continental manuscripts and added to the first printed edition of the very popular late fourteenth- or early fifteenth-century pastoral manual *Speculum Christiani*, printed by William de Machlinia *c.* 1484 (*STC2* 26012): '*Fiat voluntas tua s. in c. et in t.* scilicet cordis simplicitate, corporis castitate, oracionis veritate et operis sanctitate' (p. 99).

ASPECTS OF THE 'PUBLICATION' OF WYCLIF'S LATIN SERMONS

Anne Hudson

The most important manuscript of Wyclif's Latin works now surviving in England, Cambridge, Trinity College, MS B.16.2 (abbreviated as C), contains a list of its contents in a medieval hand on a flyleaf at the front.[1] The contents are divided into four blocks: the first two are of philosophical writings, the third of sermons and the fourth containing the late *Opus Evangelicum*. The manuscript is an extremely complicated one in makeup, and has lost a number of leaves by excision; none of the folio numberings are complete, and those that are most prominent are incorrect; the numbers I shall give are those found in Thomson's catalogue of Wyclif's writings but are certainly wrong.[2] But the third block of material is relatively straightforward and nothing is lost. The initial list of contents divides this section again into four: the first containing 57 sermons on the Sunday gospels, the second 64 on the Sanctorale (actually in the order Proprium followed by more extensive Commune), the third 59 on the Sunday epistles, and the fourth 64 'de epistolis in sanctorum festiuitatibus cum aliis diuersis sermonis'; a total of 244.

Loserth, in his edition of the sermons for the Wyclif Society for the most part followed the Trinity manuscript both in order and in readings: the first 57, the first 61 and all 59 in volumes 1–3 respectively correspond with the order in this manuscript. But Loserth unfortunately reassigned the final three sermons of the Sanctorale as that appeared in C, and more drastically confused the fourth group of that manuscript.[3] The changes were designed to take into account the evidence of the Hussite manuscripts of the sermons in Vienna, but Loserth apparently failed to understand all the details; he also did not know of the two important

[1] This list, together with a description of the manuscript and its contents, is to be found in M. R. James, *The Western Manuscripts in the Library of Trinity College Cambridge*, i (Cambridge, 1900), pp. 513–15. The description is not in every respect accurate, and I hope to publish a more detailed account of the manuscript elsewhere. I am indebted for much help with this manuscript, as with so many others over the past twenty years, to the unfailing generosity and expertise of Dr Ian Doyle.
[2] W. R. Thomson, *The Latin Writings of John Wyclyf* (Toronto, 1983), includes references to the manuscript under the works which it contains; for a summary see p. 311. Thomson lists each sermon separately, his numbers 54–298; these numbers will be used here, prefixed by 'T'. I suggested to the Librarian at Trinity College that a new foliation should be entered, leaving gaps in the numeration for folios which had been excised; unfortunately, though the principle was agreed, only a handful of numbers have been entered in the manuscript, and those so inconspicuously as to be easily overlooked.
[3] J. Loserth, *Johannis Wyclif Sermones*, i–iv, Wyclif Society (London, 1887–90); the three reassigned sermons are T112–114, numbered in C as 62–64 of the Sanctorale, all for feasts connected with the dedication of a church, which Loserth included at the end of his first volume, the rest of whose contents are the sermons on the dominical gospels.

Wolfenbüttel manuscripts, also of continental origin.[4] My chief interest in this paper is the fourth group of sermons; the problem of the conclusions of the three first sets is complicated, revealing that neither the Trinity manuscript nor Loserth's modifications to its ordering can be regarded as authoritative, and must be left for another place.

All four groups of sermons contain within them a number of cross references to material elsewhere in the sermons. These usually take the form either of *ut patet sermone – huius* (or comparable wording) when the cross reference is within the same group and the gap is filled by the sermon number, or *ut patet sermone – – partis* when the reference is to a sermon in another set and the numbers first of sermon and then of part are both provided.[5] In theory, of course, there is no reason why these cross references should not be scribal rather than authorial. Indeed, four marginal references of this or similar kind in C might suggest that all began as scribal additions in the margins that were only subsequently incorporated into the text; the fact that some of the references lack the provision of the number might seem to confirm the secondary nature of the information.[6] But checking the other manuscripts seems to point against this interpretation: the four marginal notes in C are not replicated elsewhere, but almost all those references incorporated into C's text are found in all other copies at the same places, even if the numbers given sometimes vary.[7] These other copies are not in other readings particularly close to C, and were certainly not copied from C; at times incorrect numbers in C can be corrected from the other copies, and notably from Wolfenbüttel 565.[8] It is clear that, to put it at the least, these cross references must go back to the hyparchetype of all extant manuscripts.

That in the case of the first three groups of sermons they go back to Wyclif himself is suggested by the fact that the cross references in the Sunday gospel sermons refer only to that group, those in the Sanctorale refer to that group but also to the preceding Sunday gospel sermons, whilst those in the Sunday epistle sermons refer to all three groups.[9] In the preface to the Sunday gospel set (a preface oddly missing from C), Wyclif describes what follows as *sermones rudes ad populum colligendi*, written *in illo ocio quo a scolasticis ociamur*

---

[4] Chiefly Vienna, Österreichische Nationalbibliothek, MSS 3928, 3931, 3934, and 4529; Wolfenbüttel, Herzog August Bibliothek, MS Cod.Helm.306 contains primarily the Sunday epistle sermons (T176–234) and may be of Polish origin, whilst MS Cod.Helm.565, the more important of the two, contains this same set preceded by the Sunday gospel sermons (T55–111).

[5] For instance, *ut patet . . . sermone xxi* (*Sermones* ii.176/8), and *ut exponitur sermone xxxvi partis prime* (*Sermones* ii.227/20).

[6] For the four marginal references in C see Loserth's notes to *Sermones* ii.13/11, 107/31, iii.27/29 and 110/31; for the incomplete references for example *Sermones* ii.288/3, 323/23, 371/27.

[7] There are 23 cross references in the Sunday gospel set, all found in MSS Vienna 3934, 4529 and Wolfenbüttel 565; 40 in the Sanctorale sermons, all save two found in MSS Vienna 3928 and 3931; 14 in the Sunday epistle sermons, all save one found in MSS Wolfenbüttel 306 and 565. The references of the fourth set will be considered below.

[8] Thus MS Wolfenbüttel 565 corrects *Sermones* i.260/11 from 34 to 37 (the allusion is to sermon 37, i.248/3), *Sermones* iii.148/17 from 19 to 17 (reference to sermon 17, iii.133/14), and fills the gap left by C at iii.145/4 with the correct number 5 (referring to sermon 5, iii.32/26).

[9] For references to sets other than that in which the reference appears see *Sermones* ii.203/38, 227/20, 285/3 and iii.26/29 (as corrected, see below n.12), 139/5 (as corrected by Wolfenbüttel 565 to *sermone 33* [Wolfenbüttel 306 erroneously *34*] *partis secunde*).

(i.*v).[10] From this it has usually been deduced that the three sets of sermons that make up Loserth vols. 1–3 were composed *as we have them* after Wyclif's retirement to Lutterworth in the summer of 1381. Though the makeup even of these sermons is more complicated that this easy summary would imply, the organization of the material seems correctly assignable to the period between 1381 and 31 December 1384 when Wyclif died.[11] The preface implies that the Sunday gospel set was written first; the opening sentences of the ensuing two groups likewise imply their second and third positions. If a scribe had intended to add cross references to aid consultation of this large body of preaching materials, there seems no reason why set 3 should not be alluded to in set 1. But the absence of such cross references is entirely intelligible if the author were inserting them as he went along. Since all the 77 cross references that are found in these three sets allude to sermons *earlier* in the sequence than the sermon in which they occur, it would follow that the implication of this evidence is that Wyclif composed each set sequentially exactly in the order in which it now stands.[12]

This point becomes important when we turn to the fourth group of sermons, a group that has so far not been precisely described. The scribe in the Trinity manuscript who wrote the list of contents evidently did not understand this assemblage, and the fact that the main scribe of this section provided no headings at all to any sermon in it (though he numbered its sequence – not quite correctly at the end) cannot have helped him. Loserth divided the material into two groups, the *Sermones Quadraginta* and the *Sermones Mixti*. To the second, which was a fictional title that has confused everyone attempting to use Loserth's fourth volume, I will return later. The first of these titles is certainly correct: the group is found in the same order, and as a separate entity, in Lambeth Palace 23 (henceforward L) where it is incomplete, and in two Vienna manuscripts, 3928 (V) and 3932 (X). The Hussite cataloguer whose work survives in three early fifteenth-century manuscripts likewise recognized this as a separate group: he gives the information that *Sermones XL compositi dum stetit in scolis* begins with the words *Hora est.*[13] In all the surviving copies of the group, this is indeed the opening sermon (T257, *Sermones* iv.197); all these copies likewise agree in their ordering of all the sermons that they preserve. Although neither of the Vienna manuscripts of the *Sermones Quadraginta* are absolutely complete and both lack any heading to the group, knowledge of the fact that it should contain 40 sermons is shown by one scribe's marginal note at the end of the 38th in V *hic desunt duo sermones.*[14] The index that precedes the sermons in the Lambeth

---

[10] *Sermones* i. unnumbered page containing *Praefatio* lines 11, 9 respectively.

[11] A study of the background to these three sets of Wyclif's sermons is being made by Pamela Gradon.

[12] As printed by Loserth, the reference at iii.26/29 (T179) *dictum est sermone lxxx* appears to be an exception, but the two Wolfenbüttel manuscripts correct to *sermone 60 prime partis* (correctly i.401/21).

[13] The catalogues are printed, not entirely accurately, by R. Buddensieg, *John Wiclif's Polemical Works in Latin*, Wyclif Society (London, 1883), i.lix–lxxxiv; they appear in Vienna, Österreichische Nationalbibliothek, MSS 3933, 3935, 4514 and in the later 7980 (of which Buddensieg only transcribed a part). I plan to publish a new study of these catalogues elsewhere.

[14] The whole is in V fols 193ra–253rb, in X fols 92va–152vb; X contains sermons 1–39 (T257–95), V only 1–38 (T257–94).

manuscript, itself now incomplete, includes sermon numbers up to 41; but it seems probable that the apparent extra sermon results from a misnumbering in the presentation of the usual material somewhere amongst the lost sermons rather than from the intrusion of another sermon – material said in the index to be sermon 41 actually occurs in regular sermon 40.[15]

The *Sermones Quadraginta* have long been recognized to date from a much earlier period of Wyclif's career than the longer sets that make up Loserth's and Trinity's first three groups.[16] The fifteenth-century Hussite catalogues' note *dum stetit in scolis* is shown by internal references in most of these sermons to be essentially correct. Quite apart from the more tempered tone of allusions to the religious orders and the papacy than is normal in the productions of Wyclif's last years, and the absence of any reference to heterodox notions of the eucharist, a few precise indications of date make it possible to suggest dates between January 1375 and September 1379 for many of the sermons. Where these sermons were preached is less clear: *dum stetit in scolis* may be correct as a dating indication, but several of the sermons may have been preached in London rather than in Oxford – they would then be examples of the sermons which Walsingham alleged Wyclif had delivered in these years, 'running from church to church around London'.[17] Almost simultaneously in 1966 two scholars, William Mallard and Gustav Benrath, produced a closer analysis of the *Sermones Quadraginta*, assigning precise dates and an order to several of the sermons.[18] On eleven of the forty they agree; Mallard with varying degrees of hesitation placed twenty more, and assigned six further doubtful dates.[19] More important for the present purpose is the fact that the ordering of the sermons that can be established from internal references cannot, even on the more conservative listing agreed by both Benrath and Mallard, be reconciled with the manuscript order. Using the sermon numbers as these appear in the surviving manuscripts, but arranging them in the order agreed by these two scholars, with those only dated by Mallard in italics, the following sequence is established:

---

[15] L's copy of the sermons is fols. 258ra–280vb breaking off in sermon 28 (T284); the index is on fols. 256rb–257ra. The quiring at the end of the manuscript is very difficult to check because the volume is too tightly bound; the surviving sermons seem to be in two quires originally of twelve leaves each, but the final leaf of the second is lost. The index numbering seems to be correct against the usual text up to sermon 32, whilst references to sermons 34–41 correspond to material in the usual texts numbered 33–40; the index includes no references to a sermon 33, and it thus seems likely that the scribe of this manuscript erroneously advanced the numbers after 32.

[16] See, for instance, Loserth Sermones iv.v, or H. B. Workman, *John Wyclif* (Oxford, 1926), ii.206–7.

[17] Thomas Walsingham, *Chronicon Anglie*, ed. E. M. Thompson, Rolls Series (London, 1874), p. 117, dated 1377.

[18] W. Mallard, 'Dating the *Sermones Quadraginta* of John Wyclif', *Medievalia et Humanistica*, 17 (1966): 86–105; G. A. Benrath, *Wyclifs Bibelkommentar* (Berlin, 1966), pp. 378–85. I have substituted the manuscripts' sermon numbers for those derived from Loserth's muddled edition in vol. iv; Loserth's numbers are used by Mallard and Benrath, but can be translated from Thomson's listing.

[19] Some of the second category seem reasonable, but I am not sure that his assumption that Wyclif would never have preached more than a single sermon on one Sunday is unchallengeable – indeed, does Walsingham's derogatory comment imply that Wyclif broke that convention in his evangelical zeal?

*6; 9, 12–13, 16–17; 37, 33–5, 40, 38, 1; 4; 7, 8, 10–11;
14–15, 19, 22–23; 39, 2–3; 18, 20, 24–25; 29*[20]

As is clear, not merely are sermons 1 and 2–3 late in the chronological sequence, but there is no pattern of rearrangement; only in one case are more than two sermons found together *both* in chronology and in manuscript sequence.

The rationale behind the manuscripts' *re*organization of these 40 sermons is easy enough to see: from sermon 1 to sermon 36 they have been arranged into the sequence of a single liturgical year, though the sermons vary in their use of gospel or epistle lection, and sometimes a Sunday is doubly provided whilst others are entirely omitted.[21] Sermon no. 37 (T293) backtracks from 22 Trinity to 19 Trinity, whilst no. 38 (T294) is for 25 Trinity; the full quota of forty is made up by a sermon on the lection for a virgin and martyr from the Sarum Commune Sanctorum and by one for the dedication of a church. But this secondary organization was not the only 'editorial' change. Cross references were also provided. Four of these are in the same format as those already described in the other sets: *ut patet sermone* – with a number inserted finally. These numbers are found in all copies, but can only be correct on the liturgical arrangement that the manuscripts follow – they cannot be correct chronologically.[22] It should be noted that, unlike those in sets 1–3, these are all four *forward* references in regard to manuscript position. More of the cross references are of the form *ut dixi sermone proximo* or *proxima dominica* (*proximus* in Wyclif regularly means previous, not following) and these are more puzzling. Some are, of course, indecisive: *proxima dominica* at the start of sermon 17 (iv.321/14), alluding to sermon 16 (iv.320/3ff.) is correct by Mallard's extended chronology, since these two are dated by him 11 and 6 April 1376 respectively, and by manuscript order where they are for Good Friday and Palm Sunday. Others are correct only by the rearranged liturgical order of the manuscripts: thus the reference to *in sermone proximo* in manuscript order 20 (iv.349/10), alluding to the matter of 19 (iv.340/13) does not work for the chronological order at least on Mallard's arrangement, since 20 is there separated from 19 by six other sermons.[23] Such references must have been added after the reorganization. Yet others, however, cannot work on the manuscript order: most of these are in the opening sentence of sermons, where the preacher makes plain his intention of continuing a previous discourse to the same congregation – this evidence is, indeed, the major plank in the case by which

---

[20] Sermon 1 (T257) is dated by Benrath to 30 November 1376, Advent Sunday and St Andrew's day (see iv.197/23 and 198/36), and that is accepted here; Mallard thinks the bulk of the sermon from that date, the remainder from three years later. The semi-colons mark breaks in the dating of the sermons, for which see summaries in Benrath p. 386, Mallard p. 105.

[21] Thus, for instance, there are two sermons, nos. 8–9 (T264–5), on the gospel for Sexagesima Sunday, two, nos. 15–16 (T271–2), on the epistle for Palm Sunday, three, nos. 17–19 (T273–5) on the gospel for Good Friday; but the fourth to the ninth Sundays after Trinity lack provision of any kind. No. 26 (T282) for the Assumption is places between sermons for the third and tenth Sundays after Trinity, a common but not invariable position for the feast.

[22] *Sermones* iv.202/6 referring to sermon 38 (iv.468/2) in no. 1, iv.213/4 to sermon 39 (iv.476/20) in no. 3, iv.432/14 to sermon 37 (iv.464/1) in no. 33; the form of reference at iv.309/5, no. 14, is different in form *sermone de dominice 19* (to no. 37, again iv.464/1), but must have been inserted after a liturgical arrangement had been settled.

[23] Mallard dates 20 as 18 April 1378, 19 as 27 March 1377 (pp. 94–97, summary p. 105).

Mallard and Benrath have been able to build up their chronology. Thus what is now sermon 38 refers twice (iv.469/38, 474/14) to material preached *dominica proxima*, but that material is now in sermon 40 (iv.485/20, 489/6) – both Mallard and Benrath agree that these two were preached sequentially, on 23 and 16 November 1376 respectively.[24]

What are we to conclude from all this about the 'publication' of the *Sermones Quadraginta*? I would suggest that we must deduce editorial activity, putting together a round number of Wyclif's early sermons – it is highly improbable this is more than a small proportion of the total output of his preaching *dum stetit in scholis*, and parts of some other early sermons may well have been worked into the three coherent sets by Wyclif himself. A liturgical arrangement was the best way to make this material accessible to others at a later date. Some cross references were added at this stage. But no systematic attempt was made to remove the indications of the previous order. All of the surviving indications of the older order are verbal rather than numeric – that is they are of the form *sermone proximo*, *superius*, or of date, and hence might be more difficult than a sermon number for a reviser to spot and modify for subsequent copying. It would, I think, seem likely that this rather slovenly editorial activity was done by someone other than Wyclif himself. On the other hand, since the references almost without exception appear in all surviving manuscripts, whether English or Bohemian, it must have been undertaken before the hyparchetype was written.[25]

The title *Sermones Mixti* seems to have started from Shirley's listing of Wyclif's works in 1865: he recognized the 64 sermons of C's fourth section, and correctly set sixty of them against the descriptions of the Hussite catalogues; unfortunately he added a separate heading *Sermones mixti xxiv*, of which he said 'Most, but not all, of these occur in part IV', giving references to two Vienna manuscripts. Loserth, who knew the Vienna manuscripts much better than Shirley, dropped Shirley's analysis of C in favour of his second, misguided grouping; Thomson unfortunately perpetuated the title *Sermones Mixti* in his 1983 listing.[26] The best starting point here is the same medieval Hussite catalogues now in Vienna: they recognize another group of Wyclif's sermons, the *XX Sermones compositi in fine vite sue* with an incipit *Rogate que ad pacem*; the incipit is the first words of the text of sermon 3 in Loserth's volume iv, verse 6 of Psalm 121 (T237). This is sermon 3 also in part 4 of the Trinity manuscript's assemblage. Two Vienna manuscripts, V (which has appeared before) and 3931 (W), recognize the existence of a group of twenty sermons including this, though they copy them in an order that does not put this sermon

---

[24] Another instance is in sermon 16 (iv.315/34) where material in sermon 13 (iv.300/19) is stated to have been preached *proxima dominica*; Mallard dates 16 as 6 April 1376, 13 as 30 March 1376 (see summary p. 105).

[25] Lambeth omits the reference in 3 (iv.213/4), whilst in 2 (iv.206/32) and 3 (iv.217/16) the two Vienna manuscripts have less precise references. But Prague University Library V.H.27, which contains three sermons from this group (nos. 17–19, T273–5), reproduces the three references found within them.

[26] See W. W. Shirley, *A Catalogue of the Original Works of John Wyclif* (Oxford, 1865), pp. 14–15, nos. 36–7. Loserth published his revision, *Shirley's Catalogue of the Extant Latin Works of John Wyclif*, in 1924 (it was a supplement to the Wyclif Society, and includes no date); here, p. 9, he gives no details about the contents of his fourth volume of *Sermones*, but uses the term *Sermones Mixti*.

first. I will for the moment assume that it is correct to recognize such a short set of twenty sermons, and that the Vienna catalogues are correct about its first item. There are, however, complications. The Trinity manuscript (despite the muddle that Loserth made of its evidence here) from the *Rogate* opening provides in order eight sermons also found in the two Vienna copies (T237–244), followed by one not replicated in the grouping found in those manuscripts (T245), followed by a further eleven also shared with them (T246–256). It is convenient to number the shared sermons provisionally 1–8 and 9–19, but to omit the apparent intruder that would make up twenty in C. The two Vienna copies share these nineteen sermons, but they were copied by their scribes in a different order: using the Trinity numbers, in the order 15–19, followed by 1–14, without the intruding T245, but with the addition of a final sermon not found in C at all, T299. Despite this ordering, both scribes apparently had second thoughts: both add numbering which if followed would virtually replicate that of Trinity. The scribe of V numbered his sixth sermon – that which has the text *Rogate* – 1, continued the sequence through to 14, and then went back and numbered his first five sermons 15–19. The scribe of W followed a similar method, but, though he started with 1 at the same point, he included after 14 what is T299 as no. 15, and consequently renumbered his first five sermons as 16–20. W also contains a note, not by the main scribe, at the start of the group *hic sermo secundum aliam posicionem debet esse 16 in ordine, et sic sequitur ultimum huius libri.*[27] The discrepancy between V and W suggests that neither derives from the other, though they must be closely related both in original text and in the source of their modification.

If we accept the renumbering of the two Vienna manuscripts, it is possible to align Trinity and the Hussite tradition in regard to the inclusion and order of nineteen of the twenty sermons. What was the twentieth? The Vienna solution is not a happy one: T299 is described by Loserth and Thomson as 'an act sermon': this, more explicitly, is a graduation day sermon, recognized as such by the Hussite catalogues and listed as a separate item.[28] Wyclif's participation in such an academic occasion is impossible after mid 1381, and unlikely, at least in the benificent mood expressed here, for some years before that; since the Hussite catalogues are reliable in so many matters, inclusion of this sermon would go against their indication that the *XX Sermones* were written *in fine vite sue*. The fact that V does not include this sermon in its renumbering, despite its position in the manuscript immediately after 14, would seem to suggest that W's inclusion was for the sake of making up the required number rather than dependent upon any stronger justification. Trinity's sermon after no. 8 (T245) seems a better candidate: it is a gospel sermon for the commemoration of the dead, and it may be its occasion which explains why in the two Vienna manuscripts it appears at an earlier point, separated from the *XX Sermones* but attached to another sermon for the dead.[29] But, though there is a general similarity to the content of that

---

[27] Recorded by Loserth iv.147/34 note.

[28] In MS Vienna 3933 (Buddensieg i.lxi) *Recommendacio assumencium gradus*, with incipit *Dominus vobiscum* Ruth ii, and explicit *cum corpore resumendum*; the same information appears in the other copies of the catalogue.

[29] In V fols 126va–128rb, in W fols 140vb–142va, in both preceded by T236. T236 in turn appears in four manuscripts after T235, also for the commemoration of the dead; T235 belongs (despite

sermon, there is no explicit cross reference and no clear allusion to contemporary events. I am inclined, however, to think that Trinity is correct in placing this sermon where it does, and that what I numbered above 9–19 should rightly be renumbered as 10–20 with T245 as 9. If this is correct, then the archetype of V and W must already have displaced this sermon from the group.

Is there any logic behind either the arrangement that I have suggested to be original or that followed by the Hussite copyists before their renumbering? It is hard to see much. Neither order makes a single liturgical or chronological sequence, though sermons numbered here 13–20 can possibly be assigned to such a sequence between the Purification (2 February) and All Saints (1 November) 1383.[30] But sermon 11 must be dated Ash Wednesday 1383, and 12 is probably assignable to 30 November 1382.[31] Sermons 1–9 are harder to date, but there is nothing to contradict composition after Wyclif's retirement to Lutterworth.[32] It is hard, however, to understand with this group, perhaps even more than with the three larger sets, to whom Wyclif was addressing himself – more, since these sermons seem to be occasional sermons, with a specific congregation in view, rather than the preaching materials of the three long sets. Cross references are almost absent from the *Sermones Viginti*, and certainly offer no help in assessing the archaeology of this set.[33]

There are almost no references within any of the five groups of sermons to any of Wyclif's works outside the sermons themselves.[34] In this they fit in with the majority of works that the heresiarch wrote *after* his withdrawal from academic life. The earlier writings produce far more cross references from one work to another. From the earliest philosophical writings onwards, all of Wyclif's works apart from the purely occasional short piece contain considerable numbers of such specific directions. Perhaps the most extreme example is the *De civili dominio*: I would estimate that within the 1500-odd pages of its three books cross references of one kind or another occur on average every other page; some of these direct to discussion within other chapters of the same book, others to

Loserth's placing of it in vol.iv of his edition) at the end of set 3 (see cross reference at iv.6/29 to *sermone lix*, which is iii.518/10, T234).

[30] Thomson so dates 13–15 and 18; his assignment can be credibly expanded by the addition of the year 1383 for 17 (with its references to war, here the Despenser crusade), 19 (which, though it does not mention the crusade, speaks scathingly of friars and indulgences) and 20 (where the mention of fighting bishops must, *pace* Thomson, be taken as referring to the crusade). Thomson's occasion for 16 (Mass *de non Virginibus*) should be corrected to the feast of Mary Magdalen, 22 July; references to the crusade again make 1383 likely.

[31] The former was 4 February (Thomson's date is incorrect). Better reason for placing 12 as 1382 rather than 1383 is that Wyclif speaks of the issue of indulgences for the crusade, but seems to imply that the enterprise has not yet left England (see iv.117/32ff, 121/3ff).

[32] Thomson's dating of these sermons can be supplemented a little: no. 2 (T238) refers to the Earthquake Council of 1382 (iv.40/19), no. 5 (T241) to the indulgences connected with the Despenser crusade of 1383 (iv.62/26 and note the heading of this sermon in Prague University Library III.G.11 fol. 122ᵛ *Sermo optimus contra cruciatam*).

[33] The only instances are in sermons 3 (T239, iv.47/29) which seems to allude to two sermons in the first set (i.107/23 and i.210/24), and 9 (T245, iv.93/16) which declaredly refers to that set (i.272/21).

[34] T239, *Sermones Viginti* no. 3 (iv.46/9) refers to the *Trialogus*, T269, *Sermones Quadraginta* no. 13 (iv.300/34) to *in speciali tractatu istius materie*; C alone has a marginal reference to *Trialogus* book iv, cap.xxiii and xxiv beside the end of T179 (*Sermones* iii.27/29).

chapters in another book of the same work, others to different works by Wyclif.[35] Here and in other writings the fact that some of the references are incomplete, with the vital chapter number omitted, might suggest that they started as scribal additions. But the Wyclif Society variants, much supplemented by my collation of manuscripts that the Society's editors did not use, suggest that, whether original or scribal, almost every one must have been part of the hyparchetype that lies behind the transmission of all surviving manuscripts of every text.[36]

To the hyparchetype or to the author? – this is, of course, the most interesting question. At the present state of the investigation only a tentative answer can be given. There seems clear indication in the philosophical and theological works that Wyclif himself intended to facilitate reference from one of his writings to another; the relative paucity of *forward* references point to author and not editor. It seems that in the first three sets of his sermons Wyclif himself continued the method of his academic prime, and included the cross references. But the textual situation in the *Sermones XL* and *Sermones XX* suggest a rather different scenario. Here it seems most likely that an editor put together the two groups, picking up those sermons that had not been reworked by Wyclif himself into the first three sets and assigning them to two sequences according to their date of origin, early or late. The editor was sufficiently familiar with Wyclif's own habits of working to adopt, particularly in the *Sermones XL*, the system of cross-referencing his master had favoured, but without the time or perhaps inclination to engage on the rewriting necessary to eliminate the contradictions of the verbal allusions. Presentation of the output of the heresiarch in coherent groupings such as these two sets of forty and of twenty sermons is reminiscent of other aspects of activity shortly after Wyclif's departure from Oxford, the provision of summaries and indexes to the major writings.[37] It would be good to put a name to the editor of these sermons, and even better to locate his activities. But on those subjects cross references give no clue.

---

[35] *Johannis Wycliffe Tractatus de civili dominio*, ed. R. L. Poole and J. Loserth, Wyclif Society (London, 1885-1904); the edition was issued in four volumes, with the third book split between the last two.

[36] Full discussion of this evidence, together with a study of other aspects of the production of Wyclif's Latin works, will be presented elsewhere.

[37] For this see my brief summary in *The Premature Reformation* (Oxford, 1988), pp. 103-6, and references there given.

A HIVE OF INDUSTRY OR A HORNETS' NEST?
MS SIDNEY SUSSEX 74 AND ITS SCRIBES

Alan J. Fletcher

Cambridge, Sidney Sussex College, MS 74, a parchment manuscript produced professionally, though not sumptuously, *c*. 1400, is of singular interest for students of Lollard texts and history.[1] Not only is this for reasons already established: the first item it contains is a series of Sunday epistle sermons, beginning at Whitsun, that uniquely recruit the gospel sermons of the English Wycliffite cycle for their prothemes, and then follow these with epistle and pastoral commentary owing nothing to the English Wycliffite epistle series. This much is well known. Less well attended to is the fact that the content of the epistle and pastoral commentary can sometimes be strangely uneven. Although it would appear that one guiding mind may be responsible for piecing this commentary together out of various sources, it may nevertheless accommodate outspoken heresy on the one hand, as when in one sermon confession to a priest is disparaged, and on the other faultless orthodoxy, when in another sermon confession to a priest is positively recommended.[2] The reasons for this apparent

---

[1] It is described in A. Hudson (ed.), *English Wycliffite Sermons*, vol. i (Oxford, 1983), pp. 70–2. However, the following corrections should be entered. First, 175mm is a more accurate measurement of folio width than 165mm. Second, without stripping down the binding, it seems impossible to verify Hudson's collation of quires 3 and 4, but in any case, contrary to her assertion, no d signature is visible on fol. 26 whatsoever, even under ultraviolet light. This folio is therefore more likely to be the last leaf of quire 3, originally a quire of 12 but now wanting 2 before 1 and 3 after 6. Quire 4, if the lost medieval foliation in the gap between fols. 26 and 29 was accurate, originally had three foliated leaves; either fol. 29 was a singleton incorporated to complete a bifolium quire which comprised the now missing fols. 27 and 28, or a blank, unfoliated final leaf followed fol. 29, in which case quire 4 would originally have been of 4, with fol. 29 as its third folio. The addition of fol. 29 as a singleton may be more likely (and compare the now missing singleton, fol. 72, which must once have stood between quires 8 and 9). Hudson assumes misnumbering in quire 4, but this is an assumption that necessarily follows a prior assumption about the quantity of text that was originally copied. Third, the analysis of scribal stints needs revision, for which see below. Fourth, the personal name added in a sixteenth-century hand on fol. 180ᵛ is Henry Boyden, not Henry ?Boyner.

[2] Compare Sidney Sussex 74 (henceforth referred to as S in the notes), fol. 130ᵛ: 'wel Y fynde þat he [St Peter] wepte bitturly þerfore; hise teres Y rede, bote not his schrift to a prest. And þus sorwe of monnes herte doþ awey his synne whit forȝeuenesse of God þat knoweþ þat sorwe' ʿthe quotation is tendentiously retailing St Ambrose), with S, fol. 88ʳ: 'Trewe confession oweþ to be hasty, naked and hool, whit hertely forþinkynge, whit good auysement and whit ful purpose neuer more for to synne, bote schamed þerof, whit meke schewyng to a prest of good lyf þat con boþe leuse and bynde'. However, the apparent discrepancy here is perhaps a symptom of infighting within the sect over an issue on which, as on various others, it had reached no collective agreement. There are other sermons in which allusion to confession sounds quite conservative (see fol. 17ʳ: 'foly drede' or 'proude schome' is a branch of the sin of pride, whereby a man fears to worship God 'in schryuyng and in penaunce'; and fol. 41ᵛ: fornication may be purged only by 'sore forthynkyng, schryfte of

vacillation are not my immediate concern; they are best left to an extended study of these curious epistle sermons.[3] What I take to be of interest here is the element of latitude, however small, for I find it to be proleptic of a wider contradiction within the content of the manuscript as a whole, and also of one which crystalizes once we start to realize what are the sister manuscripts with which Sidney Sussex 74 affiliates. How, then, should the entire manuscript be characterized? After all, there is more to it than its first item. And how should it be located in the larger field of early Lollard texts? As is often the case, questions are liable to outstrip answers, but I hope to suggest what a few of those answers may be, even if they result merely in broaching new questions.

Particularly significant, yet hitherto unnoticed, is the existence of a set of scribal affiliations between Sidney Sussex 74 and certain other manuscripts. These affiliations may throw a little light on the questions posed earlier, and on the circumstances in which the written dissemination of radical theology could occur at a particularly sensitive moment of history. We have only to recollect that this manuscript was written around the time when the Act was passed to institute death by burning for convicted heretics to remind ourselves of that.

Whatever the theological complexion of the compiler of item 1, the Sunday epistle sermon series, is there anything to be said about the persuasions of the scribes who came to copy his work, and who must have done so in fact not long after its completion?[4] Moreover, how heterodox is Sidney Sussex 74 as a

---

mouthe, and fulle wylle neuer to sun[n]e more'). For a possible explanation of apparent discrepancies, see note 3 below.

[3] Hudson (ed.), *Sermons*, i.123, provisionally characterizes the compiler as 'a Lollard sympathizer, though not on the extreme wing of the movement'. The best account of the compiler is H. L. Spencer, 'The Fortunes of a Lollard Sermon-Cycle in the Later Fifteenth Century', *Mediæval Studies*, 48 (1986): 352–96; whether the implicit reconciliation here, pp. 380–1, of the discrepancy on confession, discussed above in note 2, is not in fact syncretistic is not clear. Further study of the compiler might explore whether a faint impression of theological unevenness, which seems to characterize the epistle and pastoral commentary generally, may not arise from differing theological sympathies in the original sources that he used. That he had access to other Lollard texts apart from the English Wycliffite cycle is clear: possibly the text *Of Antecrist and his Meynee* (Dublin, Trinity College, MS 245, fols. 117^r–24^r; relevant passages for comparison begin on fol. 118^v) may either be the inspiration behind, or the much condensed and re-worked source of, the fierce passage against abuses in the Church found in S, fol. 128^r–128^v. Also, it is possible that the compiler drew on a heterodox Decalogue commentary (see Spencer, 'Fortunes', p. 371). Some of his source material was confessionally neutral, however, as for example the tract on the three estates distributed over the Trinity 21 and 22 sermons, both imperfect. The use of the tract in the related sermon series in Oxford, Bodleian Library, MS Bodley 95 was pointed out by A. J. Fletcher, 'The Design of the N-Town Play of Mary's Conception', *Modern Philology*, 79 (1981): 166–73; see p. 170, n. 24; and its use in S by Hudson (ed.), *Sermons*, i.122). May other source material originally have been orthodox, and its orthodoxy not fully processed out? Note in this regard the sermons between fols. 3^r–47^v, whose commentary sections draw serially on what may once have been a treatise on the Seven Deadly Sins and their branches, which are not particularly extreme. Nor is there much infusion of characteristic sect vocabulary in these sections (occurrence of 'God's law' is perhaps the most suspect, and that only four times, on fols. 26^v, 31^r, 34^v and 44^v). Furthermore, their theology seems conservative (simoniacal sacrament selling, not the sacramental system, is impugned, though admittedly conservative heterodoxy could also focus on this, fol. 3; pilgrimage is implicitly endorsed, fol. 14^v; Christ feeds christians with his flesh and blood, fol. 37^r; and oral confession is necessary, though see note 2 above).

[4] The compilation must postdate the English Wycliffite cycle, which may have been composed *c.* 1390 (see Hudson [ed.], *Sermons*, i.201), and antedate the manuscript itself (s. xiv/xv).

collection generally, and what sort of readership does it seem to address? It has been said that manuscripts of the Wycliffite sermon cycle were produced for, if not necessarily by, Wycliffites.[5] Yet were this also the case of Sidney Sussex 74, then we would necessarily have to conclude that its putative Lollard audience was not quite in the first bloom of ideological purity, if indeed there ever were such a thing, and for reasons that ramify provocatively once we also take its scribal affiliations into account.

Before these are examined, however, the question of what scribes are at work in it needs close attention. Anne Hudson's is the most explicit recent investigation of its scribes, and at the end of her discussion she is uncertain about how many were involved.[6] She distinguishes a possible four hands in the manuscript, but finally collapses her distinctions with the disclaimer that these may all be 'variations in the hand of a single scribe'.[7] I think, however, that we can afford to be a little less diffident: Sidney Sussex 74 is more likely to be the work of at least three principal scribes, with the brief appearance of a possible fourth (although just conceivably, this hand is a variant of the hand of scribe C identified in the table below).[8] On the basis of a comparison of letter formation and duct, two scribes, A and B, can be confidently considered to be responsible for copying the bulk of the manuscript. Both A and B produce varieties of Anglicana Formata, with some influence from Secretary, and hence both may superficially appear similar.[9] On closer inspection, scribal habits can be discerned which effectively differentiate each hand from the other. The palographical discrimination between A and B offered here is based on a comparison of eighteen letter forms which tend to vary in small but significantly consistent detail according to which scribe is writing.[10] We can broadly characterize the net effect of these differences by saying that the appearance of

[5] Hudson (ed.), *Sermons*, i.196.

[6] A more recent, if briefer, analysis of hands is in A. McIntosh, M. L. Samuels and M. Benskin (eds.), *A Linguistic Atlas of Late Mediæval English* (Aberdeen, 1986). See *Atlas*, i.64–5. The analysis given here accords more with that of the *Atlas*.

[7] Hudson (ed.), *Sermons*, i.72.

[8] Two reasons favour identification of ?D as a distinct scribe. There are palæographical contrasts with C (for example, the addition of a hairline stroke to the 2-shaped **r**, which is not present in C; compare Plate 2b, line 12, corde with plate 2a, line 5, þerwit), and linguistic ones (for example, ?D spells shall/should with an sh-, not an sch- as does C; ?D spells þe whiche, as opposed to þe wiche [and variants] in C; etc.). The linguistic profile of C is given in *Atlas*, iii.367–8, LP 705. But both the palæographical and linguistic contrasts are small.

[9] Palæographical terms follow M. B. Parkes, *English Cursive Book Hands 1250–1500*, rpt. with minor revisions (London, 1979).

[10] These are: **a** (A tends to tick the tail of the **a** more noticeably than B); **b** (in A the downstroke on the **b** ascender has a more rounded and downward curve than in B, where it projects out at a wider angle to the ascender); **d** (in A it has a more rounded back than in B, where this is more upright and its top flatter; also, a **d** variant in B doubles back the stem more noticeably than does the comparable variant in A); **e** (the splay of the **e** lobe in B is much wider than in A, where it also occasionally may feature an otiose flourish in word final position); **f** (A tends more noticeably than B to extend the cross stroke each side of the letter shaft, and the head of the **f** in B tends to project out at a wider angle to the shaft); **g** (in A the right of the under lobe normally never joins the body of the upper lobe); **h** (in B the head of the **h** tends to project out at a wider angle than in A, where it often curves back towards the ascender; also, in A the **h** descender swings more prominently beneath the letter towards the left); **I/J** (in B, upper case **I/J** tends to feature a distinctive approach stroke not found in A); **k** (in A, the head of the ascender tends to project beyond the lobe, while in B it falls before the lobe); **m, n, u/v** (their minim feet have more pronounced ticks in A than in B); **Q** (in A the lobe of

proue þis false or aȝeynes goddes lawe þat I haue sayde nowe
here · I wole reuoke hyt mekely · but wel I marke þat þis
gospel sayth þat god ȝaf suche power to men but þis gospel sayth not þat god ȝafe þysse power to men & þfore
preye we Jhū crist of helpe And grace to vnderstonde þe
holy sentence of hys lawe to fulfille it in oure lyfe &
So to come to heuene blysse & c̄ · Loquimini veritatem vnus
quisq̄ cū proximo suo · v̄ ḡ · Speke ȝe treuthe veche con wyth
hys broþ ¶ Bycause þat trewe speche & grace maketh loue
among neyȝeburs & false speche & vnel speche maketh
also wrathþe & moste of alle monnes lymes þe tunge mi-
keth loue or wrathþe & þfore tat þat we speke to goode
non or to ynel · we schulden be war what we speke and
byfore kepe oure tunge & þfore sayde þe prophete in þe same
boke · Posui ori meo custodiam cū consistet pðr ad mē i me
I putted keppyng to my mouthe when þe synful schulde in-
stonde me · but when auȝ schal speke loke he speke þe
treuthe · but ȝet nē neden not alle tyme forto telle þe tru-
the · ffor þe as hyt myȝte do harme & þfyte vnto noone or
elles þe as it myȝte do more harme þen gode þe vs awe to
be war & holde oure tunge stylle · & when þat þou may þle-
se god & þfyte wt þi speche · þenne owe ȝe not to helde þe
stylle · but sayth forthe þe treuthe · for if þou holde þe stylle & wilt not speke þe treuthe for to helpe þin neyȝebure
when þat he hath nede ffor ryȝte or for preyer for drede or for
fleschely loue · for wrathþe or for hate þat þou haste vn to hym
þou consentest to þat wronge · þat me þi neyȝebure done
·inuesse more þenne synneth he þat spekeþ falsely i wyte
nesse or inqueste hys neyȝebure to harme wyth lesynges or
wt lyes & oþ false wordes · for þe lawe sayth / Qui tacet
consentire videt / & also sayth Seynt Jule þnle ynis in hys
Epystle / Qui talia agūt digni sūt morte · nō solū q̄ ū fa-
ciūt ea s̄ eciā q̄ ū consentiunt facientibz / þat is he þat
holdeth hym stylle consenteth to þe dede · and onely þey þt
done suche thynges ben wurþi þe deth · but also þey þat
consenten to hem þat done þese dedes & þfore speke ȝe
þe treuþe · Whenne þat it may þfyte & drede more god of

heuene þen any erþly þing & þey war eñ wt ȝoure speche
þt it nys paye not god Bote stoke ȝe vefe on treuþe wt
his neyȝbore for dauid þe p̄phet askeþ of god almyȝthe
wñe gs hit° & c° Lord who schal dwelle i þi dwellyng pla
ce or lord who schal reste in þin holy hul/ þat is for to
saye i þe blisse of heuene And god onswereþ þeyn by þe
same p̄phete & suþ he þat entreþ wt outen fulþer & wiþ
cher riȝtwisnesse he þt spekeþ treuþe i his herte & he þt
dyde not dysseyt wt his tunge ny aȝeyn his neyȝbore
dyde no wykednesse ny aȝey his neyȝbore took no vi
lenye þe wykede spirit in his siȝt is broȝt vnto noȝt
onely god glorifieþ hem þt dreden by he þt sweteȝ
to his neiȝbore & desteyneþ hym not & he þt ȝaf not
his good vnto vsiure & he þt tok not ȝifte on þe innocet
Iñ þise sixe vers is muche witt schewed & namely hou
þt mon schal haue hym to his neyȝbore Bote for to
declare þis noȝ þe tyme is to schorte Bote y schal her
aftr ȝef god wul ȝeue me grace & noȝ wul y tellen
ȝou forþ þe furste comaundemet of þe loue of god as y seu
de on sonenday Loue is likened vnto fuyr for þynde
þat hit haþ as we rede on whitsonenday iþe churche
¶ Aduenit ignis diuini ñ cõbuies ß illuminac
& ffuyr ȝeneþ his hete on foure ptes comunely Aluer
Buſteþ comuly þe fuyr brenneþ vpward & aftr þat hit
brenneþ hoot on euer ptie & leste of alle pties is þe he
te souþward/ þus schulde oure loue be reulyd i þis
world/ moste brennyg of alle oure loue schulde be to god
for he kyndeleþ i oure soule/ þe coles of his loue wt þe
blast of his loue breth Houeynge on þe croc whene he
arede for oure loue øbuinac & Aftr schulde oure loue
be hoot to oure frendes & loue he as þu doid vs as cristi
taiȝte his apostelis sayng/ hoc & p̄ceptu meū þis is
my comaundemet þt ȝe loue to ȝesdur þe toþr loue al
so schulde be hoot to oure enemyes/to loue he for go
sesake as he bradey ȝou so aþt vto Dico vo vost Dileg̃ inim
te inncoe vñs & Bifuiate þis q' voz oderuᵗ liy oure s
þely to ȝou Loue ȝe ȝoure enemyes & Dop wel im to he
þe wucke haþ ȝou hated for alle maner men & wynne

Item siknes ofte to agaste oþer men left þey foloweden hey
synnes. As þe sikenes of antiochie whom god smote with
suche a sikenesse þat wormes startiden oute of his body
while he leued in so feyfory þat he stanke so foule þat alle
his weyene heny þei with and myzt nouzt acorden þer wyth
And at last þat he ne myzt nouze hym self suffre his
owene stenche. And þan he gan to knowe hym self and
said it is to be ytfille ouzette to god. And a deeth hum
nouzt to hole hym self euene to god. and ye euery say
þat he axid mich of god of whom he schulde no haue. and
made avowe to god þat he schuld make ye citee of ierlm
fiee. And ye ielkes to make hem also fiees as men of athe
ins and þat he wold hous goddis temple with precious
aray. and multiply ye holy vessellis and fynde of his
owene ierte coste and spenas preymynge to ye sac
fiees. And he wolde by come a iew And goo one al the
londe and preche goddis myzt. And god zit zaf hym no rid
as he desyredey. And I trow certayne þat was, for he axid it to litte.
What nede was it to hym to forsake his wickednesse
whan he was ynnunzty to done gode oþer ille, and by
this vengeaunce þat god toke of yis kynge schulde
me see what it es to bee ynobedient to god. and also it
es to take hede þat whennes so euere it otheskit þat he
suffrit it es feskly. and þat he schalle nede deye. for þou
he may skape his sikenesse art may he nost skape dey
and so þꝰ most nedis come to þm iekeynge ¶ ye secounde
synnony þat schal clepe ye to þis partunke, doþ is olde
and ye condicion of þis is this þat þou he tarry with ye
he wole nouzt tene ye til he bryng ye to ye thyrd þat is
deey. but þer beey many þat þou þei haue þis synne whi
hem þer takey none hede. he seey his heed hory. his bak
cokit. his bretthe stynky his teer falliy his eyen sizty.
his vissage ienelit hys eiene wext heny to heyp. What
meney al this. but þat elde synny to ye dome. but what
more madнes may be þan Almit be clepeð and deaffe to þ
þes fulle þiekenyng þeie. but he milwey wette he for
fetiy boye body and owule so dampnacion for eneye. if he
seyng aftrello ineрthe on the wey he penkiy so myzit þei
on þat he forzetiy. Who diskiy hym or wiþдy he schаtt

neuerþeleſſe I trowe he was not damagd in as muche he had ſuch
ſuch repentauns. for repentauns in þis lyfe cometh neuer to late if it be
true, but

so doþ he þat is smyten with age and liþy so on þe false þeef
his welthe · þat he forgetiþ whidir he is awey · her fore say
and holy doctours þat among alle abusions of the world
most is of an olde man þat is obstynate · for he penkiþ nouȝt
on his owne goyngis of this ne of his passynge into þe liff
þat is to come · he heriþ messangeris of deeþ · and he leueþ
hem nouȝt · and þe cause is this for the yresolde corde þat
suche a nolde man is bounden with is harde to breke · þis
corde is custom þat of thei þaties þat is of idelle poynte · In
honest speche · And þinkes þe . þe þynche ȝif they growiþ
a man from þe childehod into mannys age yei makiþ a
treble corde to bynde þe olde man on custume of synne · hei
fore say ysaye breke þe bondis of synne · yeui herfore who so
euere þat þt be þat art þus comed þat þt myȝt nouȝt skape
þat þu ne schalt ȝelde þe rekenynge of þi bailie · The þird
de sinony to þis rekenynge is deeþ · and þe condicion of þis
is þis þat whanne euere he come fist ouer þe secunde or þe
þe laste · he ne spareþ neyþer pouere ne ȝonge ne he dredeþ no
þretenyng · ne he ne takeþ hede of no praiere ne of no ȝifte
ne he grauteþ no respyt · but þuy oizen delay he bryngeþ forþ to
þe dome · herfore say seynt austyn wel auȝte euery man dre
de þe day of his deeþ · for in what staat so euere a mannys
laste day fyndeþ hym whan he goþ out of þis weild · on þe
same staat he bryngeþ hym to his dom · herfore say þe wise
some penk on þi laste day and þu schalt neuere synne · herfore
y rede penk þat þt schalt ȝelde þe rekenynge of þi bailie · J
seide al so þat yeie schulde be anoyer dom to þe whiche alle
men schulden come to gedre · and þis schal ben comyneual · and
þat as to þat oþer dom euery man schal be clepid þuy þise
þree comunys · so to þis dom al þe weild schal be clepid þuy
þise general clepyngis · And þat as þe oþere þree messager
a mannys ende · so þise telliþ þe ende of þe weild · þe fyste is
þe weildis sikness · þe secunde is febilness · and þe þridde is
his ende and his · The sikness of þe weild þt schalt
knowbe by charites acoldynge · his elde and his febilnesse þu
schalt knowbe by tokenes fulfillynge · and his ende þu schalt
knowbe by anticristis þsprynge · fist y sere þt schalt knowbe
þe weildis sikness by charites acoldynge · deþis þat þeny
of þyndis sery þat a body is sik whanne his kyndely hete

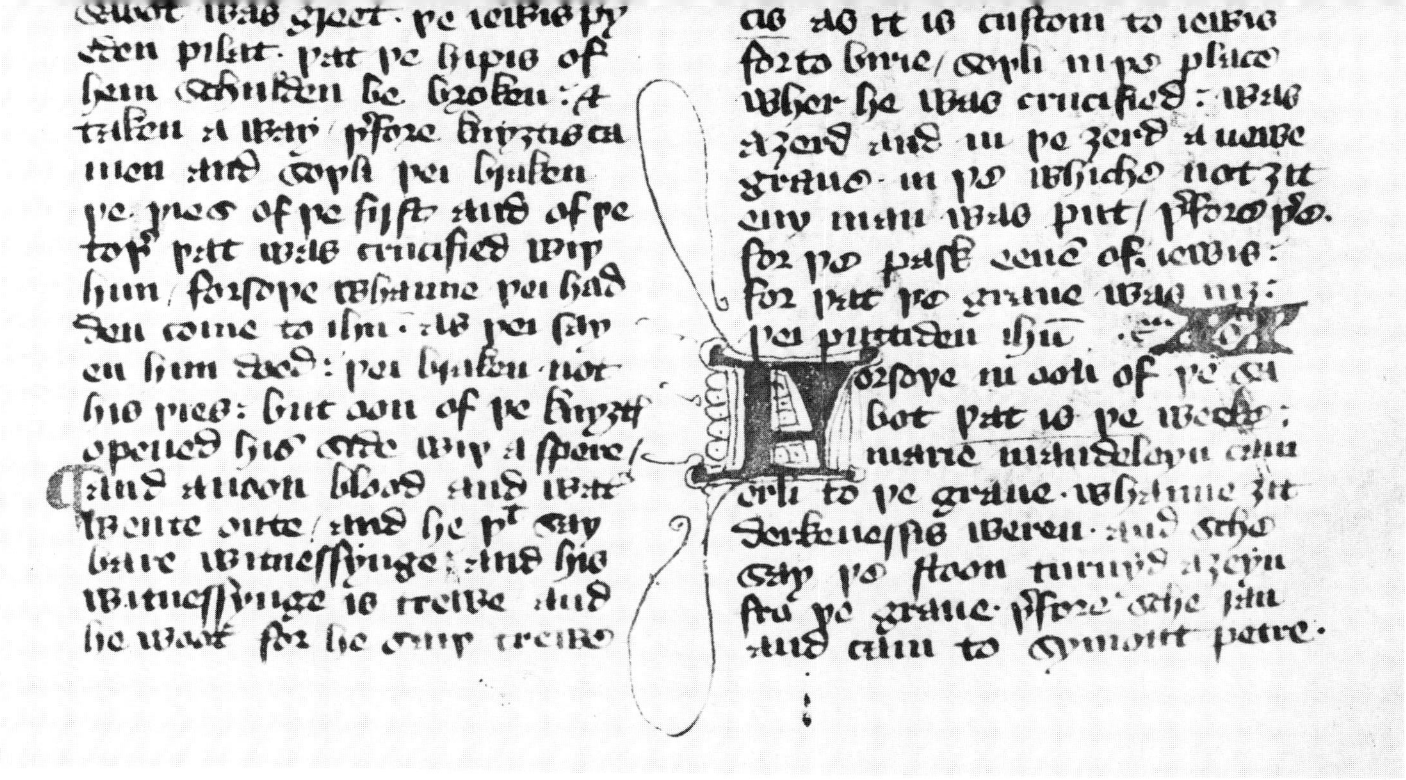

Plate 3   Dublin, Trinity College, MS 74, fol. 94ʳ

penie of þe money & þei offred
to hym a peny & þhe seiþ to hem
whos is þis ymage & þe writ
yng aboue þei seie to hym
Of cesar þene he seiþ to hem
þerfore ȝelde ȝe to cesar þo þin
ges þat ben cesares & to god
þo þinges þat ben of god And
þei heryng wondreden & lefte
hym þei wente awey In þat
day Saduceis þat seien þer is
no risyng aȝen come nyȝ to
hym & askeden hym sayinge
maister moyses seide ȝef any
mon be ded hauyng a do
ne þat his broþer wedde his
wyf & reyse seed to his broþ
þerfore Seuene breþeren were
ren at vs & þe furste a wif
weddid is ded & he not hauyng
seed lefte his wif to his bro
þer Also þe secounde & þe prid
te til to þe Seuene þerfore
þe laste of alle & þe woman is
ded þerfore in þe risyng aȝen
whos wif of Seuene schal
sche be for alle hadden hire
Sopely þe onswerynge seiþ to
hem ȝe erre neiþer knowyng
þe scriptures neiþ þe vertu of
god for in þe risyng aȝein
neiþ þei wedde neiþ ben wed
did bote þei ben as angeles of
god in heue Sopely of þe risyng
aȝein of dede men ȝe han not
red þt is i seid of þe lord sayin
ge to ȝow I am god of abraham
& god of ysaac & god of iacob
he is not god of dede men bote
of lyuyng men And þe aspyin
ges of pepul seyyng wondrede
i his techyng Forsoþe pha
riseis heryng þat he hadde put
silence to Saduceis comen

to gedir in to on & on of he
a techer of þe lawe askedeis
temptyng hym maistir whi
che is a gret comaundement
i þe lawe ihc seide to him þou
schalt loue þe lord þi god of
al þin herte & in al þi soule
& in al þi mynde þis is þe
furste & þe moste comaundemet
forsoþe þe secounde is lik to þis
þou schalt loue þi neȝebore
as þi self In þese two maunde
mentes hongeþ al þe lawe &
prophetes Sopely þe phariseis
gederid to gedir ihc askede
hem sayinge what semeth
to ȝow of crist whos sone is
he þei seien to him Of dauiþ
ihc seiþ to he þerfore hou i spirit
cleper Dauiþ him lord sayinge
þe lord seide to my lord sitte on
my riȝt half til þat i putte
þine enemyes a fool of þi feet
þerfore ȝef dauiþ cleper him lord
hou is he his sone & no man
myȝte ouswere a word to him
ne any man was hardy fro
þat day to asken him more

Þene ihc spak VIII
to þe companyes of pepul
& to his disciples sayin
ge vpon þe cheier of moyses
scribes & phariseis seten prof
kepe ȝe & do ȝe alle þinges whit
euer þei schulle seie to ȝow soþe
nyl ȝe do aftir soure werkes
Sopely þei seien & don not Sope
ly þei bynde to greuouse char
ges & vnportible or þt mowe
not be boren & putte into þe
schuldres of men bote wiþ þn
ue fyngre þei wol not meuen
hem þerfore þei don alle þinge

Plate 4   Dublin, Trinity College, MS 74 fols. 23ᵛ–24ʳ

werkes þat þei be seien of me
forsoþe þei alargen hire phi
lateries þat ben fimbrie of cloþer
& magnifien hire hemmes.
Soþely þei louen þe firste sit
tyng places in soperes & þe
firste chaieres in sinagogis
& salutacouns in þe chepyng &
to ben clepid of men maistres.
Soþely nyl ȝe be clepid maistr.
for on is ȝoure maister forsoþe
alle ȝe ben breþeren & nyl ȝe
clepe to ȝou a fadur on erþe.
for on is ȝoure fadur þat is in
heuenes neiþ be ȝe clepid mai
stres. for on is ȝoure maister
crist. he þat is more of ȝou
schal be ȝoure mynistre forso
þe he þat schal hiȝe hym self
schal be meekid & he þt schal
meeken hym self schal be en
hauncid. Soþely wo to ȝou
scaribes & phariseis ypocritꝰ
for ȝe closen þe kyngdam of he
uenes bifore men. soþely ȝe
entre not nyþ suffre men entre
ynge for to entre. Wo to ȝou
scaribes & phariseis ypocritꝰ
þat eeten þe housees of widue
wes in longe praier preiyng
for þis þing ȝe schule taken
þe more dom. Wo to ȝou scri
bis & phariseis ypocritꝰ þt
cumpasen þe see & þe lond. þat
ȝe make on proselite þt is on
turned to ȝoure ordre & whanne
he is schal be maad ȝe make
hym a sone of helle double mo
re þen ȝou. Wo to ȝou blynde
ledueres þat saien. whoeuer

schal swere by þe temple of
god no þing is. soþely he þat
schal swere in þe gold of þe tem
ple oweþ or is dettour. ȝe fooles
& blynde forsoþe wher is more
þe gold or þe temple. þt halewiþ
þe gold And who eu schal swere
in þe auter noþing is. bote he
þat schal swere by þe ȝift þat
is on þe aut oweþ. Blynde me
forsoþe what is more þe ȝift or
þe aut þt halewiþ þe ȝift. for
soþe he þat swereþ in þe auter.
swereþ in hit & in alle þingꝰ
þat ben vpon. And he þt swereþ
in þe temple swereþ in hit & in þt
þat dwelliþ in þe temple. & he
þat swereþ in heuene swereþ in
þe trone of god & in hym þat
sittiþ on it. Wo to ȝou scribes
& phariseis ypocritꝰ þt riȝt þat make
of þe cuppe & of þe plater þat clene
is wiþ outen forth. forsoþe wiþ
inne ȝe ben ful of rauenie &
vnclennesse þou blynde phari
se. clanse first þat þing of þe
cuppe & plater. þat is wiþt in ne
forþ þt & þat þing þt is wiþ ou
ten forþ be maad clene. Wo to
ȝou scribes & phariseis ypocritꝰ
þat ben lik to sepulcres maad
white. þe whiche wiþ oute forþ
semen faire to men. Soþely wiþ
inne þei ben ful of bones of de
de men & al filþe. So & ȝe forsoþe
wiþ oute forþ apperen iust to
men. bote wiþ inne ȝe ben ful
of ypocrisie & wickednesse. wo
to ȝou scribes & phariseis ypo
critꝰ. þt buylden sepulcres of
pfetes. & maken faire þe biriels
of iust men. & saien. ȝef we ha
den ben in þe daies of oure

Wo to ȝou scribes & phariseis ypocritꝰ þt tiþe mynte & anete & comyn &
han laft þo þingꝰ þt ben greuouser or of more charge of þe lawe. ꝥ do
axioun & feiþ. & þise þingꝰ it bihoueth for to do & not to leue
þe blynde ledueres & strainynge þe gnatte. bote swolowinge a camel

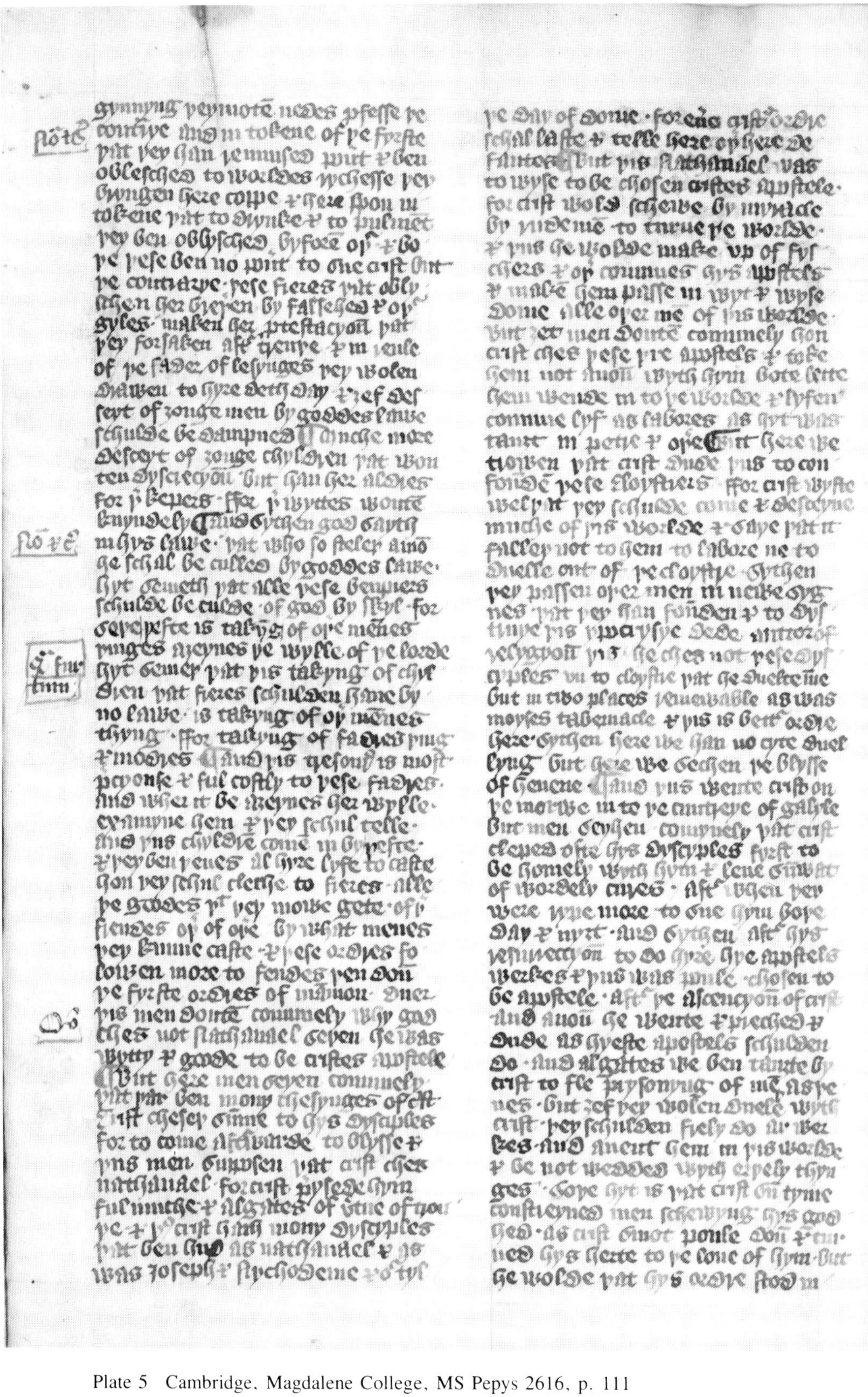

gynnyng þey mote nedes professe þe
contrarye þing in tokene of þe fyrste
þat þey han renuised wiþ & ben
oblesched to worldes rychesse þey
bryngen here coppe & here spon in
tokene þat to drynke & to puisnet
þey ben oblysched byfore oþer & bo
þe þese ben no þing to one crist but
þe contrarye. þese freres þat obly
schen her breþeren by falsehed & oþer
gyles maken her professyon þat
þey forsaken alle þinges & in rense
of þe fader of lesynges þey wolen
drawen to here deth day & ȝef des
sert of ȝonge men by goddes lawe
schulde be dampned myche more
desert of ȝonge children þat won
ten dyscrecyon but þan her elders
for þe leuers ffor þe wyttes wonte
kyndely. And syþen god sayth
in hys lawe. þat who so steleþ and
he schal be cursed by goddes lawe.
hyt semeth þat alle þese begyners
schulde be cursed of god by skyl. for
þeþefte is takyng of oþer mennes
þinges aȝeynes þe wylle of þe lorde
hyt semeþ þat þis takyng of chil
dren þat freres schulden haue by
no lawe is takyng of oþer mennes
þyng. ffor takyng of faders þing
& moders. And þis tresoun is most
peryouse & ful costly to þese faders.
And whan it be aȝeynes her wylle.
cyrnmyne hem & þey schul telle.
And þis chylde come in byleste.
& þey ben þeues al here lyfe to caste
hou þey schul clerke to freres alle
þe godes þat þey mowe gete of þ
frendes or of oþer by what menes
þey kunne caste & þese ordres fo
lowen more to fendes þen don
þe fyrste ordres of mankinde. Ouer
þis men donte commenly why god
chees not Mathie whan he was
wytty & goode to be cristes apostele
But here men seyen commenly
þat þer ben mony chesynges of crist
Crist chesiþ summe to hys dysciples
for to come afterwarde to blysse &
þus men supposen þat crist chees
Mathie. for crist pyseche hym
ful muche & algates of vertue of þou
þe & þat crist hadde mony dysciples
þat ben hyd as Mathie & as
was Joseph & Nychodeme & oþer

þe day of dome. for ech crist ordre
schal laste & telle here of here de
fautes. But þis Mathie was
to wyse to be chosen cristes apostele.
for crist wolde schewe by myracle
by nombre to true þe worlde.
& þus he wolde make up of hys
chees & oþer commnes hys apostels
& make hem þusse in wyt & wyse
dome alle oþer men of þis worlde.
But ȝet men donte commenly hou
crist chees þese þre apostels & toke
hem not anon wyth hym bote lette
hem wende in to þe worlde & syþen
commune lyf as labores as hyt was
tauȝt in petre & oþer But here we
trowen þat crist dude þis to con
founde þese cloysterers ffor crist wyste
wel þat þey schulde come & deceyue
muche of þis worlde & saye þat it
falleþ not to hem to labore ne to
dwelle out of þe cloystre syþen
þey passen oþer men in newe sygnes
nes þat þey han founden & to dys
tinge þis priuat syte dede autor of
relygyoun þus he chees not þese dys
cyples in to cloystre þat he dwelte ine
but in two places remevable as was
moyses tabernacle & þis is better ordre
here syþen here we han no cyte dwel
lyng but here we seken þe blysse
of heuene. And þus wente crist on
þe morwe in to þe cuntreye of galyle
But men seyen commenly þat crist
cleped ofte hys dyscyples fyrst to
be homely wyth hym & leue summe
of worldly cures. After when þey
were more to one hym hope
day & nyȝt. And syþen after hys
resureccyon to do here hye apostels
werkes & þus was Mathie chosen to
be apostele. After þe ascencyon of crist
And anon he wente & preched as
dude as þe fyfte apostels schulden
do. And algates we ben tauȝte by
crist to fle prysonyng of mannes per
nes. but ȝef þey wolen dwelle wyth
crist þey schulden frely do her wer
kes and ancrit hem in þis worlde
& be not wedded wyth erþely thyn
ges. Hope hyt is þat crist on tyme
confermed men schewyng hys god
hed. as crist smot poule don & tur
ned hys herte to þe loue of hym. But
he wolde þat hys ordre stod in

Plate 5 Cambridge, Magdalene College, MS Pepys 2616, p. 111

scribe B's work is far more angular than scribe A's. In A, two of these eighteen letter forms are especially interesting, because they provide a reliable quick check on which scribe is writing at any one time: two-compartment **g**, which in stints by scribe A consistently tends not to join its under lobe to the body of the upper lobe on the right hand side (see Plate 1b, line 4, dwelly*n*g), and **s**, which in word-final position is often formed quite idiosyncratically somewhat like a Greek epsilon (see Plate 1b, line 4, q*u*is).[11] The third scribe, C, distinct again from A and B, copies most of item 3, the sermon *Redde racionem villicacionis tue* of Thomas Wimbledon. His is a hand strikingly different from A and B, and is a good Anglicana variety of about the same date (see Plate 2a).[12] The scribal stints are set out in the table below.

Scribal stints	*Contents*
Scribe A, fols. 3r–18v	Sunday epistle sermons: from Whitsun to Trinity 6 [first sermon acephalous; excision of leaves in some others].
Scribe B, fol. 19r	Continuation of Trinity 6.
Scribe A, fols. 19v–29v	Remainder of Trinity 6 to Trinity 9 [excision of leaves in some sermons].
Scribe B, fols. 30r–54v	Trinity 10 to Trinity 19 [excision of leaves in some sermons].
Scribe A, fols. 54v–142v [A resumes half way through the penultimate line of fol. 54v.]	Trinity 19 to Sunday within the Ascension octave [excision of leaves in some sermons].
Scribe B, fols. 143r–66v [Fol. 167r–v blank.]	*Pater noster* of Richard Ermyte.
Scribe C, fols. 168r–76r	Thomas Wimbledon's sermon *Redde racionem villicacionis tue*.
Scribe ?D, fols. 176r–78v [?D resumes after C part way through line 11 of fol. 176r.]	Continuation of Wimbledon's sermon.
Scribe A, fol. 179r [Fol. 180r–v blank.]	Remainder of Wimbledon's sermon.
Scribe A, fols. 181r–91v	Decalogue treatise [fols. 181r–89v] and a commentary on the *Ave Maria* [fols. 189v–91v].

upper-case **Q** is circular, while in B it is either indented or angular); **r** (in B, 2-shaped **r** is not flourished with a hairline as in A); **s** (**s** in word final position in A is formed somewhat like a Greek epsilon); **þ** (A displays a certain tendency to tick the foot of the descender); **w** (in B this is much more angular than in A, which also uses about three **w** variants, as opposed to B's essentially consistent shape). The ampersand in A and B is distinctive in small ways, and B favours biting more than A.

[11] Only once, in the *Puer natus est nobis* sermon, does scribe A abandon this s for a more cursive and standard Anglicana variety; for an explanation of his altered practice, see note 14 below.

[12] Compare Parkes, *Book Hands*, plates 2 (i) and (ii).

Scribe A, fols. 191^{v}–92^{v}	Sermon on theme *Puer natus est nobis*.
Scribe B, fols. 194^{r}–204^{v}	Six sermons on respective themes: *Diliges Dominum Deum tuum* [fols. 194^{r}–96^{r}]; *Estote prudentes et vigilate in oracionibus* [fols. 196^{r}–98^{r}]; *Sana, Domine, animam meam, quia peccaui tibi* [fols. 198^{r}–200^{r}]; *Hodie oportet me in domo tua manere* [fols. 200^{r}–2^{r}]; *Mortuus viuet* [fols. 202^{r}–4^{r}]; *Christum sanctificate in cordibus vestris* [fol. 204^{r-v}, unfinished].
Scribe A, fols. 204^{v}–7^{v} [A resumes at line 34 of fol. 204^{v}].	Sermon on theme *Ememus panes* [atelous].

This analysis is also supported by linguistic evidence.[13]

It is clear that the manuscript is chiefly alternating between the stints of scribes A and B. This kind of alternation is a pattern commonly met with elsewhere, where it tends to characterize manuscripts that are in some measure planned, rather than those that are random assemblages of booklets. This is the first point, then, that can be made about Sidney Sussex 74, that in spite of the subsequent excision of many leaves, it originally had a certain integrity as a collection; it seems to have been a planned ensemble. I will return to the implications of this and of the manuscript's contents later. Another conclusion seems to be that scribe A is keeping an eye on the overall shaping of the compilation; he completed the stint of scribe C (the Wimbledon sermon) and probably added the sermon on fols. 191^{v}–92^{v} later in a spare space after the material that immediately precedes and follows it had already been copied up.[14] Furthermore, A, B, C and ?D appear to have been working in association.

Let us now turn to the first of the scribal affiliations which may help to locate this manuscript in a wider context of manuscript production. Dublin, Trinity College, MS 74 contains two items. The first is a brief list of gospel and epistle readings for the Commune and Proprium Sanctorum, followed by another brief

[13] The linguistic profiles of portions of S which the *Atlas* did not analyse can be shown to match portions which it did. Thus, fol. 179^{r} (the remainder of Wimbledon's sermon) matches the language of my scribe A elsewhere, just as fols. 194^{r}–204^{v} (six sermons on various themes) match the language of my scribe B elsewhere. The *Atlas* editors, possibly influenced by Hudson (ed.), *Sermons*, i.72, were not absolutely certain about whether my scribe A is palæographically distinct from B. They give a full linguistic profile of fols. 1(*recte* 3)–50, differentiating with the numerals 1 and 2 respectively forms characteristic of their ?A scribe from ones characteristic of their scribe B (*Atlas*. iii.550–1). It should be noted, however, that the language of fols. 194^{r}–204^{v}, an analysis of which they did not publish, in fact duplicates almost exactly the variant forms characteristic of their scribe B. Similarly, the language of this portion matches that of fols. 143^{r}–66^{v} (Richard Ermyte's *Pater noster*), a stint, in my view, also in the hand of B (though given as ?D in the *Atlas*).

[14] Hudson (ed.), *Sermons*, i.72, thinks that the sermon on fols. 191^{v}–92^{v} is in a hand found nowhere else in the manuscript. Telling against this is the fact that its language corresponds to that of scribe A, as the *Atlas*, i.64, notes, as well as the fact that almost all the salient A features, apart from the idiosyncratic s, appear in it. The absence of the s is explained as a result of the haste with which this text, added in a spare space, was copied up; it suited scribe A to use one of his other, more cursive Anglicana s graphs here.

list of similar readings for the Temporale (some ferials are included). The second item, the bulk of the manuscript, is a Wycliffite New Testament, Later Version.[15] It is copied by four scribes, whose work is distributed as follows (*corr.* in some entries indicates evidence of Scribe A's correction):

Scribal stint	*Contents*
Scribe A, fols. 1r–6v	Gospel and epistle readings for the *Commune* and *Proprium Sanctorum*, followed by similar readings for the *Temporale* (some ferials included).
Scribe A, fols. 8ra–30ra	Matthew's gospel, followed by the opening of Mark's gospel.
Scribe B, fols. 30rb–96ra	Remainder of Mark's gospel [fols. 30rb–44vb; *corr.*]; Luke's gospel [fols. 45rb–73rb; *corr.*]; John's gospel [fols. 73vb–96ra; *corr.*].
Scribe C, fols. 97ra–108rb	Rom [fols. 97ra–106ra; *corr.*]; I Cor [fols. 106ra–08rb; *corr.*].
Scribe A, fols. 109ra–30vb	Remainder of I Cor [fols. 109ra–15va]; II Cor [fols. 115vb–21vb]; Gal [fols. 121vb–25ra]; Eph [fols. 125ra–28ra]; Phil [fols. 128ra–30rb]; Col [fol. 130rb–vb].
Scribe D, fols. 131ra–48vb	Remainder of Col [fols. 131ra–32rb]; I Thess [fols. 132rb–34ra]; II Thess [fols. 134rb–35rb]; I Tim [fols. 135rb–37vb]; II Tim [fols. 137vb–39va]; Tit [fols. 139va–40va]; Philem [fols. 140va–41ra]; Heb [fols. 141ra–48ra]; Prologue to Jas [fol. 148va–rb].
Scribe B, fols. 149ra–206rb	Prologue to Jas repeated [fol. 149ra–rb]; Jas [fols. 149va–52rb]; I Pet [fols. 152va–55rb; *corr.*]; II Pet [fols. 155rb–57rb]; I Jn [fols. 157rb–60va; *corr.*]; II Jn [fols. 160va–61ra]; III Jn [fols. 161rb–va]; Jude [fols. 161va–62va]; Acts [fols. 163ra–92rb; *corr.*]; Rev [fols. 192va–206rb; *corr.*].

Though most of this manuscript is written by scribe B, it is clear from the many corrections entered in scribe A's hand that the latter had a superintending role (see Plate 3, where in column a, lines 1–12, scribe A enters a palimpsest correction to a stint by B); like scribe A of Sidney Sussex 74, scribe A of Dublin, Trinity College, MS 74 too has kept an eye on the overall compilation of the manuscript. Moreover, there is little doubt but that both scribes are one and the

---

[15] The New Testament is complete, though Acts are located before Revelation.

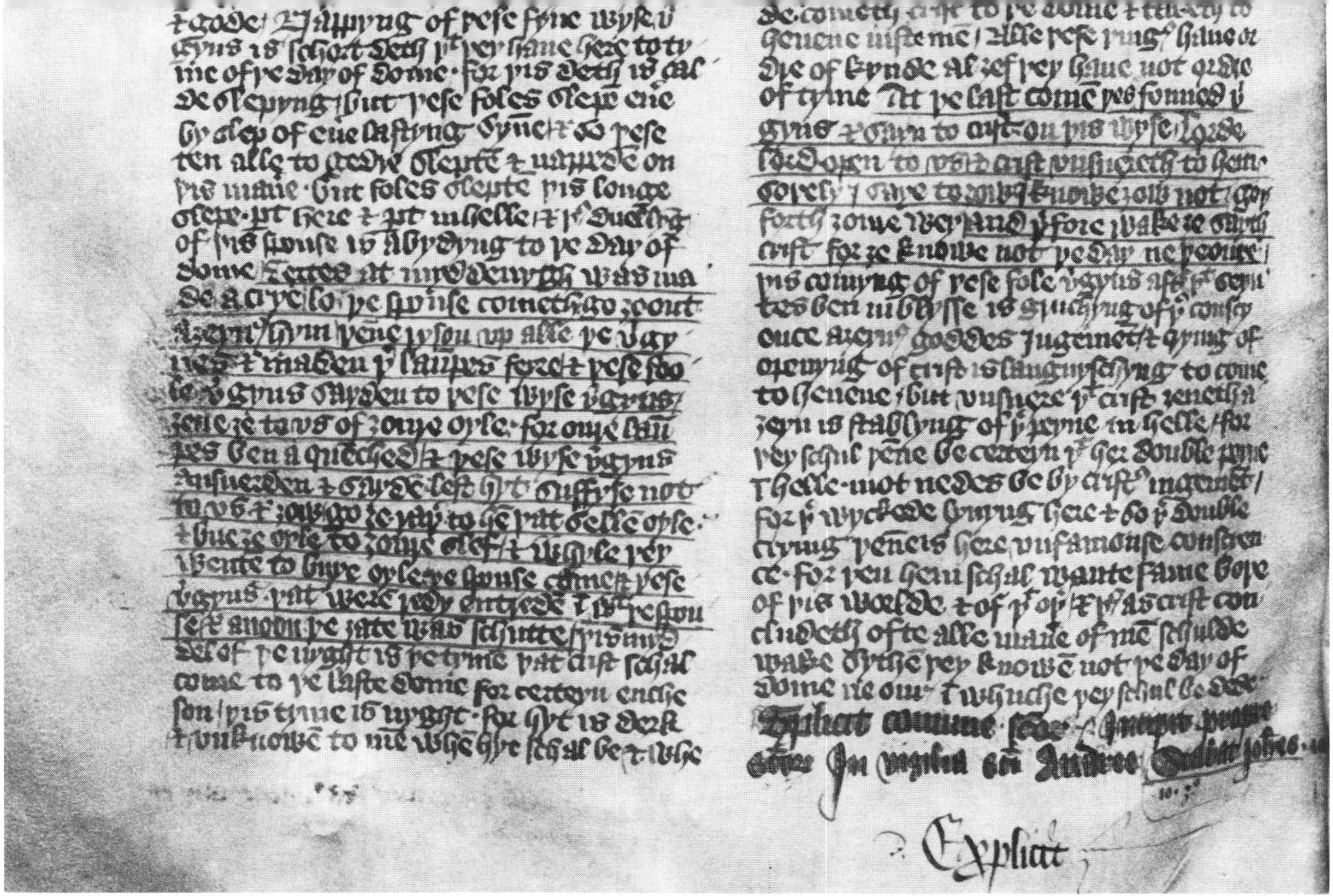

Plate 6 Wisbech and Fenland Museum. MS 8. fol. 87ʳ

pre zeer sch co seide ẏ offrede to
non oper ping bote my self to
herye god do he wt his sacri
fice what hym self likep/ for
pene you schalt not grustche
what so euer he do wt his on
ne ping / þ bote you parte ine
wille sory penke i to be þ glad
zef you do for what day you
hast pie wille pon hast pe
blessyng pat crist zeuep to pe
poure i spirit þ pe kyndam
of hene is pin And sope book
is lerned bonzt þ sold for pou
hast bonzt crist wt forsaking
pinte and you art maad a
plime of cristes religion pat
holy writt spekep of þ sey
pat per was a multitude pt
leuede i crist per abbot of oo

7a

Plate 7   London, British Library, MS Egerton 826, fols. 20ᵛ–21ʳ

herte ⁊ oo soule· And þis is þe
bettur· þen for to haue þe man
tel ⁊ þe ryng· þe wympul ⁊ þe
veyl· whit þurte for crist lo
neþ no þurte· ⁊ so crist ⁊ þei
hau not oon herte ⁊ oo soule
⁊ þis was openly schewed whã
ne petre awsude ananye ⁊
saphire his wyf· for þei haden
þurte ⁊ gret multitude is
now· of þis secte sane hem lak-
keþ oon herte ⁊ oo soule· And
alle suche þou þei euer semē
to hem self oþer to foles· þat
demen aftur hire wittes not
aftur resou· tofore god þei bē
apostataes· of þe wrreligiou
of þe grete ãticrist· þat is
luafer· þat wolde haue had
þurte i heuene bote seynt

7b

same, as a comparison of the stint of scribe A in Plate 1b with Plate 4 should demonstrate.[16] So here, then, is the first of the manuscript affiliations to be established: Sidney Sussex 74 associates, through its scribe A, with a copy of the vernacular New Testament. Such an affiliation might seem natural to anyone eager to appropriate to the heterodox cause Sidney Sussex 74; a connection between it and *scriptura sola* would seem in this regard entirely apt, whatever approval or hostility attended English translations of the Scriptures before 1407, the year in which Archbishop Arundel's Constitutions settled that issue decisively.[17] Was scribe A, then, who was evidently a practised fellow capable of assuming responsibility in the scriptorium in which he worked, himself a Lollard or a Lollard sympathiser, and to put the question raised earlier again, what about those for whom he was writing his manuscripts? Scribe A will be revisited later, and answers deferred till then.

Scribe B of Sidney Sussex 74, who had a share in copying the Sunday epistle sermon series with scribe A, also worked on items 2 (the *Pater noster* of Richard Ermyte) and 6 (a set of sermons on various themes). How heterodox was scribe B? If we were to judge by what he was prepared to copy, we would have to conclude not very, or at least, not very consistently. Let us look at item 6, the sermons on various themes. In four of them, the recommendation of oral confession for the soul's health is so routine as to sound routinely orthodox; there is nothing heterodox here.[18] One of these four sermons, on the theme *Mortuus viuet* and doubtless for use at funerals, goes further. Not only does it commend oral shrift, but also enjoins the duty of praying for the dead.[19] In fact this sermon is a translation from a Latin source, a version of which may be found in a manuscript in Hereford Cathedral Library.[20] The Hereford manuscript is not well known (it was never put on the map in the works of Owst, for example), yet its inclusion of *Mortuus viuet* endorses what the content of that sermon has already suggested, namely, that the sermon is impeccably orthodox. The

---

[16] Plate 1b is S, fol. 55^r; Plate 4 is Trinity College Dublin MS 74, fols. 23^v–24^r. I would like to thank Professor Michael Benskin for supporting my opinion that the stints are the work of one and the same scribe, and also Professor John Scattergood, who by happy chance brought this manuscript to my attention.

[17] See A. Hudson, 'The Debate on Bible Translation, Oxford 1401', *English Historical Review*, 90 (1975): 1–18 (reprinted in A. Hudson, *Lollards and their Books* [London and Ronceverte, 1985], pp. 67–84); also, the modifications thereto in A. Hudson, *The Premature Reformation* (Oxford, 1988), p. 417; for Arundel's Constitutions, see D. Wilkins (ed.), *Concilia Magnae Britanniae et Hiberniae* (London, 1737), iii.314–19. A. Hudson, 'Some Aspects of Lollard Book Production', *Studies in Church History*, 9 (1972): 147–57, claims (p. 155) that one of the English Wycliffite sermon scribes (in BL MS Harley 2396) turns up in part of a Wycliffite Gospels, Later Version (Gonville and Caius College Cambridge MS 179/212). The present study justifies her forecast in the same article, that more overlapping would probably be found; a systematic search may well reveal even more.

[18] See in the sermons *Estote prudentes et vigilate in oracionibus*, fols. 196^v–97^r; *Sana, Domine, animam meam, quia peccaui tibi*, fol. 199^r; *Hodie oportet me in domo tua manere*, fol. 200^v (this sermon, fol. 201^r, seems also of orthodox belief that the bread and wine of the Eucharist are the body and blood of Christ); and *Mortuus viuet*, fols. 202^v–3^r. There is also a singular absence of characteristic sect vocabulary in these sermons.

[19] *Mortuus viuet*, fol. 202^r; three lines of text originally referring to purgatory have been erased by some (Reformation?) reader (see Spencer, 'Fortunes', pp. 355–56, on this).

[20] Hereford Cathedral Library, MS O.III.5, fols. 104va–106vb. Other manuscripts may yet come to light.

Hereford manuscript was probably assembled under the aegis of the Augustinian canons,[21] themselves strenuous Lollard opponents, and indeed in two other of its sermons the Lollards are roundly, if briefly, attacked.[22] There seems little doubt, then, but that scribe B's *Mortuus viuet* was theologically blameless. Prayer for the dead found no favour with Wycliffites, that is if the English Wycliffite sermons may be taken as the yardstick of their opinion.[23] Yet on another occasion and in a different manuscript, it is precisely these English Wycliffite sermons that our scribe B *is* prepared to copy. The man who produced Cambridge, Magdalen College, MS Pepys 2616 (see Plate 5), and the second copyist of Wisbech Museum, MS 8 (see Plate 6), have been declared to be one and the same.[24] These manuscripts largely contain the English Wycliffite sermons.[25] His similarity to our scribe B has also been remarked on.[26] I think we can go further than this, however, and say with some confidence that the Pepys/Wisbech scribe is none other than our Sidney Sussex scribe B again. To prove this, I would draw attention first to the palographical similarities that unite the various stints of B in all three manuscripts.[27] Second, it should be noted that the linguistic fit of the Middle English that scribe B writes in Sidney Sussex 74 against that of the Pepys 2616 scribe is remarkably close.[28]

Anne Hudson's endeavours to locate Sidney Sussex 74 in the field of Lollard texts have excluded it from the scriptorium or centre which is likely to have

---

[21] Several of the sermons are for visitations and synods, and may reflect the professional interests of the compiler. Judging by content, he may have been an Augustinian canon. For example, the visitation sermon on the theme *Videbo templum* (Hereford Cathedral Library MS 0.III.5, fols. 38rb–40vb) refers to a monastery, brothers and canons, and the rule of 'beatissimus pater noster Augustinus' (fol. 40ra). Also, compare the visitation sermon on the theme *Visitabo in virga iniquitates eorum* (fols. 85vb–86vb), where the community addressed is called a *collegium*, and the visitor has come 'ad reformandum . . . mores et vitam regularium canonicorum' (fol. 86ra).

[22] Hereford Cathedral Library MS 0.III.5, fols. 57ra–60va, in a sermon on the theme *Benedicite, sacerdotes Domini, Domino* which seems to have intended a clerical audience, censures Lollards as 'heretici ypocrite' who strive to deceive 'per pravam doctrinam mites ac simplices in ecclesia' (fol. 59va). The next sermon, probably for Lent 4 on the theme *Abiit Ihesus trans mare* (fols. 60va–68rb), condemns the teaching 'alicuius magistri erroris seu Lollardi' (fol. 64vb). This sermon attacks *curati* who violently remove the right of preaching and teaching from the mendicants *per illud statutum noviter editum*, possibly in a reference to the repressive legislation of Arundel's Constitutions (see note 17 above). If so, it would date the sermon to sometime after 1407–9. (For the mendicant reaction to the Constitutions, see B. Z. Kedar, 'Canon Law and Local Practice: The Case of Mendicant Preaching in Late Medieval England', *Bulletin of Medieval Canon Law*, n.s. 2, (1972): 17–32.) The hand of this portion of the Hereford manuscript appears to date from the first half of the fifteenth century.

[23] See A. Hudson (ed.), *English Wycliffite Sermons* iii (Oxford, 1990), p. 312, ll. 4–15.

[24] Hudson, *Sermons* i.83 and 93.

[25] See Hudson, *Sermons* i.82–4 and 92–4 respectively for their contents and descriptions.

[26] Hudson, *Sermons* i.72.

[27] Comparison of Plates 1a, 5 and 6 should make this clear, in conjunction with the analysis of B forms given in note 10 above.

[28] The linguistic profile of Pepys 2616 is given in the *Atlas* iii.511–12, LP 676, and located in north Warwickshire, no more than six miles from my scribe B (see *Atlas* iii.512–13, LP 677). Of particular interest is the unusual spelling 'þoused' (THOUSAND) shared between scribe B in S and in Pepys 2616 (only once in S in a stint by scribe B, fol. 19r, does a more standard spelling, thousonde, appear). In the entire printed *Atlas* corpus, 'þoused' is recorded only for these two manuscripts (see *Atlas* IV, 266), which might in itself begin to suggest a kinship between them more particular than the merely regional.

produced the manuscripts of the English Wycliffite cycle.[29] But in view of its connection, via scribe B, with two other manuscripts which have been admitted to this scriptorium or centre, it would seem that the case for its exclusion demands to be reviewed. Were we to shave away hypotheses with Ockham's razor, we would be left with the economically bald conclusion that it would be perverse to dismiss Sidney Sussex 74 from the scriptorium or centre that produced the English Wycliffite cycle itself. But what are the consequences of admitting it?[30] Have we a rogue scribe in scribe B, an orthodox fifth-columnist, a subversive at party headquarters? I rather doubt it; that would depend on what view of the scriptorium or centre we entertain. The truth may be more prosaic, that we are simply dealing with someone who copies what he is given to copy, both heterodox material and material unassailably orthodox, and that he has no hard and fast scruples about doing so. Nor will it do to dismiss him merely by explaining him away as idiosyncratic in this respect.

Let us call scribe A of Sidney Sussex 74 to the witness stand again, for as was said earlier, we have not finished with him yet. It will be recalled that he copied parts of the Dublin, Trinity College, MS 74 Wycliffite New Testament, an activity that would certainly not be out of keeping with a scribe of Lollard leanings. I come now to the final manuscript affiliation that I want to establish. London, British Library, MS Egerton 826 is of a small, portable format, written by three scribes.[31] The first of these, its scribe A, is also likely to be the scribe A of Sidney Sussex 74. One conspicuous difference of his Egerton work, it must be admitted, is its enhanced formality: here, it shows much stronger influence from Textura (compare Plates 1b and 7). However, there were moments in Sidney Sussex 74 when scribe A similarly showed an inclination for producing the kind of script that I believe he deployed in Egerton: witness the variety of display script that he sometimes used to make Bible lemmata more notable in the epistle sermon series.[32] Notice too in Plate 7 the recurrence of the familiar **g** and **s** graphs. As well as these, there is a group of smaller palæographical features all of which are consonant with scribe A's work as we know it in Sidney Sussex 74.[33] In a case like this, where the palæographical link with Sidney Sussex 74 is nevertheless not so readily apparent, it would be interesting were a linguistic link demonstrable. In fact, one is. The *Linguistic Atlas of Late Mediæval English* locates the written dialect of scribe A in Egerton 826 in north-west Warwickshire, and that of scribe A in Sidney Sussex 74 in north east

---

[29] Hudson, *Sermons* i.201–2. By 'centre' she seems to intend a place of copying not as clearly demarcated as the word 'scriptorium' would suggest, yet a place which at least corresponded to the same town or area (p. 201).

[30] Hudson, *Premature Reformation*, p. 424 remarks on the inclusion of orthodox texts into compilations essentially Lollard; indeed, she cites an example from the English Wycliffite cycle itself, Cambridge, Trinity College, MS B.14.38. She neglects, however, to address possible implications such an amalgam may have for understanding the nature of the scriptorium/centre, other than to venture, (p. 425) that Lollards may have been less 'narrow-minded' in their reading habits than modern critics might imagine. But see further on this below.

[31] I am happy to thank Dr A. I. Doyle for drawing this manuscript to my attention.

[32] Though found *passim*, a conspicuous example of B's display script appears on fol. 139ʳ, at the reiteration of the sermon's epistle theme *Vir oblitus est qualis fuerit*.

[33] A tendency to tick the foot of the descender of þ, to flourish final -e with an otiose stroke, and to treat the ampersand comparably.

Worcestershire; both are actually plotted no more than eight miles apart.[34] What is the text that scribe A copies in Egerton 826? It is the long Middle English prose work, incomplete here through loss of leaves, known as *Book to a Mother*, ostensibly a manual of spiritual exhortation addressed by a priest to his aged widowed mother.[35] It is an interesting text: intruded in the ninth article of its Creed exposition, 'I beleue in . . . holy Chirche' is a suspicious gloss, 'þat is, alle þat schulle be saued'.[36] This sounds like the *Ecclesia* as *praedestinatorum Universitas* characteristic of Lollard thought.[37] Also, the *Book* is many times an explicit supporter of the 'dominion of grace' theory (essentially, this held that no one in mortal sin could legitimately exercise dominion over anyone or anything).[38] Again, this is typically, though not exclusively, Wycliffite.[39] Finally, the *Book* seems close to heterodoxy in its attack on female religious, although a difficulty here is that it is not entirely clear whether the actual institution of 'private religion', rather than delinquency within the institution, is the target.[40] So, was the *Book to a Mother* the work of a Lollard or Lollard sympathiser? Its author certainly seems to have skirted unorthodoxy.[41] Yet if he were seriously unorthodox, how would that be reconciled with the teaching of the *Book* that Christ himself substantiates the consecrated bread and wine, that each of the Church's seven sacraments is extolled without qualification, that images are holy in as much as they betoken holy saints, and that the value of oral confession to a priest is axiomatic?[42] All these doctrines, contrarily, are perfectly orthodox; on balance, if these things can be weighed in quantities, the author was far more a conservative than a radical. Indeed if the *Book*, as its editor believes, was composed *c.* 1370–80, it was in any case written either before Wyclif had been officially censured, or just conceivably at about the same time;

---

[34] See *Atlas* iii.523–24, LP 4682 and iii.550–51, LP 7591 respectively.

[35] A. J. McCarthy (ed.), *Book to a Mother: An Edition with Commentary*, Salzburg Studies in English Literature 92, Studies in the English Mystics 1 (Salzburg, 1981).

[36] McCarthy, *Book*, p. 2, ll. 1–2.

[37] Compare Wyclif's view in his *Opus Evangelicum*, ed. J. Loserth, *Johannis Wyclif Operis Evangelici* (London, 1896), p. 22, ll. 31–35: 'per *regnum celorum* intelligitur sancta mater ecclesia. Cum enim regnum communiter accipitur pro suis civibus et predestinatorum conversacio secundum Apostolum sit in celo, racionabiliter vocatur ecclesia regnum celorum' (discussing the Apostles' question, Matthew 18.1, of who will be greatest in the kingdom of heaven).

[38] Compare, for example, McCarthy, *Book*, p. 73, ll. 16–18 and p. 75, ll. 17–21.

[39] On the 'dominion of grace' theory, see M. Wilks, 'Predestination, Property and Power: Wyclif's Theory of Dominion and Grace', *Studies in Church History*, 2 (1965): 220–36; J. D. Dawson, 'Richard FitzRalph and the Fourteenth-Century Poverty Controversies', *Journal of Ecclesiastical History*, 34 (1983): 315–44.

[40] The matter is discussed by McCarthy, *Book*, p. lvi. An outspoken attack against corrupt religious includes a mention of 'false, feigning nuns, flattering friars' (p. 194, ll. 14–20; also, note the ranking of reprobate clergy, p. 90, ll. 15–17). Though reminiscent of Wycliffite polemic, the expression is not exclusively so, and is otherwise without parallel in the *Book*.

[41] Apart from the suspicious material noted above, there is little in the way of sect vocabulary, though a couple of times Antichrist is referred to (for example on p. 123, ll. 24 and 25; other references, pp. 158, 162, 166 and 182, arise naturally as a consequence of Bible translation), and a small cluster of references to God's law occurs (p. 51, l. 6, p. 65, l. 25, p. 75, l. 8, p. 76, l. 5, p. 77, l. 3 and p. 77, ll. 9–10). In regard to the author's possible heterodoxy, McCarthy, *Book*, p. xlvi, rightly observes that 'unorthodox views usually enjoy a limited acceptance by the unwary before the Church declares them heretical'.

[42] See McCarthy, *Book*, p. 147, ll. 1–10; p. 15, ll. 9–12; p. 39, ll. 10–12; and p. 38, ll. 21–22, p. 43, l. 3, p. 57, ll. 9–10, p. 61, l. 2, p. 64, ll. 3–6, p. 144, ll. 21–22, for coverage of these issues.

whichever way, the *Book* would seem rather early to coincide with the fuller exfoliation of Wycliffite thought.[43] But again, via its scribe A, Egerton 826 connects with Sidney Sussex 74, which in turn, via its scribe B, connects with manuscripts deemed to have originated at the heart of Lollard book production. Could Egerton 826 also have been a product of the same scriptorium or centre?

If it was, then perhaps it only exemplifies at large what Sidney Sussex 74 may exemplify in small, namely, that our concept of what the scriptorium or centre was like must also accommodate the capacity of that centre to turn out not only Lollard work, but also that very orthodoxy which Lollardy found so inimical.[44] Whatever the 'centripetal' implications, as Anne Hudson elegantly puts it, of the extraordinary textual supervision of the English Wycliffite sermon cycle, it cannot equally be said that the scriptorium or centre that produced it was as comparably controlled in respect of what other texts it was prepared to copy.[45] To opine that early Lollards were not so 'narrow-minded'[46] in their reading tastes as might be expected is to court a contradiction if, that is, one is also anxious to maintain that theirs was a consistent creed; imputations of latitudinarianism are scarcely advantageous to such an argument.[47] Some of our putative early Lollards, if they indeed were the recipients of certain of the manuscripts discussed here, would presumably have experienced a little dilution of the coherence of their characteristic creeds through reading them. Current Wycliffite scholarship should perhaps adjust to the prospect that the scriptorium or centre responsible for the English Wycliffite sermon cycle may itself have been more a site of conflicting ideology than that scholarship has been prepared to acknowledge. The scraps of evidence that I have assembled here seem to suggest that such was the nature of a corner of it, around about the year 1400 at any rate, when not everything it was producing was being processed and doctrinally homogenized.

But as mentioned earlier, surprise about inconsistency surely depends upon the presuppositions we have formed about what the scriptorium or centre was like. If we grant that its output was to an extent ideologically mixed, then any scriptorium convened specifically for the purpose of disseminating Lollard

---

[43] On the date of the *Book*, see McCarthy, *Book*, pp. xxx–xxxiv. Wyclif's first official censure came in 1377; he was forced to quit Oxford in 1381.

[44] Similarly, origin in a scriptorium in which scribes simply copied what was made available without troubling to scrutinize the contents would explain some of the manuscripts in which both orthodox and heterodox texts have been compiled (for some examples, see Hudson, *Premature Reformation*, p. 425). It is harder to imagine such nonchalance after about 1407, and certainly not in Oxford, when Arundel moved to censor what the scriptoria there could copy (and see further below on this).

[45] Hudson, *Sermons* i.196; the apparent lack of control over what texts the scriptorium or centre copied is perhaps congruent with the lack of supervision exercised over the format of the English Wycliffite sermon cycle manuscripts, and which has perplexed their editor (Hudson, *Sermons* i.193). One could perhaps make a case for some partisan ethos present in the scriptorium or centre by pointing out that as well as its few radical nuances, the *Book* contains much vernacular Bible translation that might have made it an attractive copying proposition; indeed, a characterization of the scriptorium or centre put no more strongly than that seems a possibility. Nevertheless, allowing the *Book* to be copied still compromised important Lollard tenets in other respects.

[46] Hudson, *Premature Reformation*, p. 425.

[47] Hudson, *Premature Reformation*, pp. 382–89. In her anxiety to reject the view of Margaret Aston that Lollardy was a variable creed, may Hudson have veered too far the other way?

writing becomes an unlikely home for some of the manuscripts discussed here: the awkward corollary of believing that would be that the organizers of such a scriptorium were nevertheless careless of examining the content of what their scribes were copying. What seems clear is that we are dealing with a scriptorium or centre not only well placed to acquire Lollard texts, but orthodox ones too. If, as seems conceivable, the inconsistent output of this scriptorium may be regarded as a barometer of the cultural context that it existed to serve, then we may also be dealing with a context in which the boundaries of theological acceptability had not yet been tightly drawn, or at least, not yet legally enforced to any formidable extent. Whether the scribes themselves were partisan in any clearly definable sense either one way or another is less apparent. Some may have been, but others manifestly were not; copying was their job, and they simply got on with it.

So where did the manuscripts come from? Given the implications of inconsistency, the Braybrooke theory, that they originated at the Northampton-shire seat of the notorious Sir Thomas Latimer, would not seem to fare well.[48] Yet if the scriptorium or centre were already well established before the Lollards arrived on the scene, we could make more sense of the situation. It has not been noticed that the sixth of Arundel's Oxford Constitutions could be interpreted as addressing just the sort of circumstances for book production that seem to be at issue here. This constitution required that before any work of John Wyclif could be copied, a committee of at least twelve approved University men should vet it.[49] When they had cleaned it up, an official exemplar of it could then be lodged with the University stationers. Evidently there was no question simply of leaving theological censorship up to the initiative of the stationers themselves; their job, like that surmised for some of the scribes discussed earlier, was just to get on with copying what they were given to copy. After 1407, the difference was that whereas before what they were given to copy was not carefully supervised, even though the copying process itself may have been, now they could copy only what came to them 'universitatis nomine ac auctoritate'. Oxford makes an excellent claim for being the home of the scriptorium or centre.[50] Whether this scriptorium or centre, in the early years of the Lollard movement, should be characterized less as a hive of orthodox industry than as a heterodox hornets' nest is another matter, however. Perhaps we would falsify what some of the evidence seems to be saying if we seriously imagined that this question, at least, was one that we should expect to resolve.

---

[48] Hudson, *Sermons* i.197–98, reviews the Braybrooke claim.
[49] See Wilkins, *Concilia* iii.317. They also had to be unanimous in agreement.
[50] Hudson, *Sermons* i.201, also considers the claims of Oxford to be 'strong'.

THE TRANSMISSION AND AUDIENCE OF
OSBERN BOKENHAM'S
LEGENDYS OF HOOLY WUMMEN

A. S. G. Edwards

London, British Library, MS Arundel 327 is a parchment manuscript of one hundred and ninety six leaves. It contains the only complete surviving text of Osbern Bokenham's *Legendys of Hooly Wummen*, comprising a collection of thirteen female saints' lives in verse, mainly in rhyme royal or couplets, but some excursions into other forms, chiefly the *Monk's Tale* stanza. The lives are those of Saints Margaret, Anne, Christina, the 11,000 Virgins, Faith, Agnes, Dorothy, Mary Magdalene, Katherine, Cecilia, Agatha, Lucy and Elizabeth. These lives all appear to have been written between 1443 and 1447[1] while Bokenham was resident in Clare, Suffolk. To the lives proper Bokenham added various prologues and dedications giving details of the circumstances of composition and the various patrons for whom some of these lives were written. This manuscript has not been much studied. The only modern description of it of which I am aware appears in Mary Serjeantson's Early English Text Society edition in 1938.[2] It is possible to add a little to her summary account and, through an examination of the manuscript to suggest some of the contexts that are relevant to our understanding of Bokenham's work.

The most immediate context is that of the production of Bokenham's text. According to its colophon the Arundel manuscript was copied either by, or more probably for, one 'Frere Thomas Burgh' in Cambridge in 1447, for presentation to a 'holy place of nunnys',[3] quite possibly, as Dr Doyle has suggested, for the Franciscan nuns of Aldgate and Denny.[4] But the manuscript contains the work of three different scribes. The first twenty-eight leaves, consisting of Bokenham's Prologue and Life of St Margaret, were copied by the first of these; and the next

---

[1] Bokenham states that he began the first legend, St Margaret, in 1443 (ll. 187–88). The 'prolocutorye in-to Marye Mawdelynes lyf' is dated 1445 (l. 4982). And the colophon states that the manuscript was copied in 1447 (p. 289). All references to Bokenham's text are to the edition by Mary S. Serjeantson, EETS, OS 206 (London, 1938).

[2] The description appears on pp. xxiv–v.

[3] The relevant phrase of the colophon states that the manuscript was 'doon wrytyn . . . by . . . Frere Thomas Burgh'. Dr Doyle has pointed out to me that the form of words suggests that Burgh caused the manuscript to be copied rather than that he copied it himself; see also M. C. Seymour, 'The English Manuscripts of *Mandeville's Travels*', *Edinburgh Bibliographical Society Transactions*, 4, part 5 (1966): 188. The view that Burgh was the scribe is expressed in C. E. Wright, *English Vernacular Hands from the Twelfth to the Fifteenth Centuries* (Oxford, 1960), p. 20.

[4] A. I. Doyle, 'Books Connected with the Vere Family and Barking Abbey', *Transactions of the Essex Archaeological Society*, n.s. 25, part 11 (1958): 236, note 8.

legend, St Anne, was copied by a second scribe (fols. 27–39).[5] The transcription of the chief scribe[6] did not begin until fol. 39[v], about a fifth of the way through the manuscript.

The first twenty-eight leaves form a distinct codicological unit. In addition to being in a different hand, the ruling is quite different from that in the rest of the manuscript as are the forms of decoration. In this section there are several gilt initials of varying size, between two and four lines, with purple penwork, as well as small initials in either red with green pen work or blue with red penwork (Plate 8). And the quire signatures in this part form a distinct sequence unrelated to the collation of the rest of the manuscript.[7]

The second part of the manuscript, that is, that which begins on what is now numbered fol. 27, evidently constitutes a fresh start, one very probably separated in both time, and in place from the production of the first part of Bokenham's work. This portion is signalled by both a change of scribe and of decorative pattern. On fol. 27 the beginning of the Life of St Anne is marked by an elaborate 10-line gilt initial (Plate 9)[8] This more elaborate decoration is abandoned after the brief stint of the second scribe ends on fol. 39[r], at the end of the Life of St Anne. When the main scribe begins his transcription the decoration settles into a modest, but generally consistent pattern of large blue initials, with red penwork and rubricated titles at the beginning of each legend, and simple blue or red initials alternating at the beginning of each rhyme royal stanza.[9]

But there are other variations within particular legends. Thus two, the Lives of Saints Anne and Christina, lack the characteristic rubricated title headings (on fols. 27[r] and 39[v] respectively), while for another, the Life of St Agatha, rubricated side headings have been inserted.[10]

There is also evidence of some confusion within this longer section of the manuscript. The evidence of quire signatures suggests that there were unforeseen problems in the apportioning of copy within an already established quire sequence. The sequence of these signatures suggests that two additional quires had to be inserted after the gatherings had been initially quired.[11]

These data seem to suggest that the creation of this manuscript was, in some respects a rather piecemeal affair. The autonomy of the first part of the manuscript, the elaborate but swiftly abandoned decoration of the next legend, the variations in format within other individual legends in the rest of the second

---

[5] The discrepancy between the foliation and the actual number of leaves is due to the fact that the final two of the first twenty eight leaves are blank and hence were unnumbered by the British Museum. I have, nonetheless, followed this modern foliation throughout.

[6] Facsimiles of this scribe's hand appear as frontispiece to Serjeantson's edition (fol. 74[v]) and in Wright, Plate 20, fol. 91[v].

[7] The collation of this portion is, by the quire signatures: c–e[8], [f][4].

[8] There is a similar 8-line initial on fol. 28[v].

[9] These initials do not appear in those legends which are written in couplets, i.e. those of Saints Katherine, Cecilia and Lucy (fols. 116[v]–172[r]).

[10] These headings appear on fols. 153[r], 153[v], 161[r], 161[v] and 162[r].

[11] A new sequence of signatures begins on fol. 27[r]; signatures are still visible on a number of leaves, although the lower margins have been cropped. In describing the collation inferred signatures have been placed in square brackets while the letters *Y* and *Z* denote gatherings that appear to have been added after the manuscript was intially quired. The collation appears to be: a–b[8], [c]–[d][8], *Y*[8], e[8], *Z*[8], f[8], [g]–[h][8], i–1[8], [m]–[t][8]; see also below note 13.

part, the problems with the quiring there, as well as the brief interpolation of a further scribe for the space of a single legend, suggest a series of ad hoc engagements with Bokenham's text that, in turn, suggests that the planning of the manuscript had not been fully thought out prior to its execution. That this is so seems curiously at odds with the evident technical competence of those involved in the manuscript's preparation.

This seeming contradiction can be resolved by a series of hypotheses concerning the development of the manuscript that is now London, British Library, MS Arundel 327, drawn in part from codicological and in part from internal evidence. The initial stage evidently comprised what is now the first section of the manuscript: the preamble and Life of St Margaret. This was very probably both written and executed at Bokenham's residence at Clare. It is from Clare (120) that he 'directe[s]' this part of his work to Burgh 'at hoom at Caunbrygge in yowr hows' (207). The decoration of this part, Kathleen Scott advises me, is consistent with a Clare provenance.

It must be stressed that there is nothing in this first part of the manuscript to suggest any larger design or plan. What Bokenham had copied, decorated and conveyed to Burgh was seemingly what he at that stage conceived as a one-off job. Whether it was Burgh's response, local pressures, Bokenham's evident facility in this form of composition, or some combination of these factors, clearly Bokenham was subsequently disposed to compose more of these legends. And, we gather, to transmit them to the seemingly eager Thomas Burgh for wider dissemination. It is this process of transmission that merits some consideration. For there appears no controlling schematic or other necessity to the sequence of legends as we now have it. But at one point Bokenham does enumerate what has accreted. About half way through the manuscript he lists the legends he has so far composed.[12] Although the order in which he lists them is not the actual order in which they appear, it is necessary, of course, that they should all precede the point in the manuscript at which they are enumerated. The legends already completed – those of Saints Anne, Mary, Margaret, Dorothy, Faith, Christina, Anne, and the 11,000 Virgins – are cited on fol. 92^v. It is in the portion of the manuscript preceding this point that Burgh evidently had problems with his quiring and had to insert the additional gatherings into his already planned sequence.[13]

This fact, in its turn, suggests something about the nature of the exemplar received. Or, more accurately, exemplars. For it seems that the piecemeal accumulation of legends from Bokenham's facile pen, was reflected in a parallel accumulation of separate legends on the desk of the eager Burgh. Thus, what he had before him when he planned the transcription of Arundel 327, was not a single exemplar, but a series of separate quires or booklets containing Bokenham's fair copies. Evidently only the first of these, the Life of St Margaret, was prepared in a form Burgh felt appropriate for circulation, and to it

[12] He describes them as 'dyuers legendys . . . of hooly wummen . . ./ As of seynt Anne, to blyssyd Marye / The modyr, of Margrete & of Dorothye, / Of Feyth & Crystyne, & of Anneys þer-to, / And of þo Eleuene thowsend uirgyns al-so' (5038, 5040–44).

[13] The first of these inserted gatherings (*Y*) appears to comprise fols. 59^r–66^r; the second (*Z*), fols. 75^r–82^r. This suggests that the legends that had to re-positioned were those of St Faith (fols. 66^r–74^r) and St Dorothy (fols. 87^r–91^v).

Two thyngys / owyth euy clerk
To aduertysyn / begynyg a werk
If he procedy wyl ordeneelly
The fyrste is what / the secude is why
In wych two / as it semyth me
The foure caulys comprehendyd be
Wych as philosofyrs vs do teche
In the begynnyg / men owe to seche
Of euery book / and aftyr ther entent
The fyrst is clepyd cause effityent
The secunde they clepe cause materyal
formal the thrydde / the fourte fynal
The effityent cause / is the auctour
Wych aftyr hys cunnyg doth hys laboure
So acomplyse the begunne matere
Wych cause is secude / and the more dere
That it may be / the formal cause
Settyth in dew ordre / clause be clause
And these thre thyngys longyn to what
Auctour matere and forme ordinat
The fynal cause declaryth pleynly
Of the werk begune the cause why
That is to seyne / what was the entent
Of the auctour fynally / & what he ment
So thus ye seen mowen compendyously
How in these two wrdys / what & why
Of eche werk the foure caulys aspye
When mowen requyryd be philosophye

Plate 8   London, British Library, MS Arundel 327, fol. 1ʳ

Vita Sctae Anne matris Sctae Marie

Prologus

If I hadde cunnyng and eloquens.
My conceytes craftely to dilate.
As whilom hadde the fyrth rethoryens.
Gowere. Chaucer & now lytgate.
I wolde me begyn to translate.
Seynt anne lyf in to oure langge.
But lekyr I. fere to gynne so late.
Lest men wolde ascryuen it to dotage.
ffor wel I. know that fer in age.
I. am runne & my lyues date.
Approchith faste & the fers rage.
Of cruel deth so wyl my fate.
Ineuytable hath at my gate.
Set hys carte to carye me hens.
And. I. ne may ne can thau I hy hate.
Ageyn hys fors make resistens.
Wherfore me thinkyth & lothe it ys.
Best were for me to leue makynge.
Of englysh & suche as ys amys.
To reformyn in my hymyng.
ffor that ys a ryght coueyn cunnynge.
A man to knowen hys trespace.
Wyth ful purpos of amendynge.
As ferforth as god wyl graunte hys grace.
ffor whil a man hath leyser and space.
Here in pis wordlys abydyng.
Or thau that deth hys brest enbrace.
To ransake hys lyf in alle thynge.

Plate 9 London, British Library, MS Arundel 327, fol. 27r

he appended the transcriptions of his amanuenses. The planning of the manuscript had apparently proceded apace until Bokenham's own enumeration of the sequence of legends was remarked, a discovery which entailed some quick rejigging of the already-established quire sequence.

The existence of a series of discrete exemplars may also explain the variations in the layout of the text that occur within particular legends. These variations presumably reflect those of individual exemplars.

The circulation of such pious booklets, at times probably amounting to no more than a quire, seems consistent with other indications of the circulation of devotional and other works in East Anglia and elsewhere in the mid fifteenth century.[14] One might assume that certain of Lydgate's shorter religious poems would have had some circulation in such a form for presentation to particular dedicatees, works like his 'Fyftene Ioyes of Oure Lady' done for Isabella Despenser, Countess of Warwick[15] or his *Legend of St Margaret*, commissioned by Ann, lady March;[16] or various of his shorter saints' lives, such as his Legends of St Austin or St Giles, which would each fit neatly into a single quire.[17] But such quires or booklets containing relatively short works were, of course, by their nature, notably fragile.[18] The closest actual parallel I can find is the quire of Lydgate's shorter religious poems made nearly contemporaneously by Richard Fox of St Albans and which is now appended to his collection of the works of Eleanor Hull in Cambridge University Library, MS Kk.1.6.[19] But it seems most likely, from the physical evidence, that Arundel 327 derived from such a mode of circulation.

In addition, there is external evidence to support the hypothesis of this booklet method of transmission and compilation for Bokenham's *Legends*. London, British Library, MS Addit. 36983 is a large, mid fifteenth century compilation including, *inter alia*, the *Cursor Mundi*, *The Three Kings of Cologne*, *The Abbey* and *The Charter of the Holy Ghost* and various Chaucer lyrics.[20] It also includes,

---

[14] On such forms of booklet circulation see Julia Boffey and John J. Thompson, 'Anthologies and Miscellanies: Production and Choice of Texts', in Jeremy Griffiths and Derek Pearsall (eds.), *Book Production and Publishing in Britain, 1375–1475* (Cambridge, 1989), esp. pp. 288–91.

[15] The text (196 lines) is printed in H. N. MacCracken (ed.), *The Minor Poems of John Lydgate*, Part I, EETS, ES 107 (London, 1911), pp. 260–67.

[16] 539 lines; printed in MacCracken, pp. 173–192.

[17] As they do, for example, in London, British Library, MS Harley 2255, a collection made for presentation to Lydgate's Abbot at Bury, William Curteys, fols. 24ʳ–32ʳ and 95ᵛ–l03ʳ respectively.

[18] See, for example, the comments of Anne Hudson, 'A Lollard Quaternion', *RES*, n.s. 22 (1971): 435–42. There are other recorded instances of such quires; for example, Robert Norwich bequeathed 'one little quire of paper, with the kings of England versified' in 1443 – see *Norfolk & Norwich Archaeological Society*, 4 (1855): 332; the will of John Goodyere in 1504, includes, among other books a 'quere of phisik of the secrets of women' – see F. C. Cass, 'Books in Wills and Inventories', *Notes and Queries*, 7th series, 9 (1890): 271 (I owe this reference to the kindness of Dr Julia Boffey). There is, of course, abundant evidence of the existence of fascicular manuscripts in England in the fifteenth century, and it seems highly likely that, in a number of cases, the individual fascicles circulated separately for periods of time.

[19] On Fox see G. R. Owst, 'Some Books and Book-Owners of Fifteenth-Century St Albans', *Transactions of the St Albans and Herts Architectural and Archaeological Society* (1928): 177–88. On CUL Kk.1.6 see, most recently, Alexandra Barratt, 'Dame Eleanor Hull: A Fifteenth Century Translator', in Roger Ellis (ed.), *The Medieval Translator* (Woodbridge, l989), pp.87–101.

[20] For a brief description see Sarah M. Horrall (ed.), *The Southern Version of the Cursor Mundi* (Ottawa,1978), i.16–17.

on the verso of the final leaf (fol. 305^v), the beginning of Bokenham's *Legend of St Dorothy*. It seems that the manuscript once contained a complete text of just this one of Bokenham's Legends. And the textual variants for even the small portion that survives suggest that the process of transmission had been quite extensive.[21] It seems that Burgh may not have been the only person to whom Bokenham transmitted his Legends.[22]

There is, moreover, an explicit link in the Arundel manuscript with Clare. On fol. 39^r there is an erased inscription that is partially legible under ultra violet light. It reads:

> Thys to[?] tretyse [. . .]made y^{23} mayster osberne[?]/ of the conuent of Clare

Once again, one must assume that the initial transcription of this note was a carrying over from Burgh's exemplar similar to the local variations in format. Its deletion was presumably felt to be consistent with Bokenham's stated desire for anonymity in his preamble (ll. 31–40).

The picture I have sketched postulates Clare as the originating centre for the circulation of Bokenham's works. A number of other contemporary mansucripts have been associated with Clare, some of them in Middle English, most of which have been assigned to the Bokenham canon.[24] These include the unique Middle English translation of the *De Consulatu Stilichonis*, London, British Library, Additional 11814, described in its colophon as written at Clare in 1445,[25] and the so-called Clare Roll, a Middle English verse dialogue between a Secular and a

---

[21] The full list of the variants for the small portion of the text (ll. 4736-4770) that survives is as follows (the Arundel text provides the lemma): 4742. compere in malyhs] cruell compere; 4743. oþir] many o.; 4744. dwellen] duell; 4753. vynys] v. and; 4754. feyr] full f.; 4756. Hyht þat oon] The toone hight; 4758. þat] the; 4761. clepyd] did clepe; 4762. & in pryuy wyse] whom did Baptyse; 4763. bysshop] hooly b.; hyr dede baptyse] in preuy wise; 4766. synguler] specyall; 4768. And] And all; eek] *om.* ; 4770. þe] *om.*

[22] The Additional MS seems to be the only other surviving witness to Bokenham's text. N. Toner, 'English Augustinian Writers of the fifteenth Century', *Sanctus Augustinus Vitae Spiritualis Magister* (Rome, 1959), ii.501-2, claims there was a further, incomplete manuscript, now untraced, but once in the library of Gresham College. His authority for this is an entry in Edward Bernard, *Catalogi librorum manuscriptorum Angliae et Hiberniae* (1697), ii, part I, p. 81, 3214.315, which describes '*Tho. Burgh's* Lives of the Saints, translated by *Osbern Bokenham*'. The entry goes on to enumerate 10 of the 13 Lives (omitting the 11,000 Virgins, Cecilia and Agatha). But since the Gresham College manuscripts went (as Toner notes) to the Royal Society, and subsequently (as he does not note) to the British Museum to form the Arundel collection, it seems most likely that this reference is to what is now Arundel 327. The omission of several of the Legends in the Bernard description seems most explicable as incomplete cataloguing.

[23] Or possibly, 'þe' as Dr Julia Boffey has suggested to me. I am indebted to Dr Boffey for her help in reading this erasure.

[24] The fullest account of the Bokenham canon appears in Francis Roth, *The English Austin Friars, 1249-1538*, Cassiciacum, vol. VI (New York, 1966), i.515-17.

[25] For a facsimile of this manuscript see Wright, Plate 19; the text is edited by E. Flügel, *Anglia*, 28 (1905): 255-99. On Bokenham's authorship see, most recently, Douglas Gray (ed.), *The Oxford Book of Late Medieval Verse and Prose* (Oxford, 1985), pp. 470-71. A subsequent attempt has been made to challenge both the date of the work and Bokenham's authorship; see John Watts, '*De Consulatu Stiliconis*: texts and politics in the reign of Henry VI', *Journal of Medieval History*, 16 (1990): 251-66, esp. 252, 258 and note 34. But the argument for re-dating it to 1454 or 1455 rests on insubstantial palæographical arguments and the writer is unaware that Bokenham was still alive in 1464 (see the following footnote).

Friar,[26] as well as several other manuscripts that seem to have been decorated and/or illustrated there.[27] Clare seems to have been one among a number of such centres in fifteenth century East Anglia that seem to have catered to appetites of readersfor vernacular works, often lay readers. As was apparently the case with Clare some of these centres were linked to the works of a particular author. One thinks most obviously of Bury St Edmunds and Lydgate or King's Lynn and Capgrave, both of which have been extensively studied.[28] A part of the context of Bokenham's work is his awareness of these other centres of local literary activity and the chief figures associated with them. Thus, the only vernacular works specifically mentioned by him are 'owre ladyes lyf Ihon lytgates booke' (2007), Lydgate's *Life of Our Lady*, and Capgrave's *Life of St Katherine* which he cites in his own life of the saint.

Reference to either poem is unsurprising in a work that addresses itself primarily to a lay female pious audience of the period. Both were by authors particularly well known within East Anglia,[29] and seem to have appealed particularly to a female readership. Capgrave's *Life of St Katherine* survives in four manuscripts, at least two of which can be clearly linked to such readership: in London, British Library, MS Arundel 168 it appears as part of another anthology of female saints's lives, including Lydgate's *Life of Our Lady*;[30] and London, British Library, MS Arundel 396 was owned by an Augustinian nun, Katherine Babington, sub-prioress at the priory of Campsey in Suffolk. Lydgate's *Life of Our Lady* was a far more popular work than Capgrave's. Composed in 1415–16,[31] it circulated widely during the fifteenth century. About

---

[26] College of Arms MS Muniment Room 3/16. For a facsimile of this manuscript see *Heralds Commemorative Exhibition, 1484–1934. Enlarged and Illustrated Catalogue* (London, 1936), Plate xlii; the text is edited by C. Horstmann, *Osbern Bokenam's Legenden* (Heilbronn, 1883), pp. 269–74. As pointed out by M. B. Hackett, 'A note on Osbern Bokenam', *Notes and Queries*, 206 (1961): 246–47, the fact that Bokenham was alive in 1464 makes him a candidate for the authorship of this work.

[27] For a list of manuscripts that seem circumstantially connected with Clare see Kathleen Scott, 'Lydgate's Lives of Saints Edmund and Fremund: A Newly-Located Manuscript in Arundel Castle', *Viator*, 13 (1982): note 68.

[28] On Lydgate and Bury see Scott (note 27 above); on Capgrave and King's Lynn see P.J. Lucas, 'John Capgrave O.S.A. (1393–1464), Scribe and "Publisher"', *Transactions of the Cambridge Bibliographical Society*, 5 (1969): 1–35.

[29] Bokenham probably knew both authors personally. Capgrave was a fellow Austin friar. He refers to Capgrave's work as 'My fadrys book, maystyr Ioon Capgraue, / Wych þat but newly compylyd he' (6356–57). And Bokenham alludes to Lydgate several times in his *Legendys* (see ll. 417, 1404, 4058, 10532). Bokenham is also linked to Lydgate indirectly through the will of John Baret of Bury, who had been Lydgate's co-pensioner, who in his will of 1463 included a bequest to 'Maister Osberne frere of Clare iij s. iiii d.'; see S. Tymms (ed.), *Wills and Inventories from the Registers of the Commissary of Bury St. Edmunds*, Camden Society 49 (London, 1850), p. 35. Baret was evidently a man of marked literary interests: his will also includes bequests of a number of books. It may not be coincidental in the present context that Baret's niece by marriage was Katherine Denston; see Gail McMurray Gibson, *The Theater of Devotion* (Chicago, 1989), p. 195, note 22.

[30] For a brief description see J. A. Lauritis *et al.*, *A Critical Edition of John Lydgate's Life of Our Lady*, Duquesne Studies, Philological Series, 2 (Pittsburgh, 1961), p. 48.

[31] On the dating of Lydgate's poem see J. Parr, 'The Astronomical Date of Lydgate's *Life of Our Lady*', *Philological Quarterly*, 50 (1971): 120–25.

fifty copies survive (as opposed to only four of Capgrave's *Life*).[32] It does appear in one manuscript, Arundel 168, as I have already mentioned, with Capgrave's *St Katherine* and in another, Harley 4011, with Bokenham's unique prose *Polychronicon* translation,[33] collocations which may reflect some form of regional compilatio. Several of the manuscripts of Lydgate's poem have connections directly with female readers or with families known to have included such readers.[34]

Two such families have links to Bokenham's works. As I have mentioned a number of the legends are addressed to individuals, mainly female; these include: Katherine Denston in the *Life of St Anne*, and again, with Katherine Howard in the *Life of St Katherine*; John and Isabel Hunt in the *Life of St Dorothy* and Agatha Flegge for the *Life of St Agatha*. The conjunction of these figures becomes explicable by reference to a further figure who significantly enlarges our sense of the context of Bokenham's literary activities.

Bokenham's *Life of Mary Magdalene* is dedicated to Isabel Bourchier, Countess of Eu. Isabel was, of course, sister to Richard, duke of York, to whom Bokenham alludes briefly, if admiringly in the course of his work (5018ff.).[35] Both the Flegge and Denston families were among Richard's retainers.[36] And Richard was apparently the dedicatee of the Claudian translation sometimes claimed for Bokenham's *oeuvre*, the manuscript of which contains his badges.[37] His badges and those of his wife Cicely also appear in the unique manuscript of the Clare roll mentioned above.[38] He also appears to have owned other books both pious and secular.[39] Another versifier, Benedict Burgh was among the

[32] For the fullest listing of the manuscripts of Lydgate's poem see A. Renoir and C. D. Benson, 'John Lydgate', in A. E. Hartung (ed.), *A Manual of the Writings in Middle English* (New Haven, 1980), 6.2128–29; see also A. S. G. Edwards, *Notes and Queries*, n.s. 32 (1985): 450–52.

[33] For a brief description see Lauritis, pp. 32–33. The *Polychronicon* translation was edited by C. Horstmann in *Englische Studien*, 10 (1887): 6–34.

[34] Professor George Keiser has in hand a full study of the manuscripts of Lydgate's poem.

[35] Richard evidently had other, more formal links with Clare. A document of 22 July, 1454 describes him as 'patronus noster' of O.E.S.A. – Clare; see Francis Roth, *The English Austin Friars, 1249–1528*, Cassiciacum, vol. VII (New York, 1961), ii.334, no. 830. Richard's patronage extended to other religious houses. He and his wife Cecily are named in the prayers for patrons in a manuscript of the Requiem Offices owned by Sion Abbey (*olim* Bute MS 171, sold Sotheby's, 13 June, 1983, lot 14). On Cecily herself as patron and boook owner see C. A. J. Armstrong, 'The Piety of Cicely, Duchess of York: A Study in Late Medieval Culture', reprinted in his *England, France and Burgundy in the Fifteenth Century* (London, 1983), pp. 135–156.

[36] See P. A. Johnson, *Duke Richard of York, 1411–1460* (Oxford, 1988), pp. 63–64, 159, 232.

[37] The claim for Bokenham's authorship is advanced by N. Toner, 'Augustinian spiritual writers', ii.503.

[38] Roth, i.516.

[39] These include London, British Library, MS Royal 19 A. XIX, a copy of Christine de Pisan's *Livre de Cité des Dames*, on which see G. F. Warner and J. P. Gilson, *Catalogue of Western Manuscripts in the Old Royal and King's Collections* (London, 1921), ii.322–3; Bibl. Municipale de Rennes 22 (Books of Hours); on which see M. Rickert, 'The So-Called Beaufort Hours and York Psalter', *Burlington Magazine*, 104 (1962): 238–46; and Ushaw College 43 (Book of Hours). I owe my knowledge of this last to Dr Doyle *via* Dr Kathleen Scott; see now N. R. Ker and A. J. Piper, *Medieval Manuscripts in British Libraries, IV: Paisley-York* (Oxford, 1992), pp. 549–51. I am also grateful to Dr Carol Meale for her help on Richard's books. Richard may also have been the owner of one of the so-called Kerdeston Fragments of hunting tracts (sold Sotheby's, 12 March, 1946, lot 2255, now in the possession of H.R.H. the Duke of Gloucester). One of the fragments (fol. 3r) contains an historiated initial that may have been a portrait of Richard; see further, Bror Danielsson,

beneficiaries of his patronage.[40] The Bourchier family itself seems to have included book collectors, possibly over more than one generation.[41] Among the books in the family's possession is a copy of Lydgate's *Life of Our Lady*, now Oxford, Bodleian Library, MS Ashmole 39. The name 'Isabell' appears on the inner back cover together with the signatures of Anne and Sir Thomas Bourchier.[42]

To compose his *Life of Mary Magdalene* for Isabel, Bokenham tells us that he had to interrupt the composition of another female saint's life, for another female patron: the *Life of St Elizabeth* which he had agreed to undertake for Elizabeth de Vere, countess of Oxford.[43] (This ultimately appears as the final one of his legends.) Although Bokenham has sometimes been credited with Yorkist sympathies,[44] the de Veres were a family of Lancastrian bias. Katherine Howard was probably also a relative of Elizabeth's who came from the Howard family.[45] The de Vere's were also a notable family of book collectors, whose activities have been documented at length by Dr Doyle.[46] In addition, Elizabeth de Vere's own circle of acquaintance included such book collectors and literary patrons as the Pastons, Sir John Fastolf and Miles Stapleton.The family's own books included another copy of Lydgate's *Life of Our Lady*, London, British Library, MS Harley 3862. Unfortunately, for my purposes, the arms it includes are those of Elizabeth's son, the thirteenth earl of Oxford. But, given the literary interests of his parents, which may have included ownership of the Ellesmere Chaucer,[47] one has at least grounds for hoping that it may have been in the family earlier.

Bokenham's lives of female saints can be placed with the broad context of East Anglian literary patronage in the mid fifteenth century, outlined many years ago by Samuel Moore.[48] Such patronage was pious, local, and emulative. What

---

'The Kerdeston "Library of Hunting and Hawking Literature" (early 15th c. fragments)', in *Et Multum et Multa . . . Festgabe für Kurt Linder*, herausg. Sigrid Swenk, Gunnar Tilander and Carl A. Willemsen (Berlin, 1971), pp. 47–59, esp. p. 50. (I owe this reference to the late Dr Sarah Horrall.)

[40] See Samuel K. Moore, 'Patrons of Letters in Norfolk and Suffolk, c. 1450', *PMLA* 27 (1912): 93–94.

[41] Other books in the family's possession at various time include Oxford, Bodleian Library, MS Lyell 25 (Book of Hours), Huntington Library, HM 19920 (Statutes) and Princeton, University Library, MS Garrett 150 (*Brut*).

[42] It may also be noted that the Bourchier family was evidently among the patrons of Clare. The monastery established a chantry from the family in 1463 'in return for their numerous benefits' (Roth, ii.347, no. 868 where the date is erroneously given as 1463; the error is corrected by Hackett, p. 247). The document confirming this was signed by, among others, Osbern Bokenham.

[43] Bokenham describes the interruption to this plan in ll. 5045–5117.

[44] See, for example, Roth, ii.334. But it seems at least, if not more likely that Bokenham's regard for Richard stemmed from his role as 'patronus' of Clare, which, as the earliest Englsh Augustinian house (founded in 1248) had a tradition of noble and royal patronage; see further, Roth, i.259–62.

[45] She is presumably the same person who was granted a letter of confraternity to Clare in 1445; see Roth, ii.327, no. 804, and Predendary Clark-Maxwell, 'Some Letters of Confraternity', *Archaeologia*, 75 (1924–25): 19–60, especially p. 59 where this letter is described briefly by C. L. Kingsford, who notes that 'the prettily illuminated border suggested that it had been specially written for Katherine Howard'. I have not seen this letter which was then in the muniments of Lord De L'Isle and Dudley, but it seems likely that this was another Clare production.

[46] In 'Books Connected with the Vere Family', pp. 222–39.

[47] The most recent discussion of the Vere's connection with the Ellesmere manuscript (Huntington Library, MS EL 26 C 9) is in C. W. Dutschke *et al*, *Guide to the Medieval and Renaissance Manuscripts in the Huntington Library* (San Marino, Calif., 1989), i.49–50.

[48] See note 40 above.

distinguishes Bokenham's work is the range of female patrons he was able to draw upon. Both his major contemporaries Lydgate and Capgrave seem to have undertaken their works primarily either for male patrons or for institutions. (Capgrave appears to have undertaken only one work for an unnamed female patron, his *Life of St Augustine* and none of Lydgate's major works were written for women.[49]) Bokenham stands apart in the frequency and particularized focus of his efforts to address the literary needs of a distinctively female audience. We glimpse in his activities an interface between poet and patrons that demonstrates a widening of the literary audience in terms both of class and gender.

But Bokenham was, whether by design or accident, not simply meeting the demands of a localized lay female audience for vernacular religious verse to an unusual and perhaps unprecedented extent. His various works were compiled by Thomas Burgh into a larger work for professed female religious. The regional adaptability of it probably did not stop there. As I have tried to suggest, portions of it may have achieved a wider circulation. The *Life of St Dorothy* in London, British Library, MS Add. 36983 is seemingly of Bedfordshire provenance.[50]

But the adaptability of Bokenham's work may be seen as, in some sense, a reflection of the versatility of its author. The final context the *Legends of Hooly Wummen* invites us to consider is that of his own literary career. For Bokenham is rather more than a minor literary hack, an equivalent of (say) a Burgh or a Metham. The balance of probability adds the Claudian translation to his poetic oeuvre and might also credit him with the authorship of the 1438 *Gilte Legende*.[51] One of a number of factors that strengthen his claim to the latter work is that it is the only other collection of Middle English saint's lives to include all those that appear in the *Legends*. This, together with other unambiguous evidence of his activities as a prose translator establish Bokenham as a versatile writer, one whose range of accomplishments both pious and secular, verse and prose,[52] merits fuller appreciation than it has received.[53]

---

[49] Lydgate did write a few works, usually fairly short, for women patrons; these include, *Guy of Warwick* for Margaret Talbot, countess of Shrewsbury; 'The Invocation to St Anne', for Ann, Countess of Stafford; 'The Virtues of the Mass', for Alice Chaucer, Countess of Suffolk; the *balade* 'That Now is Hay Some-Tyme was Grase' made apparently for Katherine Valois, Henry V's queen; and the 'Treatise for Lavenders' and the 'Epistle to Cibille' both for Lady Sibille Boys. See also p. 162 and fns. 15–16.

[50] Robert E. Lewis and Angus McIntosh, *A Descriptive Guide to the Manuscripts of the Prick of Conscience*, Medium Ævum Monographs, n.s. 12 (Oxford, 1982), p. 155.

[51] The arguments for and against Bokenham's authorship are conveniently summarized by Charlotte D'Evelyn, 'English Translations of Legenda Aurea', *A Manual of the Writings in Middle English*, general ed. J. Burke Severs (Hamden, Conn., 1970), ii.434–35. Since then see Manfred Görlach, *The South English Legendary, Gilte Legende and Golden Legend*, Braunschweiger Anglistische Arbeiten, Heft 3 (Braunschweig, 1972), pp. 82–86, who argues against Bokenham's authorship. I omit from the present discussion the problem of the authorship of the *Liber de Angelis*, surviving apparently uniquely in Cambridge, University Library, MS Dd. xi. 45, fols. 134ᵛ–139ʳ, and there ascribed to one 'Bokenham'.

[52] One may also add 'in Latin as well as Middle English'. Bokenham claims in his *Legendys* to have written a Latin verse life of St Anne (ll. 2081–3).

[53] I am particularly indebted to Dr Julia Boffey for her assistance, as well as to Professor Sheila Delany, Dr Carol Meale, Professor Derek Pearsall, Dr Kathleen Scott and (*ut semper*) Dr Doyle.

ANOTHER LOOK AT THE RELIGIOUS TEXTS IN LINCOLN, CATHEDRAL LIBRARY, MS 91

John J. Thompson

The frequency with which references to Robert Thornton and his texts are made in modern studies of Middle English religious and romance writings is eloquent testimony of the importance modern scholars attach to both the man and his books for our understanding of certain aspects of English literary history. Thornton was the mid-fifteenth-century Yorkshire copyist who gathered up an impressive array of Middle English prose and verse items, and some short Latin pieces, in Lincoln, Cathedral Library, MS 91 (the Lincoln Thornton Manuscript). Broadly speaking, he organised these into 'romance' and 'religious' sections in gatherings A–K and L–P of the manuscript.[1] A third and final 'medical' section contains the Thornton copy of the *Liber de Diversis Medicinis*; another cluster of Middle English verse writings by the same copyist makes up a second volume, now London, British Library, MS Addit. 31042 (the London Thornton Manuscript).[2] Shared paper stocks provide the clearest indication that Thornton probably worked on both his 'religious' and his 'romance' quires over a similar period of time.[3] A mixture of physical and textual evidence also supports the view that the London Thornton MS was, or

---

[1] For a summary description of the Lincoln Thornton manuscript see Gisela Guddat-Figge, *Catalogue of Manuscripts Containing Middle English Romances* (Munich, 1976), pp. 135–42. For the 'romance' section see also my 'The Compiler in Action: Robert Thornton and the "Thornton Romances"', in Derek Pearsall (ed.), *Manuscripts and Readers in Fifteenth-Century England* (Cambridge, 1983), pp. 113–24; for a more sanguine recent account of Thornton and his 'religious' section than I offer here, see G. R. Keiser, ' "To Knawe God Almyghtyn": Robert Thornton's Devotional Book', in James Hogg (ed.), *Spätmittelalterliche Geistliche Literatur in der Nationalsprache*, Analecta Cartusiana, 106 (Salzburg, 1984), pp. 103–129. Other recent general studies which refer to Thornton's likely interests in Middle English religious literature include Vincent Gillespie, '*Lukynge in haly bukes*: *Lectio* in some Late Medieval Spiritual Miscellanies', also in *Spätmittelalterliche Geistliche Literatur in der Nationalsprache*, pp. 1–26; Felicity Riddy, 'The World of the Book', in her *Sir Thomas Malory* (Leiden and New York, 1987), pp. 1–30; and my 'Textual Instability and the Late Medieval Reputation of Some Middle English Religious Literature', in *TEXT: Transactions of the Society for Textual Scholarship*, 5 (1991): 175–94.

[2] For the special place of the *Liber de Diversis Medicinis* as a separate small 'book within a book' in the two-volume Thornton collection see my note in *Transactions of the Cambridge Bibliographical Society*, 8 (1982): 270–75; for an account of the second Thornton volume, see my *Robert Thornton and the London Thornton Manuscript* (Cambridge, 1987); also Ralph Hanna III, 'The Growth of Robert Thornton's Books', *Studies in Bibliography*, 40 (1987): 51–61.

[3] Of the five types of watermarked paper surviving in Thornton's 'religious' section, three (containing watermarks iii, v, viii) are also found in both the 'romance' section of the Lincoln manuscript and also, in smaller quantities, in the London Thornton manuscript. The two other small stocks of paper in the 'religious' section of Lincoln (containing watermarks xiii, and xiv) are not found elsewhere in Thornton's collection. For revised identification of the paper stocks and further details see *Robert Thornton and the London Thornton Manuscript*, pp. 71–3.

became, an overflow volume, which Thornton had commenced before completing the tripartite Lincoln collection. This second volume has its own 'shape' as a miscellany of religious and moral poetry in English, but this seems to have evolved in an ad hoc fashion as Thornton obtained the written materials that enabled him to continue his copying activities.[4]

The present state of our understanding of the Thornton manuscripts and Robert Thornton's life and times is not unknown to Dr Doyle. He has examined and discussed Thornton texts on a number of occasions, initially in his doctoral thesis, but also in his recent work on vernacular writings in late medieval manuscripts, particularly manuscripts containing Middle English alliterative verse.[5] Before Doyle, critical interest in Thornton's religious texts had been largely editorial. Nineteenth-century scholarly landmarks include G. G. Perry's 1866 and 1867 editions of Thornton religious pieces for EETS and, just under 30 years later, Carl Horstman's monumental edition of *Early Yorkshire Writers, Richard Rolle of Hampole and His Followers*.[6] The latter includes, in Horstman's first volume, his transcriptions of material from Thornton's 'religious' section. Almost a century after its first publication, *Early Yorkshire Writers* remains a storehouse of information, often providing modern scholars with readily accessible texts of key Middle English religious items taken by their nineteenth-century editor from a select few of the manuscript copies known to him.

Today there are other useful markers for students of Thornton's religious items. Nearly thirty years after Dr Doyle's stimulating comments on Thornton and his desire to see demonstrated 'the character of Thornton's literary supplies', many of Thornton's items, and both his manuscripts, have been subjected to repeated modern scholarly scrutiny.[7] Research on Thornton has frequently been conducted by critics who know well the value of checking Doyle's unpublished Cambridge thesis for promising scholarly leads – the present writer is no exception. Seen from this perspective, the publication of the Scolar Press facsimile edition of the Lincoln Thornton manuscript in 1975 might be said to have marked the successful coming of age of the codicological approaches and interests pioneered by Doyle.[8] More recent years have also seen the publication of a small number of modern critical editions of Middle English

---

[4] In the course of preparing this paper for publication, I have been prompted to develop some of the views expressed at the York conference in the light of Phillipa Hardman's unpublished lecture on the London Thornton manuscript, delivered at the second Early Book Society Conference, Trinity College, Dublin (August, 1991).

[5] 'A Survey of the Origins and Circulation of Theological Writings in English in the 14th, 15th, and Early 16th Centuries with Special Consideration of the Part of the Clergy therein', Ph.D. dissertation, Cambridge, 1954 *passim*; also 'The Manuscripts', in David Lawton (ed.), *Middle English Alliterative Poetry and Its Literary Background* (Cambridge, 1982), pp. 88–100. My debt to Doyle's unpublished work throughout this paper will be immediately apparent to the many scholars who have had occasion to consult his thesis.

[6] For Perry, see *English Prose Treatises of Richard Rolle of Hampole*, EETS OS 20 (London, 1866, revised ed., 1921); *Religious Pieces in Prose and Verse*, EETS OS 26 (London, 1867, revised ed., 1914); Horstman's *Early Yorkshire Writers* was published in two volumes (London and New York, 1895, 1896). For the Thornton material, see i.184–337 and 363–411, ii.334–39. In the following account where I use Horstman's text, I have occasionally also silently emended it.

[7] For Doyle's original comment, see his 'Origins and Circulation', ii.277, note 26.

[8] *The Thornton Manuscript*, introd. D. S. Brewer and A. E. B. Owen (London, 1975, revised ed., 1977).

religious prose material also found in Thornton, with the promise of others soon to follow.[9] As this paper will demonstrate, the accompanying scholarly apparatus in these modern editions can enable us to locate a 'Thornton' version of a Middle English religious item within a broader complex of fifteenth-century manuscript networks. By identifying important textual features in some of the extant manuscript copies, modern scholars can begin to recover aspects of the late medieval reputations of frequently recopied texts. This seems a necessary prerequisite for any attempted reassessment of the roles likely to have been played by individual copyists such as Thornton in the transmission history of the Middle English religious prose pieces discussed below.

Robert Thornton remains an attractive figure for modern scholarship, however, not only because of the relative accessibility of much of his written material in these modern forms, but also because he is readily seen as an individual who is representative in some way of the fifteenth-century lay reading public. Dr Doyle has made this point in his own work and other recent studies, most notably by George Keiser, have attempted to identify the particular strands in the complex web of fifteenth-century literary culture that the Thornton copyist can be said to represent.[10] While we now know much more than hitherto about Thornton's likely identity as a member of the North Yorkshire minor gentry, we have far from exhausted the search for other important aspects of Thornton's identity as an individual late medieval reader, copyist, and book producer. In the general context of current scholarly interest in late medieval English texts, manuscripts and their earliest readers, this may seem like a relatively minor desideratum.[11] But it seems worthwhile returning to the Thornton example because it usefully illustrates the generally fragile state of our current knowledge concerning the activities, interests, and habits of even the best known late medieval copyists or those of their earliest likely listeners and readers.[12]

It is not clear, for example, whether Thornton worked on his two-volume literary collection for a single intended audience, perhaps comprised of members of his own extended household, or, indeed, whether this work preoccupied him

---

9 Toshiyuki Takamiya (ed.), 'Walter Hilton's "Of Angels' Song"', in *Two Minor Works of Walter Hilton* (Tokyo, 1980), originally published in *Studies in English Literature* (Tokyo), English Number, 1977; Sr. Mary Luke Arntz (ed.), *Richard Rolle and þe Holy Boke Gratia Dei*, Salzburg Studies in English Literature, Elizabethan and Renaissance Studies, 92.2 (Salzburg, 1981); S. J. Ogilvie-Thomson (ed.), *Walter Hilton's Mixed Life*, Salzburg Studies in English Literature, Elizabethan and Renaissance Studies, 92.15 (Salzburg, 1986); S. J. Ogilvie-Thomson (ed.), *Richard Rolle: Prose and Verse*, EETS OS 293 (London, 1988). For this study, I have also consulted the unpublished edition of *The Mirror of St Edmund* in its Middle English prose version by Clare Rosemary Goymer, MA thesis, University of London, 1961; and the unpublished edition of *The Abbey of the Holy Ghost* by D. Peter Consacro, Ph.D. dissertation, Fordham University, 1971.

10 'Lincoln Cathedral Library MS 91: Life and Milieu of the Scribe', *Studies in Bibliography*, 32 (1979): 158–79; 'More Light on the Life and Milieu of Robert Thornton', *Studies in Bibliography*, 36 (1983):111–19.

11 It is salutary to note, nonetheless, that the example of Robert Thornton and/or his collection is cited in no less than five chapters of the most recent general survey of late medieval English book production procedures; see Jeremy Griffiths and Derek Pearsall (eds.), *Book Production and Publishing in Britain, 1375–1475* (Cambridge, 1989), pp. 16, 26, 234, 297–302, 310, 314, 341.

12 The better-documented but still problematic case of the Londoner John Shirley (a fifteenth-century copyist associated with the metropolitan book trade) offers another not dissimilar case in point.

for his entire writing career, or, alternatively, for just the latter part of a busy life. Apart from the fortunate survival of his two manuscripts, no other examples of Robert Thornton's handwriting have yet come to light which would perhaps help clarify other unsettled issues regarding his amateur or professional scribal status. Despite the promising and important pioneering work by Angus McIntosh, we also know disappointingly little about shared linguistic features, particularly the dialect layers in Thornton's 'religious' and 'romance' material (both manuscripts) and their possible significance.[13] Nor can we do much more than speculate about what is likely to have happened, in the short term, to quires that Thornton had already completed while his work on a larger collection was continuing. Thornton's first readers may well have had access to early portions of his work in progress and could easily have helped shape the collection in ways which have not been fully appreciated.[14] This likelihood, coupled with our remaining uncertainty about the precise nature of some of Thornton's most important sources, complicates much of what we might also want to say about the reading tastes represented by one or other, or both, 'Thornton' volumes.

From a late twentieth-century perspective, it is interesting to observe that there are no works by Chaucer, Gower, or Langland in either of the two surviving literary miscellanies now associated with Thornton. The Yorkshire copyist instead gathered up a small number of short religious and didactic pieces by the prolific fifteenth-century English poet John Lydgate and set these alongside other anonymous short religio-didactic verse texts in the London Thornton manuscript.[15] This is a 'Thornton' volume, where no obvious attempt is made to maintain an artificial distinction between 'religious' and 'romance' material – a suspiciously modern generic distinction that Lydgate himself may not even have recognised. The London Thornton manuscript and Thornton's 'romance' section are, however, both relatively mixed collections, written in English, and mainly (in the case of the London manuscript, exclusively) in verse. Taken together, they possibly represent their compiler's eclectic tastes for religious and moral stories, exemplary biographical writings often loosely based on historical themes, and short poems dealing variously with a wide range of commonplace

---

[13] 'The Textual Transmission of the Alliterative *Morte Arthure*', in N. Davis and C. L. Wrenn (eds.), *English and Medieval Studies Presented to J. R. R. Tolkien* (London 1962), pp. 231–40. Although McIntosh has argued that the Thornton source for his texts of the alliterative *Morte* and *The Privity of the Passion* was the work of a single Lincolnshire scribe (S), that anonymous scribe's exemplar for the alliterative *Morte* (M1), unlike the *Privity* exemplar (B1), seems to have been a dialectally-mixed text. The full significance of this evidence, and other signs that Thornton had access to dialectally-mixed sources from the same general area, invite further scholarly investigation.

[14] See also my comments in 'Collecting Middle English Romances and Some Related Book-Production Activities', in Maldwyn Mills *et al* (eds.), *Medieval Romance in England* (Cambridge, 1991), pp. 17–38.

[15] The Lydgate items are *The Passionis Christi Cantus* (IMEV 2081); *Verses on the Kings of England* (IMEV 3632); *The Dietary* (IMEV 824) and *The Virtues of the Mass* (IMEV 4246). All IMEV refererences in this paper are to both *The Index of Middle English Verse*, by Carleton Brown and Rossell Hope Robbins (New York, 1943) and also its *Supplement*, by R. H. Robbins and John L. Cutler (Lexington, 1965). For further discussion of the present manuscript context of Lydgate's verse in Thornton's collection, see *Robert Thornton and the London Thornton Manuscript*, esp. pp. 42–46. In her unpublished lecture (referred to in note 4 above), Phillipa Hardman has satisfactorily and fully explained the curious 'false start' to Thornton's text of *The Passionis Christi Cantus*.

religio-didactic topics. As I have shown elsewhere, this material occasionally also suggests its compiler's particular brand of simple – some would say naïve – piety.[16] On the other hand, however, Thornton's 'religious' section in the Lincoln manuscript became the sole repository in his two-volume collection for some characteristic short English writings by Richard Rolle and Walter Hilton, also for other Middle English religious prose, including *The Mirror of St Edmund, John Gaytryge's Sermon, The Abbey of the Holy Ghost*, the loosely-structured *Gratia Dei* compilation, and a number of short related tracts. The prose pieces I have just described make up the bulk of the distinctive 'religious' section in Thornton's collection and determine its essential character. (See the summary diagram below, pp. 180–1.)

Many unanswered questions remain about the manner in which Thornton is likely to have approached the task of copying, and presumably using, some of the items now extant in this 'religious' section. Were items like *The Mirror of St Edmund*, and *John Gaytryge's Sermon* (also familiar to modern readers as the *Lay Folks' Catechism*) intended for purposes of practical religious instruction, possibly for members of the scribe's family instead of, or as well as, the scribe himself?[17] Or were these items, together with the short texts by Rolle, Hilton and other related religious writings represented in the same section of his collection, primarily intended to facilitate prayer, penance, and contemplation among enthusiasts for the 'mixed life', among whose number might be included Thornton?[18] And, did Thornton prepare carefully 'edited' copies of this material for his intended audience, perhaps acting as his own spiritual adviser or that of other members of his household? Or, by contrast, was Thornton an enthusiastic advisee, someone who was granted privileged access (presumably by his own family counsellor or director in spiritual matters) to different versions of *Gaytryge's Sermon, The Mirror of St Edmund*, and these other important and characteristic English devotional works? One of the delights of such speculations is that it is possible to construct a picture of Thornton that reflects many or all of these possibilities. On the occasion of a York manuscripts conference in honour of Dr Doyle, it seems worthwhile bringing together some of the remaining scraps of manuscript and textual detail that enable us to continue the process of exploring and testing the 'Thornton' evidence.

---

[16] A good example of this is the inordinate care with which Thornton placed the Middle English Infancy narrative he carefully entitles 'the Romance of the childhode of Ihesu Criste þat clerkes callys Ypokrephum' next to *Richard Coer de Lyon* (London Thornton manuscript, fol. 163ᵛ). See details and plate in *Robert Thornton and the London Thornton Manuscript*, pp. 47–48, pl. 34.

[17] The Thornton incipit for *Gaytryge's Sermon* on fol. 213ᵛ describes this item as a 'sermon . . . þe whilke teches how scrifte es to ᵇᵉ made & whareᵒᶠ and in scrifte how many thynges solde be consederide' . Doyle's interesting point that this *Gaytryge* heading emphasises simultaneously both the public and private aspects of the ways in which the 'sermon' may have been used ('Origins and Circulation', 1, pp. 33–4) has been taken up and developed in David Lawton, 'Gaytryge's Sermon, *Dictamen*, and Middle English Alliterative Verse', *Modern Philology*, 76 (1979): 329–43; also Vincent Gillespie, '*Doctrina and Predicacio*: The Design and Function of Some Pastoral Manuals', *Leeds Studies In English*, n.s. 11 (1980): 36–50, esp. pp. 43–6. Thornton's late minor insertions in this incipit (indicated by the superscript text) perhaps argues for some degree of scribal inattention on his part while copying this item (cf. note 27 below).

[18] This point is vigorously pursued in George Keiser, 'Þe Holy Boke Gratia Dei', *Viator*, 12 (1981): 289–317, at pp. 306–8; for a more cautious estimate, as part of a larger survey, see Vincent Gillespie, '*Lukynge in haly bukes*', esp. p. 1. I discuss the *Gratia Dei* material in 'Textual Instability', pp. 180–82.

It may well be that the act of copying material for Thornton's 'religious' section was, or became, a devotional exercise of some kind. Suspicions that this may have been the case are raised by the survival of a penitential commonplace bearing Thornton's family name in the head margin of fol. 278ᵛ in quire P. This scribal tag reads: 'Thornton misereatur mei dei/ miserere mei deus'. It accompanies a short Latin prayer cluster on fols 277ᵛ–279ʳ that Thornton is likely to have copied from an illustrated *Horae*, but the full extent of the tag's likely significance for the scribe is now lost to us.[19] Added to this are possible signs of Thornton's quasi-proprietary regard for some of the items copied in both his manuscripts, hinted at by his occasional use of other conventionally pious scribal tags, including the characteristic *Robertus Thornton qui scripsit sit benedictus amen.*[20] Perhaps of greater significance for the purposes of this paper is that Thornton added his own Christian name at appropriate places in one of the Latin prayers he copied as a filler item on fol. 176ᵛ at the end of his 'romance' section, thereby simply but effectively making it his own. The English instructions accompanying this Latin prayer charm are intended for busy men and women of the world: women in childbirth, travellers, those about to go into battle, or to seek grace and favour from kings, princes and other temporal authorities. Texts of this kind were presumably intended to be recited frequently, and many similar prayers were probably either memorised or else carried around on scraps of paper until they were read to pieces.[21] The Thornton prayer on fol. 176ᵛ presupposes, moreover, that its readers will have some knowledge of, and will themselves recite, *Deus in nomine tuo* (Vulgate Psalm 53), *Deus misereatur* (Vulgate Psalm 66); *De profundis* (Vulgate Psalm 129) and *Voce mea* (Vulgate Psalm 141). By copying this Latin prayer and identifying himself so closely with it, therefore, Thornton may have been endorsing the assumptions of earlier English and Latin writers that *their* intended readers would have ready access to the familiar recommended psalms in their own Psalters or Books of Hours.

These are slender signs of Thornton's 'personality', but one of the frustrating aspects of the search for Thornton's likely motives and methods is that the most interesting potential sources of information are often found in manuscript and textual features that would not otherwise merit much scholarly attention. My discussion of Thornton's Latin filler items is a typical case in point. Many of these late additions are potentially interesting, I maintain, precisely because they

---

[19] Thornton's source must have contained material which was not unlike the set of indulgenced Latin devotions in an early fifteenth-century York Psalter (Cambridge, Trinity College, MS O.3.10). The latter manuscript preserves a less garbled version of much of Thornton's Latin material on fol. 278ᵛ, with accompanying illustrations and descriptive rubrics which promise protection for the reader who peruses them and and repeats the prayers devoutly. Full details and identification of the Latin material can be found in my unpublished D.Phil. thesis, University of York, 1983, pp. 63–66, 446–7.

[20] This personalised form of the tag may well also be a mark of ownership. It survives once in the London Thornton manuscript, on fol. 66ʳ, and twice in Lincoln, on fol. 98ᵛ in the 'romance' section, and on fol. 213ʳ in the 'religious' section.

[21] Compare also the preceding filler item on fol. 176ᵛ which is another Latin prayer charm assumed to have similar qualities. I briefly discuss the survival of a fragmentary Middle English version of this item in Edinburgh, NLS, MS Advocs' 19.3.1 in 'Collecting Romances in the Later Middle Ages', p. 28, note 37.

were probably derived from a thoroughly conventional prayerbook source. It seems reasonable to assume that Thornton and some members of his family possessed their own prayerbooks (or at least had relatively unrestricted access to one), so it is not difficult to imagine that Thornton could have exercised a degree of personal selectivity in choosing the hymns, prayers and other short scraps that became filler material in his own collection. These items are best described as 'fillers' because Thornton probably added them at a late stage in the history of his collecting activities, after he had already brought together his 'romance' and 'religious' sections to form a major single one-volume household library.

Such assumptions can provide a possible context in which to consider the disrupted sequence of short Latin texts now surviving on fol. 178ᵛ at the end of quire K in the Thornton 'romance' unit. On this page, Thornton suddenly abandoned the task of copying a prayer describing the seven gifts of the Holy Ghost after the description of the first gift (the gift of understanding); the defective Thornton copy is then followed by a prayer to the Virgin and two other short prayers, including, as a final item in the sequence, Latin prayers to St Leonard and St Eustace. At an earlier stage in their textual history these items were derived from antiphons and collects usually associated with the service books of the medieval church.[22] In the Thornton copy, the two prayers neatly fill the limited remaining writing space on his crowded page. But why should Thornton have interrupted his account of the seven gifts, and why might he have been particularly attracted to prayers for some saints rather than others in his search for filler material?

Some testamentary evidence suggests that the beginnings of a possible answer to the latter question might be found in Thornton family history. One William Thorneton of York, gent (probably the scribe's son), will proved 17 March 1488/9, requested to be buried in St Cuthbert's church, York, but he also left 6s 6d for 'þe reparacion of the yle in Steyngrave kyrk' and 'my newe Messe buke to the Maner of Newton in Rydale to serve in Seynt Peter Chapell to the Worlde end'.[23] In 1572, just over a century after the Thornton scribe is known to have been active, the will of another Robert Thornton of East Newton was proved which throws further light on the continuing interests of Thornton family members in their parish and local church. The later Robert states his wish that his body be buried in Stonegrave, at the end of St Leonard's altar, 'nyghe wheras my father and other my ancestors do lye and ar buryed'.[24] The Thornton tomb in

---

[22] Versions of the 'Thornton' prayers to individual saints can also be identified in the published York Breviary, for example; see S. W. Lawley (ed.), *Breviarium Secundum Usum Ecclesie Eboracensis*, Surtees Society, 75 (London, 1882), cols. 668–69 (Eustace), 671–72 (Leonard).

[23] Borthwick Institute, Prob. Reg. 5, fol. 353ʳ. I am very grateful to Dr David Smith of the Borthwick Institute for assisting me with the references to the Probate Register cited in this paragraph. The detail of William's new mass book is also noted by Keiser, 'To Knawe God Almyghtyn', p. 121, as part of his speculation that Robert Thornton's two-volume collection may have been held by the family in the chapel at East Newton. A generation earlier, of course, William's father may well have used another Yorkshire 'mass book' as one of his own major Latin sources.

[24] Borthwick Institute, Prob. Reg. 5, fol. 353ʳ. The sustained interest of the Thorntons of East Newton in St Leonard's altar and the aisle containing the Thornton tomb is confirmed by other scattered references in later wills. The tomb itself was moved during the 1862 renovation of the church at Stonegrave before which it was reported that 'the north aisle was raised by the vaults in it nearly to the level of the tops of the pews in the church, and that steps led up from the nave to this

Stonegrave still exists and dates from 1418. It is also situated near an altar which, since at least the fourteenth century, has been dedicated to St Leonard. It is inviting to assume, therefore, that a prayer to St Leonard would have held some particular attraction for a fifteenth-century scribe and book producer who was also a member of the Thornton family at East Newton. Robert Thornton's choice of filler prayer on fol. 178ᵛ may well be another very minor vestige of what, in a different context, Malcolm Vale has described as the late medieval gentry's 'proprietary attitude towards the places in which they were buried'.²⁵

By turning to other religious material in the Lincoln Thornton manuscript, it is also possible to suggest likely reasons for the scribe's obvious failure to complete his copy of a prayer enumerating the seven gifts of the Holy Ghost. Among the cluster of short items ascribed to Richard Rolle, on fols. 192ʳ–96ᵛ in quire L, Thornton copied in full a Middle English version outlining all seven gifts of the Holy Ghost (fols. 196ʳ–96ᵛ); part of the Thornton copy of *The Mirror of St Edmund*, preserved on fols. 197ʳ–209ᵛ in quires L and M, also clearly enumerates the same seven gifts (fol. 201ᵛ). If Thornton had already completed his copies of both these items before adding his filler prayers, one might then begin to question whether the scribe could possibly have felt that he needed another brief item on this elementary topic, especially if, having commenced copying such a text, he discovered that his prayerbook source contained more attractive prayers which could be used to fill up some of the remaining blank space on his pages.²⁶ This attempted reconstruction of copying activities that probably took place late in the history of the collection illustrates, therefore, one aspect of Thornton's compiling instincts. It also suggests that Thornton was a book producer who gained a limited degree of 'editorial' confidence when the task of gathering up material for his collection was almost complete. My example of the incomplete 'Seven Gifts' text illustrates somewhat paradoxically, however, that even at this late stage in his compiling activities, Thornton remained attracted to writings which shared some of the same interests in elementary religious topics as several of his main prose items.

The survival of two overlapping instructional programmes in the Thornton 'religious' section is also interesting. The topics covered by both *The Mirror of St Edmund*, in quires L–M, and *Gaytryge's Sermon*, in quire M, coincide with those listed in the Peckham 1281 syllabus and, of course, Archbishop Thoresby's instructions to the clergy issued 76 years later for York.²⁷ Thornton's

platform which renders the North aisle an unsightly appendage' (detail taken from unpublished notes on the repairs kindly supplied by Mr George Morris).

²⁵ *Piety, Charity and Literacy Among the Yorkshire Gentry*, 1370–1480, Borthwick Papers No. 50 (York, 1976), p. 10.

²⁶ Thornton's obvious attraction to 'Seven Gifts' items among his Rolle-related material is also striking because it can be compared to the manner in which the anonymous compiler of Cambridge, University Library, MS Dd. 5. 64 (III) inserted an exposition of the same seven gifts as a penultimate chapter in this copy of Rolle's *Form of Living*. See the parallel-text edition in Horstman, *Early Yorkshire Writers*, i.1–49 (at pp. 45–46). The textual affiliations of the other religious material in this religious anthology offer further insights into the circumstances in which Rolle-related material circulated among clerical compilers in late medieval Yorkshire. See Doyle, 'Origins and Circulation', ii.80, and the recent account of the textual affiliations of surviving manuscripts containing Rolle's *Form*, in Ogilvie-Thomson (ed.), *Richard Rolle: Prose and Verse*, pp. lii–lxv.

²⁷ It is curious and inexplicable that the Thornton text of Gaytryge (fols. 213ᵛ–18ᵛ) should claim, erroneously, but also on three separate occasions, that the Archbishop's instructions emanated from

copies offer their intended audience self-contained and (presumably for some fifteenth-century readers, at least) predictable programmes of religious instruction in fundamental aspects of Christian belief: the Creed, the Ten Commandments, the Seven Sacraments, the Seven Works of Mercy, the Seven Virtues, and the Seven Deadly Sins. On this occasion, Thornton does not seem to have chosen between these stylistically different, parallel, treatments of familiar instructional topics, but simply copied both programmes. This brings into focus two conflicting impulses that must have been encountered on numerous occasions by some late medieval copyists and collectors of Middle English religious literature. These impulses were, on the one hand, the urge to be eclectic and reasonably undiscriminating, to gather together as much interesting written material as possible to satisfy a voracious appetite for religious and moral reading, and, on the other, the urge to be conservative, to limit and control the range of instructional and devotional material being made available to other listeners and readers. Both these impulses would seem to have played a major role in shaping the selection of material in Thornton's two-volume collection. In his individual case, of course, the conflict may have been more apparent than real if the compiling interests reflected in his 'religious' section are signs of editorial activities that had already taken place in his major sources.

The Thornton text of *The Mirror of St Edmund* also represents an attempt to expand this item in a particularly flabby but interesting way. In this version, the *Mirror*'s straightforward exposition of the petitions of the Pater Noster –extant in all the surviving manuscripts which are not fragments at this point – is supplemented, on fols. 203^r–204^v, by a second similarly literal exposition of the *Pater Noster* not found in other extant *Mirror* copies.[28] The expanded *Mirror* is then followed immediately, on fols. 209^v–211^r in quire M, by a third Middle English prose exposition of the *Pater Noster*.[29] In content, and presumably purpose, this item is not unlike the other two accounts of the same prayer now embedded in the Thornton *Mirror*.

The expanded state of the Thornton text of the *Mirror* brings to mind the so-called Lollard additions of *Pater Noster* material in some copies (not Thornton's) of *Gaytryge's Sermon*.[30] In these latter cases, the expansions do not cause the Gaytryge text to sag in quite the same way as the additions in Thornton, however, and their later inclusion is perhaps justified because of Gaytryge's unaccountable failure to include an exposition of the *Pater Noster* in his original programme. What also makes the expansions in Thornton's copy so interesting is that the English prose *Mirror* writer had already explicitly advised

'our Fadir þe byschope' (fols. 214^r, 214^v, 218^v). See the modern edition in N. F. Blake (ed.), *Middle English Religious Prose* (London, 1972), pp. 73–87, and Dr Susan Powell's paper in this volume.
[28] The 'Thornton' expansion interestingly reflects some of the religious enthusiasm for pastoral and meditative material that is often loosely associated with Rolle-related expository material, see Horstman, *Early Yorkshire Writers*, i.229–32. For a general survey of the popularity of vernacular *Pater Noster* treatments see F. G. A. M. Aarts, *Þe Pater Noster of Richard Ermyte* (Nijmegen, 1967).
[29] Horstman, *Early Yorkshire Writers*, i.261–64.
[30] See the recent account in Anne Hudson, 'A New look at the *Lay Folks' Catechism*', *Viator*, 16 (1985): 243–58; also Susan Powell's paper in this volume.

his intended readers not to worry if, in his words, they were unable to 'multyply many Pater Nosters'.[31] He had also earlier warned:

> for-thi do þay gret schame and gret vnreuerence till Ihesu goddes sone þat takes þame till wordis ry[m]and [MS: rynnand] and curius, and leues þe prayere þat he vs kennede . . . And þare-fore a hundrethe thousande er dyssayuede with multyplicacione of wordes and of Orysouns; ffor when þay wene þat þay hafe grete deuocyone, þane hafe þai a fulle fleschely lykynge, ffor-thy þat ilk a fleschely lykynge delytes þame kyndely in swylke turnede langage. And þarefore I walde þat þou war warre, ffor I say þe sykerly þat it es a foule lychery for to delyte þe in rymes and slyke gulyardy.[32]

This uncompromising attack on 'rhymes and goliardy' bears comparison to the well known attack on named Middle English romances in the much-copied *Pater Noster* verse treatment ascribed to William of Nassyngton and known as *Speculum Vitae*.[33] The *Mirror* writer's words imply that his attack was aimed at different and less specific targets than Nassyngton's, since the former was probably including in his censure some of the more expansive verse treatments of instructional and devotional topics that *he* intended to treat with the propriety he felt was due to them in his own devotional programme. His warning may once have been part of the original promotion of the *Mirror* as a self-sufficient instructional programme. In Thornton's copy, the attack on other vernacular renderings is given immediately after the intrusion into the *Mirror* text of the second exposition of the *Pater Noster*. The subsequent complex textual histories of other English versions of the *Mirror*, in many different manuscript settings, confirms, moreover, that this English writer's austere comments did not impede, and may even have encouraged, the multifarious activities of later writers and compilers who were happy to quarry his work.

Perhaps the accumulation of not one but three ME prose expansions of the *Pater Noster* around Thornton's copy of *The Mirror* can be partly excused on the grounds that these now read like completely uncontroversial later prose additions, made long after *The Mirror* writer had voiced his concerns about religious verse. The seemingly superfluous accretion of *Pater Noster* items must in some way reflect the collecting instincts of a person who is preoccupied by how one ought to pray and is seizing on three similar accounts of the same prayer

---

[31] 'Bot say all-anely þe nakede lettir with þi mouthe and thynke in þi herte of this þat I hafe said here, of ilke a worde by itselfe, and rekk noghte þof þou ne multyply many Pater Nosters; ffor it es better to say a Pater noster with gude deuocyone þane a thousande with-owttene deuocyone' (Horstman, *Early Yorkshire Writers*, i.234; Thornton text on fol. 205ᵛ). In each case where I quote from Thornton's text, similar sentiments are also expressed at the equivalent places in other surviving *Mirror* copies.

[32] Horstman, *Early Yorkshire Writers*, i.232; Thornton text on fol. 204ᵛ.

[33] IMEV 245, not in Thornton's collection, although some of the romances named in this attack certainly are (*Octavian* and *Ysumbras*). Note also Thornton's text of the Middle English verse *Tractatus . . . de Trinitate et Unitate* (IMEV 11), attributed to 'Willemi Nassynton quondam aduocati curie Eboraci' in his copy (fols. 189ʳ—91ᵛ; ed. Horstman, *Early Yorkshire Writers*, ii.334–39). Examples of other Middle English texts of spiritual instruction which originally proclaimed their self-sufficiency include the *Book to a Mother*, the *Pore Catiff* and John Mirk's *Instructions for Parish Priests*. (All three are discussed briefly in Gillespie, 'Lukynge in haly bukes', pp. 11–13.)

to work out that obsession for intended readers. This urge to 'prick heaven with a Pater noster' is not unique to Thornton's 'religious' section, of course.[34] The uniquely surviving cluster of expository material on the *Pater Noster* in his collection also betrays some signs that Thornton's likely tastes for this type of religious reading probably coincided with those of other, earlier, readers. Doyle has already noted that Thornton's copy of the *Mirror* has been adjusted by someone, twice, to address a 'dere syster and friend'.[35] These references to an implied female reader now survive uniquely in this copy. And unlike the other surviving texts of the English prose *Mirror*, both the Vernon and Thornton texts specifically address someone who is expected to 'say and do at thyne offece in þe qweire'.[36] So, in common with the other surviving English versions of *The Mirror*, the extant 'Thornton' text must reflect many different strata of late medieval reading experiences, the most important of which are likely to have been shared with the earlier compilers, owners and readers of Thornton's source.

Three short Middle English prose items by Walter Hilton in Thornton's 'religious' section offer other opportunities to appreciate the ways in which earlier owners may have affected the textual transmission of clusters of 'Thornton' religious texts before they became available to the Yorkshire scribe for copying. The texts in question are a copy of *Of Angels' Song* (fols. 219ᵛ–21ᵛ), a fragmentary copy of *Mixed Life* (fols. 223ʳ–29ʳ), and an extract from Book 1 of *The Scale of Perfection* (fols. 229ᵛ–30ᵛ). Thornton copied these without ascribing them to Walter Hilton yet in close proximity to each other in quires M and N. His texts of both the *Scale* extract and *Of Angels' Song* are addressed quite neutrally to a 'dere friend'. Although the opening of *Mixed Life* is now lost from this copy, Doyle has noted that there is a reference later in Thornton's text to a 'dere sister', and there are two further references which make specific mention of an assumed audience of women as well as men.[37] Of the eighteen surviving manuscripts containing *Mixed Life*, Thornton's copy is the only one which preserves these three readings. Some readers may be tempted to wield Ockham's razor at this point and simply claim these readings for Thornton, not a copyist in an earlier source. The corollary to this would be that

---

[34] Gillespie, 'Lukynge in haly bukes', pp. 8–10, usefully surveys the whole spectrum of paraliturgical devotions that can be associated with the *Pater Noster* prayer; see also discussion and references in Avril Henry, 'The Pater Noster in a table ypeynted', in Derek Pearsall (ed.), *Studies in the Vernon Manuscript* (Cambridge, 1990), pp. 89–113.

[35] Doyle, 'Origins and Circulation', i.44–45. Doyle's point has also been taken up in a fascinating recent historical survey of Thornton's likely points of contact with local female religious (Keiser, 'More Light On the Life and Milieu of Robert Thornton'). For the popularity of the *Pater Noster* as a prayer that could be recited by the unlettered members of some female religious communities as an alternative to taking part in the daily office, see also Aarts, *Þe Pater Noster of Richard Ermyte*, p. xcii.

[36] This Vernon/Thornton reading represents an interesting point of divergence in other surviving English prose versions of the *Mirror*. The textual tradition represented by the copy in London, British Library, MS Addit. 10053 offers the variant reading, *do þyne office in þyne herte deuoutley*, while the copy in Oxford, Bodleian Library, MS Douce 25 reads, *do þi office in þe chirche*. (textual variants quoted from Rosemary Goymer (ed.), *Mirror of St Edmund*, pp. 83–84; cf. Thornton and Vernon texts in Horstman, *Early Yorkshire Writers*, i.234, 253).

[37] Doyle, 'Origins and Circulation', i.199. The references are made at points corresponding to ll. 434, 456 and 786 in Ogilvie-Thomson (ed.), *Mixed Life*.

Middle English Religious Prose Texts and their 'Thornton' Context in the Lincoln Thornton Manuscript, Quires L–P

In the following account, quire descriptions are given in bold and quire breaks are indicated by a broken line across either both columns (if the end of a quire coincides with the end of Thornton's copy) or the first column only (if the break occurs within a text).

FOLS.	TEXTS
L²⁰ (fols. 179–198)	
179ʳ–189ʳ	THE PRIVITY OF THE PASSION
189ᵛ–192ʳ	IMEV 2616 (Rhyming tag from Rolle's *Psalter*); IMEV 11 (Nassyngton on the Trinity); IMEV 1954, IMEV 246, IMEV 1950.5, IMEV 1757, IMEV 1741 (Verse prayers to Christ and the Trinity, sometimes associated with Rolle and versions of the *Mirror* of St Edmund.)
192ʳ–196ᵛ	ROLLE-RELATED CLUSTER (all Middle English texts are in prose): Middle English tract on the Holy Name (*Oleum Effusum*); Middle English account of a vision experienced by Rolle usually conflated with *Oleum Effusum* (a Latin version is associated with the *Office* of Richard Hermit); Latin texts of *Deus Noster Refugiam* and *Ihesu Nostra Redemptio*; four Middle English exemplary tales: on imperfect and perfect contrition, on the nature of the bee (an attack on complacency in the spiritual life), and on the nature of the life led by a female recluse because of her love of Christ; two Latin extracts, the first associated with Rolle's commentary on the Canticles and the second extracted from his *Liber de amore Dei Contra Amatores Mundi*; two Middle English expositions, the first of the Ten Commandments, and the second of the Seven Gifts of the Holy Ghost; the 'Desire and Delight' tract.
197ʳ–209ᵛ	THE MIRROR OF ST EDMUND (expanded by a second Pater Noster exposition)
- - - - - - - - - -	
M²⁴ (199–221; wants xxiv?)	
209ᵛ–211ʳ	MIDDLE ENGLISH TRACT ON THE PATER NOSTER
211ʳ–213ʳ	Latin and English prayer cluster: IMEV 1692, IMEV 775; Middle English liturgical prayer to Christ; Latin devotions for the Feast of the Exaltation of the Cross
213ʳ–213ᵛ	IMEV 3921, IMEV 1674 ('when Adam delf' and a short prayer to Christ)
213ᵛ–218ᵛ	GAYTRYGE'S SERMON (*Lay Folks' Catechism*; IMEV 406)
219ʳ–219ᵛ	IMEV 1781 (a song of love to Christ)
219ᵛ–221ᵛ	OF ANGELS' SONG

N? (fols. 222, 223–236)

222ʳ–222ᵛ	IMEV 3730, IMEV 229 ('Þi Joy be like a dele'; fragment: final lines missing)
223ʳ–229ʳ	MIXED LIFE (fragment: defective opening)
229ᵛ–230ᵛ	SCALE OF PERFECTION (extract)
231ʳ–233ᵛ	IMEV 2608 (on St John the Evangelist)
233ᵛ–236ᵛ	MIDDLE ENGLISH TRACT ON PRAYER (fragmentary at end)

- -

O¹⁸ (fols. 237–253; wants i)

237ʳ–250ᵛ	MIDDLE ENGLISH GRATIA DEI COMPILATION (disarranged and fragmentary: opens abruptly)
250ᵛ–258ᵛ	REVELATION SHOWED TO A HOLY WOMAN (fragmentary copy: text missing between fols. 253–254)

- - - - - - - - - - -

P²⁴? (fols. 254–279; wants i; 3 singletons added after xv?)

258ʳ–258ᵛ	Latin texts of Vulgate Psalm 50 and *Veni Creator*
258ᵛ–270ᵛ	St Jerome's Psalter (in Latin) with accompanying Latin prayers and litany
271ʳ–276ʳ	THE ABBEY OF THE HOLY GHOST
276ᵛ–277ʳ	IMEV 3428 (extract from the *Prick of Conscience*)
277ᵛ–279ʳ	Latin Prayer Cluster: prayers on the Joys of the Virgin and the sufferings of Christ
279ʳ–279ᵛ	IMEV 704 ('Erthe upon Erthe')
279ᵛ	MIDDLE ENGLISH PRESCRIPTION FOR SCIATICA (incompletely copied)

Thornton must have been preparing this text for female readers of his acquaintance.[38]

The most unusual textual feature of Thornton's copy of *Of Angels' Song* is that it omits the short, seemingly authentic, opening section of the tract which is preserved in the six other extant manuscript copies and the one early print.[39] 'Dere Friend wit þou wel . . .', Thornton's text begins, while other copies at this point open with 'Dere brothers in Christ'. All the other extant copies then go on to explain, in Hilton's characteristically cautious manner, how the writer cannot completely reassure the enthusiastic brother in Christ that an ecstatic experience of angels' song might not simply be a distressing and evil fantasy. By its single omission, the Thornton text has lost both the reference to a male reader and to the possibility that the author 'can noght tell þe for syker þe sothnes of þis mater'. This omission seems the work of a fifteenth-century Hilton 'editor'. It reflects the likely actions of a paternalistic spiritual counsellor who may have decided to suppress the sentiments in the opening paragraph because he was reluctant to disconcert a weaker 'friend' by allowing Hilton's own brand of honest uncertainty to stand. I may be describing Thornton's own attempts to prepare his Hilton material for female readers again, but apart from the wayward 'Thornton' readings in these religious texts, there is no supporting evidence to suggest that the Thornton scribe ever took on such a role. In this case, therefore, Ockam's razor seems a very blunt instrument. It is more logical to assume that these uniquely surviving features in Thornton's written copies probably faithfully reflect similar textual details also once found in one of his 'Hilton' exemplars.

Similarly, Thornton may never have been aware that his copy of an extract from Hilton's *Scale* was once part of a much longer work. 'Wit þou wele, dere frende', the extract opens in his copy, and the item closes with a formal benediction and 'amen', making it look complete in itself. Carl Horstman did not recognise the pedigree of Thornton's text and treated it as a short self-contained item by Rolle, entitling it an 'Epistle on Salvation by Love of the Name of Jesus'.[40] The mistake is understandable and the Horstman title is apt because the Thornton copy not only looks intact but also once belonged to a version of *The Scale* that had earlier been expanded by the celebrated 'Holy Name' added passage. This late *Scale* addition offers Hilton's intended readers the possibility

---

[38] It is worth noting that these references to an audience that specifically refers to women as well as men are matched by a similarly specific, also uniquely surviving, textual reference in Thornton's copy of the *Abbey of the Holy Ghost* (fols. 271ʳ–76ʳ in quire P). Having established in its opening lines that the allegorical abbey will be founded in the human conscience, the 'Thornton' text alone sensibly asks, 'and who so will be besy to funde þis holy religione'? The encouraging answer for both male and female 'Thornton' readers is, 'And þat may ilke gud cristyne mane and woman do þat wille be besy þar-abowte'. (Thornton text and selected variants in Horstman, *Early Yorkshire Writers*, i.321–37 [at pp. 321–22]; see also text and discussion of this modest textual flourish in the unpublished critical edition of the *Abbey* by Consacro, *thesis*, esp. pp. cxii, and 2, line 4.)

[39] All references are to Takamiya (ed.), *Of Angels' Song*, esp. pp. 29–31.

[40] *Early Yorkshire Writers*, i.293–95. Horstman's title and comments suggest that he may have been misled because he was not inappropriately comparing this anonymous *Scale* extract to Rolle's *Oleum Effusum* tract. Thornton's copy of the latter (fols. 192ʳ–93ᵛ in quire L) is entitled 'Of the vertus of the haly name of Ihesu'.

of reassurance in the face of any doubts they may have experienced because of reading more widely in the enthusiastic writings of other unnamed 'holy men'. The facilitative yet cautious exposition of the Holy Name which follows is offered, we are told, because some *Scale* readers may have been made to feel unsafe (in Hilton's view), through having 'felid neuer gastely swetnes ne inly sauour in þe name of Ihesu or in þe loue of Ihesu'.[41]

Hilton's modern textual critics, including Doyle, have been perplexed by the survival of the 'Holy Name' passage in some *Scale* texts but not others, in copies which seem otherwise closely related.[42] Two of the most recent prospective critical editors of Hilton's text have conceded that, at the earliest stage in its textual history, the Holy Name passage is likely to have circulated independently of *The Scale* itself as an authentic later revision to Book 1. Many early owners of Hilton's *Scale* must have remained unaware of the existence or status of this added passage and may not even have known whether they possessed an expanded or unexpanded version. At least one reader of London, British Library, MS Harley 6579 who became aware of the short passage's existence and already had an unexpanded copy of *The Scale*, however, was able to add the 'Holy Name' addition on an extra sheet in this copy.

Such detailed textual interest in Hilton's work could only have taken place where copying conditions favoured the prospective fifteenth-century *Scale* editor. In addition to the special case of London, British Library, MS Harley 6579, quoted above, the Holy Name passage was probably added into the parent manuscript of the *Scale* copy in Cambridge, Trinity College, MS B.15.18 (354). James Grenehalgh, the sixteenth-century English Carthusian monk, and the best known of Hilton's earliest textual critics, is known to have annotated the latter manuscript and also the copy of the 1494 de Worde print (STC 14042) in the Rosenbach Foundation Museum and Library in Philadelphia.[43] Both of these are expanded versions of the *Scale*, containing the Holy Name added passage. On the other hand, in the Chatsworth copy which lacks the passage, Grenehalgh was only able to write 'there is much missing here', and was presumably not in a position to update the copy. A number of other fifteenth-century *Scale* readers show by marginal comments in their copies that they knew about the added passage's existence but, at the time of writing, were either unwilling or unable to secure a copy of the added passage in their unexpanded texts.[44] In an earlier life

---

[41] Thornton's copy also contains part of the original *Scale* where Hilton had earlier offered to assist readers who ask salvation by virtue of Christ's Passion to become 'safe as ane ankir incluse, and noghte anely þou, bot all cristene mene & wymene . . . þof it be swa þat þay hafe bene cumbyrde in syne & with syne all þaire lyfe-tyme, and neuer had felyng of gastely sauour or swetnes, or gastely knawynge of godde'. (*Early Yorkshire Writers*, i.293; Thornton text on fol. 229^v.)

[42] Doyle, 'Origins and Circulation', i.248–49. For some of the 'further investigations and fresh hypotheses' Doyle felt were necessary, see Michael Sargent, 'Walter Hilton's *Scale of Perfection*: the London Manuscript Group Reconsidered', *Medium Ævum*, 52 (1983): 189–216 (at 195–99).

[43] Details of Grenehalgh's activities in Michael Sargent, *James Grenehalgh as Textual Critic*, Analecta Cartusiana, 85 (Salzburg, 1984).

[44] From his survey of *Scale* copies Sargent has concluded that 'the scribes and annotators of nearly one-fifth of the surviving MSS seem . . . to have been aware of more than one form of the text, and to have gone out of their way to draw attention to the fact' (London Manuscript Group Reconsidered', pp. 196–97).

and different environment, the *Scale* extract now extant in the Lincoln Thornton manuscript would have been an extremely useful fragment to have had on hand for consultation, therefore, firstly, if its nature and pedigree were realised, and, secondly, if its earliest owners wished to check whether other copies of *The Scale* passing through their hands were the expanded or unexpanded versions of Hilton's work. Because of this kind of speculative possibility, one cannot automatically assume that Thornton had access to a complete copy of *The Scale* and specially selected his own extract from Book 1.[45]

The textual affiliations of these Hilton items are of most interest to Thornton scholars because they may enable us to reproduce in shadowy outline some important features of a major anthology source from which Thornton probably derived much of his own collection of Middle English religious prose. According to unpublished research by the late A. J. Bliss for his projected EETS edition, the *Scale* extract in Thornton can be classified as a Group Z text.[46] Group Z texts include those in the famous Vernon and Simeon sister manuscripts (Oxford, Bodleian Library, MS Eng. poet. a. 1, and London, British Library, MS Additional 22283); Longleat, MS 298; Cambridge, Trinity College, MS 0.7.47 (1375); London, British Library, MS Lansdowne 362; Columbia, University Library, MS Plimpton 257; Westminster School, MS 3; and Liverpool, University Library, MS Rylands F.4.10. These group Z copies also resemble Thornton's copy because they contain the Holy Name added passage, although it should be noted that the other nine members belonging to the same textual grouping do not. MS Rylands F.4.10 also preserves a more intact copy of the anonymous Middle English prose tract on prayer which, in Thornton's collection, follows almost immediately after the Hilton material on fols. 233ᵛ–36ᵛ on the last surviving leaves of quire N.[47] The short tract fits well in its present 'Thornton' manuscript setting since it stresses the virtue and sweetness of the *Pater Noster* for those who wish to pray inwardly with love and meekness. Such prayers, we are told, will make us live an angel's life.

---

[45] *Pace* George Keiser, 'To Knawe God Almyghtyn', pp. 106–7. Keiser usefully comments, however, on the fact that Cambridge, University Library, MS Ff. 5. 40 contains copies of all three Hilton works represented in Thornton's collection (including an unexpanded copy of Book 1 of the *Scale*) and that a companion religious anthology (in Oxford, Bodleian Library, MS Rawlinson C. 285) probably once did so as well; see also Doyle, 'Origins and Circulation', ii.115–7. Both these copies of the *Scale* belong to the same textual grouping in which the late A. J. Bliss has placed the Thornton *Scale* extract (see the following note).

[46] Bliss very generously communicated his unpublished findings to me in a letter dated 23 February, 1983. The 17 group Z manuscripts identified by Bliss (8 of which contain the Holy Name added passage) correspond to the 15 N-type *Scale* copies in the textual grouping also established by Rosemary Birts [Dorward] in her unpublished edition of the *Scale*, Book 1, chapters 38–52 (Oxford, 1956). Birts does not attempt to classify either the Thornton extract or the extracts from the *Scale* in Oxford, Bodleian Library, MS Rawlinson C. 894 (the latter derived from an unexpanded *Scale* copy), both of which Bliss treats as group Z manuscripts. For an account of the extensive editorial spadework necessary to support the N-type textual grouping, see Michael Sargent, *James Grenehalgh*, ii.291–329 and the useful diagram on p. 322.

[47] Fragmentary Thornton text in Horstman, *Early Yorkshire Writers*, i.295–300. This item merits closer critical attention than it has proved possible to give it in this short study; but note the partial identification in P. S Jolliffe, *A Check-List of Middle English Prose Writings of Spiritual Guidance* (Toronto, 1974), pp. 128–29 (item M 11).

Thornton's copy of *Mixed Life* has recently been re-examined by S. J. Ogilvie-Thomson in her work for a modern critical edition of the Hilton text. By her reckoning, the Thornton text belongs to the same textual tradition as the Vernon and Simeon copies but its closest textual affiliations are with the copy in Longleat, MS 29.[48] This coincidence sets off a further trail of possibilities, since the contents of Longleat, MS 29 occasionally overlap with Thornton's 'religious' section for a number of other religious items.[49] These include Richard Rolle's short *Desire and Delight* which in each manuscript is gathered up with a larger cluster of material also ascribed to Rolle. In the Longleat cluster, but not Thornton's, a copy of the Middle English lyric beginning 'þi Ioy be ilke a dele' (IMEV 3730), has been set into the same sequence. Thornton's fragment of this Rolle-related lyric is currently 'sandwiched' between his copies of *Of Angels' Song* and *Mixed Life* on a stray singleton leaf (fol. 222), once perhaps belonging to quire N, in a particularly damaged part of his 'religious' section.

The other items represented in both collections are a Middle English prose narrative usually identified as *A Revelation Showed to a Holy Woman*, and the Latin hymn *Veni Creator*.[50] The *Revelation* is the last item in Longleat MS 29. It is described as *Reuelaciones reuelate cuidam sancte Mulieri recluse* and follows a short cluster of English prose prayers and meditations, two of which are also found in Oxford, Bodleian Library, MS Lyell 30. The Longleat copy of *Veni Creator* was added as a filler item in a much earlier part of the collection. As Doyle has shown, the Thornton heading of the *Revelations* makes no reference to the protagonist being a female recluse but it retains the internal textual references to her being a holy woman. Thornton's copy is preserved on fols. 250ᵛ–58ʳ in quires O–P, as part of a carefully-tailored English and Latin cluster of material which includes Thornton's copy of the *Veni Creator* set alongside a Latin text of Vulgate Psalm 50, the *Miserere Mei Deus*.[51]

The sources lying behind both these religious anthologies were obviously documents which would have assisted our understanding of how different combinations of short items associated with the names of Richard Rolle and Walter Hilton were sent into circulation among some fifteenth-century devout and literate layfolk as far apart as London and North Yorkshire. Robert Thornton's geographical proximity to the area where Rolle is known to have lived and worked a century earlier may suggest that there was also likely to be a continuing local interest in the Yorkshire hermit-writer's works of which

---

[48] Ogilvie-Thomson (ed.), *Mixed Life*, pp. xxxiii–xli. Other *Mixed Life* copies from Ogilvie-Thomson's β textual grouping include New York, Columbia University Library, MS Plimpton 271 which originally formed a single volume with the Z/N-type *Scale* copy in MS Plimpton 257; see A. J. Bliss 'Two Hilton Manuscripts in Columbia University Library', *Medium Ævum*, 38 (1969): 157–63. The copy in CUL, MS Ff. 5. 40 (see n. 45 above) belongs to a different textual tradition which Ogilvie-Thomson describes as the 'longer version' of *Mixed Life*.

[49] See the recent description of the contents and revised account of the likely London provenance of Longleat, MS 29 in Ogilvie-Thomson, *Richard Rolle: Prose and Verse*, pp. xvii–xxxi. This intriguing religious anthology contains no other works by Hilton.

[50] Thornton text of the *Revelation* in Horstman, *Early Yorkshire Writers*, i.383–92; also discussion of the possible metropolitan provenance of this item in Doyle, 'Origins and Circulation', i.81–83.

[51] For further discussion see my 'Literary Associations of an Anonymous Middle English Paraphrase of Vulgate Psalm L', *Medium Ævum*, 57 (1988): 38–55 (at 39–40).

Thornton could hardly have remained unaware.[52] But this should not be allowed to distract attention from proper consideration of the important role also likely to have been played for Thornton by intermediary sources, several of which are likely to have belonged to clerical collectors with similar interests in gathering up clusters of Rolle-related devotional writings. This important section of the potential fifteenth-century audience for the religious works that found their way into Thornton's collection must often have enjoyed privileged access to such material by virtue of their standing in local religious communities, or because of their pastoral interests and parish responsibilities.[53] Such figures are likely to have played their part in filtering particular versions of writings by Richard Rolle, Walter Hilton, and broadly related material on similarly uncontroversial instructional and contemplative themes to the heterogeneous audience of female and male readers that also included the fifteenth-century Yorkshire copyist.[54]

If the evidence of the extant manuscripts containing the works of Richard Rolle and Walter Hilton and the other religious items I have been discussing in this paper is to be believed, it suggests just how extraordinary the combination of 'religious' and 'romance' items in Thornton's two-volume collection is likely to have been. Robert Thornton somehow seems to have enjoyed access to certain types of religious anthology sources which were either usually not made available to, or else hardly ever chosen by, other late medieval book producers also engaged in collecting Middle English metrical romances. Possible exceptions to this general rule are the Vernon and Simeon compilers who produced compendious sister volumes on the topic of *Sowlehele*, but probably also added items like *Robert of Sicily* and *The King of Tars* as moral exemplary material; the producer of Cambridge, University Library, MS Ii.4.9 where *The Abbey of the Holy Ghost* and Rolle's *Form* share company with another copy of *Robert of Sicily*; and the producer of London, British Library, MS Additional 36983 containing another copy of *The Abbey of the Holy Ghost* and the Middle English *Titus and Vespasian*.[55] The eventual tri-partite division of Lincoln MS 91 into so-called 'romance', 'religious', and 'medical' sections is, undeniably, therefore, one of Thornton's major achievements as a literary compiler. And, while these divisions were probably never clearly established or strictly adhered

---

[52] The interestingly informal manner in which Thornton's 'religious' and 'romance' sections were rubricated permits the possibility that Thornton was responsible for some of his own (occasionally suspect) 'Rolle' identifications in the rubricated headings accompanying his Rolle-related cluster. Full details in my thesis, pp. 70–86, esp. pp. 84–6.

[53] For an interesting assessment of the important role played by many such figures in the diocese of York see Jonathan Hughes, *Pastors and Visionaries, Religion and Secular Life in Late Medieval Yorkshire* (Woodbridge, 1988).

[54] In his general survey of English religious anthologies from this period, Vincent Gillespie has aptly described the nice scholarly balance that must be struck between assuming 'professional copying and promotion of such collections, and the exercise of individual initiative in the acquisition and copying of texts' ('Vernacular Books of Religion', p. 326).

[55] For all three manuscripts, see Gisela Guddat-Figge, *Catalogue of Manuscripts*, pp. 100–3 (MS Ii. 4. 9), 145–51 (Simeon MS), 166–8 (MS Additional 36983), 269–79 (Vernon MS). For Vernon/Simeon see also *The Vernon Manuscript: A Facsimile of Bodleian Library, Oxford, MS Eng. Poet. a.1*, introd. A. I. Doyle (Cambridge, 1987); A. S. G. Edwards, 'The Contexts of the Vernon Romances', in *Studies in the Vernon Manuscript*, pp. 159–70. I comment on the likely sources of supply lying behind London, British Library, MS Additional 36983 in 'Textual Instability', pp. 185–7.

to during the early production stages of Thornton's books, they were probably prompted as much by the general nature of the available exemplars, and his enviable sources of supply, as by his own compiling instincts. These latter instincts were no doubt sharpened considerably as Thornton's piles of filled and partly-filled quires continued to grow and he got a clearer sense of what he was in the process of achieving for his own intended readers.

INDEX OF MANUSCRIPTS

INDEX OF NAMES AND TITLES